P9-DNC-279

the series on school reform

Patricia A. Wasley
Bank Street College of Education

Ann Lieberman
NCREST

Joseph P. McDonald
New York University

SERIES EDITORS

This series also incorporates earlier titles in the Professional Development and Practice Series

Beyond Formulas in Mathematics and Teaching

DYNAMICS OF THE HIGH SCHOOL ALGEBRA CLASSROOM

Daniel Chazan

Foreword by Penelope Peterson

Teachers College
Columbia University
New York and London

Published by Teachers College Press, 1234 Amsterdam Avenue, New York, NY 10027

Copyright © 2000 by Teachers College, Columbia University

All rights reserved. No part of this publication may be reproduced or transmitted in any form or by any means, electronic or mechanical, including photocopy, or any information storage and retrieval system, without permission from the publisher.

Library of Congress Cataloging-in-Publication Data

Chazan, Daniel.
  Beyond formulas in mathematics and teaching: Dynamics of the high school algebra classroom / by Daniel Chazan; foreword by Penelope Peterson.
    p. cm.—(The series on school reform)
  Includes bibliographical references and index.
  ISBN 0-8077-3918-9 (pbk. : alk. paper)—ISBN 0-8077-3919-7 (cloth : alk. paper)
    1. Algebra—Study and teaching (Secondary)   I. Title. II. Series.
  QA159.C48 2000
  512′.071′2—dc21   99-053646

ISBN 0-8077-3918-9 (paper)
ISBN 0-8077-3919-7 (cloth)

Printed on acid-free paper
Manufactured in the United States of America

07 06 05 04 03 02 01 00   8 7 6 5 4 3 2 1

Contents

Foreword

What does it take to learn to teach? "Not much," some folk seem to believe these days. Witness the quick fixes suggested routinely for the problem of training and recruiting high-quality teachers to teach in our urban areas. But ask an experienced teacher, and you get quite a different story.

I heard one such story this week while driving to work and listening to National Public Radio. In a radio essay, an experienced teacher was moved to reflect on this question by the arrival in his classroom of an intern teacher to begin student teaching. Wondering what it would take for this novice to learn to teach, the teacher was reminded of a master potter in Japan who created such marvelous pots that they came to be in great demand and to fetch amazing prices. Captivated by these pots, a wealthy businessman determined not only to have one of these marvelous creations, but also to discover the secret of how the potter created them. Accordingly, the businessman traveled to the studio of the master to learn the technique. When he arrived, he learned that the potter worked only on certain days. The businessman waited and waited, and finally the day came for the potter to make pots. The master stood there surrounded by his many assistants. As the businessman watched, an assistant handed the master a newly formed pot, fashioned from a nearby potter's wheel. The master held the pot high and with a few quick strokes of his brush, he deftly painted the pot so it was a wonder to behold. But the businessman was taken aback. "Seven seconds," he exclaimed in astonishment. Turning to the master, the businessman complained, "You charge thousands of dollars for these pots, and yet it takes you only seven seconds to produce them!" "On the contrary," replied the wise septuagenarian, "it took me seventy-seven years, three months, and seven seconds to produce this pot!"

In this volume, Dan Chazan tells a similar story. Early on it becomes abundantly clear to the reader that it's taken Dan all of his forty-some years to become the kind of teacher of algebra he wants to be. And even now Dan is not done. He's still learning, and proud of it. This response may be particularly perplexing for those who believe that learning to teach involves simply knowing the subject and mastering the pedagogical skills necessary to teach it. "Since algebra is such a cut-and-dried subject, isn't the teaching of algebra a particularly certain craft?" they might ask.

"Maybe not," we come to learn. Chazan helps us understand important differences between the teaching of algebra in a Jewish Day School on the East Coast and the teaching of algebra to reluctant non-college-bound high school students, such as Callie, from working-class backgrounds in Michigan. Ably abetted by his talented and experienced colleague and teacher collaborator, Sandy Bethell, Dan teaches his students—and through them also us, his readers—to conceptualize algebra as the study of functions rather than the mathematics of "*x*'s" and "*y*'s." With a few deft strokes of his brush, Chazan sketches the complexity of what it means to learn to teach algebra to diverse learners in diverse contexts. Consider the pressures of the reform aimed at giving all students access to algebra. Add to this the challenge of learning to work with other teachers in the school's mathematics department. Figure in the need to create intellectual community among teachers where it isn't always present. What's the result?

The result is that what it takes to learn to teach algebra varies as a function of the learner, the subject matter, the context, and the teacher. Philosophers John Dewey and Joseph Schwab both knew this, and they knew that good teachers continue to develop and hone their knowledge over a lifetime. Yet only rarely are we treated to such a revealing autobiographical account of what developing such knowledge means in practice. That's what Dan Chazan offers us here. It's only on rare occasions such as these that we are able to see what goes on during those years that results ultimately in something wondrous whether it be the making of a priceless pot or the learning of a function-based approach to algebra by a reluctant Callie.

Penelope L. Peterson
John Evans Professor, and Dean
School of Education and Social Policy
Northwestern University

Acknowledgments

I wish to acknowledge the support of numerous individuals and institutions that have enabled the creation of this book and the almost decade's worth of teaching, conversation, reading, analysis, and writing that have been part of this process.

A primary debt of gratitude goes to my colleagues at Michigan State University and Holt High School and to the trustees of the Dow Corning Educational Foundation. Together these three institutions, and individuals inside them, created and supported my opportunities to work simultaneously in both university and high school settings, though it often meant that I was not as good a colleague as I might have been were my attention not split in this way. I especially would like to recognize Sandra Callis Bethell, with whom I taught for 2 years. For a host of professional and pragmatic reasons, we did not write this book together (and perhaps could not have). Had we done so, the result would have been quite a different book. While I bear responsibility for this text, it provides ample evidence of the profound ways in which my thoughts about teaching have been influenced by our association.

I also greatly appreciate the support of the Spencer Foundation in recognizing this project with a postdoctoral fellowship and Michigan State University's generous interpretation of the conditions of the fellowship. This fellowship provided me with time and opportunity to revisit the teaching experience, analyzing it for lessons of import.

My thanks as well to the large number of people who have read the complete text as it evolved—from the early reading group of Sandy Bethell, Helen Featherstone, Nan Jackson, and Susan Melnick to later readers like David Cohen, Joe McDonald, David Pimm, Bill Rosenthal, Deborah Schifter, Judah Schwartz, and Michal Yerushalmy—as well as numerous others who have read selected pieces of the text and anonymous reviewers chosen by the publishers. My thanks to all of you for your criticisms, suggestions, and comments.

And, finally, to Ronit, Bob, and Sarah (and now Jonah), thank you.

Introduction

This book is grounded in the experience of teaching mathematics to high school students. I taught Algebra One to people ages 15 through 20 who had done poorly in school. Many of these students needed to pass the course in order to graduate high school; many were openly skeptical of the reverence with which the school curriculum treats mathematics.

In the context of such teaching, the phrase "unreasonable certainties," captures two important aspects of this experience. First, there is mathematics itself. We are so used to having mathematics play a central role in schooling that we forget how "unreasonable" our views of mathematics can seem to students. Here are some illustrations.

Teachers often suggest to students that mathematical knowledge is special, different. Mathematical statements do not need to be qualified in the ways in which other statements must be. In mathematics, one can say "for all" and mean exactly that, even when talking about collections that include an infinite "number" of members and cannot be surveyed in their entirety (*all* the natural numbers, *all* right triangles, etc.). Mathematics seems to have a unique way of knowing that is different from the one utilized in other fields of knowledge. In the words of mathematician Philip Davis (1986), mathematics alone is not overthrown by experience; it can "establish beyond the question of doubt":

> History does not prove, sociology does not prove, physics does not prove, philosophy does not prove, religion (if we can forget the church's unrequited seven hundred year love affair with Aristotelianism) does not prove. Mathematics alone proves, and its proofs are held to be of universal and absolute validity, independent of position, temperature or pressure. (p. 168)[1]

And yet this "study which knows nothing of observation" and is impervious to contradiction by experience is an extremely effective and useful tool in the natural sciences.[2] It is so effective that it is given a central role in the curriculum high school students are compelled to study.

But there is another facet to "unreasonable certainties" as well. We also have a remarkably stable set of beliefs about how to teach mathematics and people's potential to learn mathematics. This set of beliefs includes constructs that underlay the description of students like the ones with whom I worked as "having low ability in mathematics," or as "unwilling to do their homework and unmotivated in school."

In this book, I bring the reader face-to-face with the predicaments that Sandy Bethell, my co-teacher, and I wrestled with as teachers of Algebra One in a particular context. In doing so, I take up both intentions of the phrase "unreasonable certainties." I examine critically key constructs used when discussing the teaching and learning of mathematics (student motivation, ability, homework, real-world problems, etc.). I also use philosophical and historical writings about mathematics to challenge the views of mathematics outlined above.

Written from the perspective of the teacher—from an acceptance of responsibility for classroom instruction, not from the perspective of a classroom observer—this book focuses on relationships between teacher, student, and subject matter. It chronicles our attempts: to create a course that focused on more than just "formulas," to engage in thoughtful, non-formulaic teaching practice, and to engage students in the study of algebra by relearning it ourselves and learning to see it in the world of our students' experience. Questions I will explore include:

- Who are my students?
- What would I really like my students to learn?
- How can I develop and use understandings of the mathematics I wish to teach and of my students and their experiences to help students become intellectually engaged in our studies?
- How do stances toward knowledge influence the nature of classroom tasks and classroom modes of interaction (between teachers and students and among the students)?

The predicaments that arise in exploring these questions are not Sandy's and mine alone. I argue that they are central to the lives of many teachers in the United States. They arise when one is asked to teach subject matter in a compulsory setting to students estranged from schooling. Secondary school teachers of core academic subjects are familiar with such assignments; in tracked settings, lower-track classes are often exclusively assignments of this kind.

Like other teachers, I have found these teaching assignments painful; they cut across the grain; they challenge my sense of what it means to be a teacher. As a secondary school teacher of mathematics, I care about the subject I teach; it forms a key part of my identity. But, as a teacher, my identity and my sense of efficacy are also bound up with my students and my capacity to aid them in their development. I want to help my students learn mathematics and value themselves as thinkers, as people with reasoned opinions. Teaching core academic subject matter in a compulsory setting to students estranged from schooling challenges this self-image. From the start, students may view the teacher as enemy, rather than ally and supporter, and the subject matter as uninteresting and irrelevant. And the relationship often goes downhill from there.

The challenge of such assignments makes high school teaching uncomfortable for many people, and is sometimes cited as a reason people leave teaching. The teacher regularly has to impose authority, often in the name of the ultimate good of the student. Yet that student often has quite a different view of his or her own ultimate good. Such conflicts make it clear that, among other things, the teacher is the larger society's agent of enculturation to majority norms. As a result, on a day-to-day basis, this sort of teaching is wearing. Many teachers, as soon as they acquire seniority, leave such assignments to younger, less experienced teachers; at the same time, for a small number of teachers, such assignments become their life's blood, a personal crusade.

Appreciating the teacher's difficulty, one might nonetheless pause and suggest that the causes of the dynamics ubiquitous to these sorts of teaching assignments arguably lie outside the classroom, if not outside the school. One might suggest that efforts to change the nature of these teaching assignments must focus on the structure of schools and that little can actually be done inside the classroom.

This is not the path that I have taken. I believe that with deeper understanding of these dynamics, even within the current arrangements, there are meaningful ways for the situation of the teacher to improve. If we, as teachers, are willing to acknowledge students' skepticism about the value of the knowledge the curriculum has to offer, the teaching of seemingly elementary mathematics can become an intellectually challenging and invigorating pursuit. In the central three chapters of the book, I will illustrate how in the course of this pursuit, both mathematics itself and the history and philosophy of mathematics become important and practical resources.

Thus, this book is a nonstandard mix of analysis of classroom episodes, curricular reasoning, and mathematics itself. However, for the most part, the book does not tackle the structure of schools or of the larger educational system; it assumes the difficulties of current organizational arrangements. Such a focus is warranted in my view for two reasons. First, it seems important to address the dynamics of a kind of teaching situation that is prevalent in schools as currently organized. Unless schooling is changed radically across the United States, these dynamics will surely continue to prevail. Thus, it seems useful to understand these dynamics deeply. Second, it remains to be established whether organizational restructuring of schools (e.g., detracking, block schedules, etc.), or of schooling as a whole, would help eliminate the dynamics I have been describing. I would argue that restructuring roles and relationships inside the classroom is a crucial part of the larger organizational restructuring needed to address the central difficulties of compulsory schooling. Simply restructuring the organization of schools, while leaving intact current modes of instruction, seems unlikely to address the alienation of some students from academic knowledge.

Though, for some readers, this book will be a trip back to what may have been a bewildering, and sometimes forbidding, place—the high school algebra classroom—the focus on the teaching of algebra is particularly illuminating for three reasons. First, mathematics is a daunting subject that for many seems to resist stubbornly all attempts to find meaning and purpose. Typical experiences as students in algebra classes leave many adults wondering what algebra is, what it might be used for, and why it is deemed so important. Concentrating on interactions inside a mathematics classroom helps one appreciate the nature of the intellectual challenges the reform of teaching poses for teachers. In particular, focusing on algebra helps one realize how differently teachers need to understand their subject matter in order to provide students with the sorts of experience reformers propose.

Second, algebra offers an important context for political reasons as well: It sits astride the high school mathematics curriculum and influences students' futures. Though there are efforts to begin the study of algebra in junior high school, or even to incorporate algebraic thinking as a strand of elementary school instruction, two years of the study of algebra is currently a central component of a traditional college-intending high school mathematics education. A tremendous portion of the mathematics component of the Scholastic Admissions Test is devoted to algebra. Thus, algebra has been described as a gatekeeping course for college admissions. But, increasingly, algebra is also a gatekeeper on the road to high school graduation. In an effort to provide equal access to a college education, algebra is now being required in many U.S. school districts for high school graduation. Thus, the teaching of algebra now affects a wider range of the high school population and becomes an important factor in attempts to reform high schools.

Third, at the same time, the traditional algebra curriculum is under strong attack for creating debilitating experiences for students. With algebra, the study of mathematics becomes more "abstract" and "academic." This change presents a clear challenge for teachers who would like to engage a wide range of students, not just the college-intending, in the study of academic content. In many lower-track algebra courses, students' motivation is poor and their achievement limited; failure rates are high. In such classes, it is especially challenging to develop students' self-confidence as reasoned thinkers.

Finally, though this book involves a return to the algebra classroom, I emphasize that it is not written from the perspective of an observer, or a student. I am inviting you to return to the high school classroom and to experience the perspective of the teacher, the active subject attempting to engage students in the study of algebra. By writing from the perspective of the teacher and asking you to appreciate the situation of the teacher, I intend to highlight the magnitude of the all-too-often underestimated challenges imbedded in reformers' calls for radical changes in teaching.

For example, in my view, the task of engaging my students in the study of algebra required that I be able to help my students see algebra in the world around them. When I began teaching at Holt High School, this task required learning about a new set of students and a new context for teaching. But it also challenged me to alter fundamentally my understanding of algebra as subject matter. I entered this teaching as an experienced algebra teacher, a novice professor of teacher education, and a regular participant in conversations about mathematics education reform. However, during these 3 years of teaching lower-track Algebra One, I came to feel that my understandings of algebra were not sufficient to the task; my ability to solve algebraic problems and to teach symbolic manipulations did not help me address the issue of student classroom engagement. In order to see algebra in the world around me and to help students identify algebra in the world around them, I needed a fundamentally different understanding of the subject matter. Greater appreciation of this dimension of the teacher's task, among others, can provide a useful antidote to the tendency to criticize teachers for their "resistance" to the visions of reformers.

In order to set the stage for my most recent teaching, the book begins with a chapter that consists of three narrative descriptions of my early attempts to teach algebra, as well as contrasting material on the teaching of geometry and descriptions of experiences that led me to seek opportunities to continue to teach high school mathematics. In the first of the early attempts to teach algebra, my teaching fits a standard picture of mathematics instruction. But, even though my students were successful on standardized tests, I was uncomfortable and skeptical. I was skeptical that my students had learned much of lasting value. I was uncomfortable that they did not exercise their own judgment in the mathematics classroom. And I was unhappy with my own understanding of the subject. In retrospect, there were commitments to mathematics and to teaching as endeavors in which reasons are provided and explored that my algebra teaching, at the time, did not respect.

With my second opportunity to teach algebra, my teaching began to change. I tried a new curricular approach and began to understand how a seemingly subtle shift in curricular approach might provide an opportunity to rethink my own understanding of the subject.

The first chapter closes with a description of my first year teaching Algebra One at Holt High School, before I began to co-teach with Sandy Bethell. Here, for the first time, I was responsible for teaching students who were not intending to go to college and who were skeptical of many of the traditional rationales for taking algebra seriously. This experience forced me to question radically my own rationales for the importance of algebra in the high school curriculum. Luckily, at Holt, I had the opportunity to examine my algebra teaching with care and to work closely with Sandy and with other colleagues in this high school's mathematics department.

After the reader is introduced in greater detail to my co-teacher, Sandy Bethell, the three central chapters of the book move back and forth between analysis of lower-track secondary school mathematics teaching and description of classes that Sandy and I co-taught. In this section of the book, three sets of issues that surface in the earlier narrative—ones I argue are at the heart of algebra teaching practice—are analyzed: student engagement with academic content, revising the algebra curriculum, and the nature of discourse in the algebra classroom.

The final chapter of the text engages the question of how mathematics teachers can participate in serious and fundamental reflection on, and change of, their practice. This discussion is grounded in a set of experiences with my colleagues at Holt High School and in the departmental atmosphere they are struggling continually to (re)create.

My Algebra Teaching Autobiography

I have had three sets of opportunities to teach algebra to middle and high school students. By recounting memorable aspects of these experiences, I will indicate key dynamics of high school algebra teaching that I examine in this book. This chapter is also designed to help readers understand the sort of mathematics instruction I would like to create and to appreciate the challenges involved in developing such instruction in many lower-track classrooms.

A NORTHEASTERN SUBURBAN PRIVATE JEWISH DAYSCHOOL

My first opportunity to teach algebra in the early 1980s was in a small, kindergarten-through-ninth-grade, private Jewish dayschool in the northeastern United States. While I had no formal classes in "mathematics methods" and no state certification, the principal of the dayschool was intrigued by my desire to teach both mathematics and Judaica subjects.

My eighth grade algebra students were eager, academically driven, college-intending students. The students, their parents, and we, their teachers, all seemed to take for granted that they would go to college. They had just finished a year with a teacher who had been fired because he rarely taught mathematics. He would come to class each day and engage students in discussion of a nuclear power plant about to come on-line in a neighboring town. The students and their parents felt they had missed a year of mathematics and would be at a disadvantage on entering high school. As a result, the students were extremely motivated in my class, relieved to have a teacher who taught math. They actively questioned me, brought in problems—both conceptual and technical—and were a joy. As a result, as a first-year teacher, I was a big success; "my" students subsequently did very well on entering the local high school.

But a decade later, in the early 1990s, teaching in a lower-track Algebra One class in a public high school (Holt High School), having grown tremen-

1

dously as a teacher and spending much more time and attention preparing a more intellectually ambitious Algebra One course, I often did not feel like a "success."[1] My students often were not motivated and their performance did not exceed the lower local standards set for them. For me, the juxtaposition of these two experiences teaching algebra points to the enormous challenges facing teachers in lower-track public high school Algebra One classrooms across the United States.

This juxtaposition of teaching experiences also helps me appreciate ways in which the structure of the dayschool solved, or perhaps obscured, challenges that were later to become central in my high school teaching. The dayschool was small, private, and organized by religious affiliation. It served mostly upper-middle-class students, though there was a small number of immigrant students on scholarship. These aspects of the school played an important role in the relationships between teachers and students, and in student motivation.

For example, I'll concentrate first on the size of the school. In a small school, students had many opportunities to learn much about me and I had similar opportunities to learn much about them. In my first year, I taught different subjects to the same students; I saw how some excelled at writing papers, though they did not do as well in mathematics. Like other faculty, I acted in the school play, along with students. In my second year on the faculty, I had the opportunity, on a regular basis, to work on mathematics with all of the students in the school, K to 9. I met my students' younger siblings and knew everyone in the school by name.

Second, the school was organized around religious affiliation. While this mode of organization leads to its own tensions, it created yet other points of contact between Jewish teachers and students. As a young man, I had a bar-mitzvah, just as the eighth grade students were to have either a bar- or bat-mitzvah (according to their sex). I had gone to the same sort of summer camp; we shared a cultural background. Students could see aspects of their possible older selves in me and I could see aspects of my younger self in both the boys and the girls. Furthermore, while perhaps not true in every single individual case, in most cases I was helping students prepare for futures about which they, their parents, and their community were in agreement. All of these factors were to be quite different in my experience a decade later.

But, though these structural elements had an impact on my experiences, while teaching at the dayschool, I was not happy with the way I taught algebra. After the first year, though my students continued to be successful, I never felt the same sense of accomplishment. The eagerness of those first students had obscured the problematic nature of teaching algebra. In subsequent classes, students did not feel the same need to know algebra and did not ask me to cover two years' material in one year.

I was teaching with the famous, and at that time ubiquitous, Dolciani and

Wooten (1970/1973) Modern Algebra text.[2] I taught students to solve linear equations (Chapters 4 and 5), to factor quadratics (Chapter 7), and to graph functions and relations (Chapter 10), and three methods for solving systems of linear equations (Chapter 11)—content still familiar to algebra teachers throughout the United States. I felt that I was teaching a course focused mainly on manipulation of symbols.

That, in and of itself, was not necessarily the problem. The problem was the ways in which these manipulations were treated. First, the rationale for our work together was always future-directed; our activity was not inherently valuable. The manipulations that I was teaching my students were included in the course because they were methods to be deployed in the solving of other problems, problems more important than the ones we were doing, problems my students would encounter in the future. For the sake of achieving mastery of component skills, the manipulations I was teaching had been disconnected from the context of later mathematical activity that would call for them.

But one then had to justify our classroom work to the students. The text attempted to do so at the start of each chapter. Here are some selections (Dolciani & Wooten, 1970/1973):

Chapter 1: Mathematics, the language of science, is the language of dreamers who plan to achieve their dreams. . . . The algebra that you will learn in this course is one of the essential foundations for the theories on which space travel is based. (p. 1)

Chapter 4: In this chapter you will study how to solve an equation by transforming it into a simpler equivalent equation. You will then be able to solve a number of interesting problems. (p. 111)

Chapter 6: You are now ready to learn how to perform operations with expressions called polynomials. You will then use these new techniques in the solution of problems more complicated than those you have solved up to now. (p. 205).

Chapter 13: As in the study of a language, mathematics becomes more interesting after the basic skills have been acquired. You will find this to be true in this chapter where you will study about quadratic equations and inequalities. With such open sentences you will increase your power to solve problems. (p. 495).

Chapter 14: As you look into your own future, can you see the role mathematics may play in it? Space engineers require a knowledge of mathematics greater than that you now possess. They did not learn their mathematics as part of their jobs. They learned it in order to get their jobs. Since many occupations which are challenging require a knowledge of mathematics, you should plan to include it in your education. (p. 523).

I was asking students to trust me; they had no way to understand why these manipulations might be considered useful or important, or how they fit into some larger mathematical activity. They had to take my word, and the authors' word, that their power to solve problems was increasing, and that this was important.

Also, as a result of this future-oriented argumentation, there was little room for students to be active as learners and to question what was being taught. They were expected to master the algorithms I was teaching. Setting aside questions about the purpose of our joint activity, they were not expected to wonder whether there were other potential methods to solve a particular problem. They were to reproduce faithfully the algorithms taught in the text. We were involved in what critics often call "rote manipulation," although the teacher's guide exhorted me to

> maintain a proper balance of emphasis on technique and on the ideas behind it. . . . Students must have the triple goal of learning "what you do," "how you do it," and "why you do it." (Dolciani & Wooten, 1970/1973, p. 37)

I did not think the text gave me the resources to do so. I thought my instruction focused almost exclusively on "how you do it."

A student, whom I'll call David, made this clear to me. He helped me understand that my teaching, at that time, focused on how you do it, and not what we were doing or why. David was a bright and often cheeky student; we had lots of contact—in fact, we ended up singing a duet in the school play. At the time, he was a short eighth grader concerned about whether he would ever grow. He was frequently disheveled and not well organized; his papers were incredibly difficult to read. In algebra, his sloppiness often created difficulties for him. He misplaced signs or could not read his own writing.

David was also an avid computer buff and had an Apple II at home. Since I was the person who coordinated use of the Apple IIs at school, David would often show me programs that he had at home and implore me to let him use the computers during school time to play video-type games. After doing poorly on an algebra test, he bought, with his parents' consent, a program to drill himself on algebra problems. The program presented an equation to solve. If the user solved the equation correctly, a video display showed flying machines of some kind being exploded by "ground artillery." After using the program at home and improving his grades, he brought the program to school and asked me if we could use the program instead of having class. He knew that, philosophically, I did not appreciate drill-and-practice computer programs, but he thought that as an algebra teacher I would endorse the program that helped improve his performance.

My conversations with David made me feel that, though they did not ask, my students wondered what it (algebra, the class) was all about. They had no broader picture of the competencies they were supposed to develop and how those might be a part of their lives, at present or in the future. Worse yet, I realized that I did not have good ideas about this myself. Their desire to have good grades, to please their parents, and to go to college kept them working at algebra. But, even though in the end they tested well by conventional standards, for me, the exercise of teaching them algebra often seemed futile and pointless. I was pretty sure that they had actually learned very little of enduring value.

I had another concern as well: I was uncomfortable with the roles the students and I had in the classroom. That said, my instruction was typical for a mathematics class. Each day, students would do a homework set that involved a series of similar problems. Students would bring their homework to class and we would "go over" problems that I thought were important or that had caused them trouble. They knew that we needed to go over a problem if they could not make headway on it or if they got an answer that was different from the answer key. Then I would introduce the new material covered in the next section, do some practice problems from that section, and assign the next night's homework. Students would usually have time to work on their homework assignment in class with my help, a very typical use of class time (see Borasi, 1992, p. 179, for a similar characterization of typical instruction).

The text and I were the authorities. The conversation, if it can be called that, was stunted. It all came through me. I told students what was right and what was wrong. That said, I did try to spice up class sessions; I sometimes tried to explain or justify why things worked in a particular way. I remember a lesson that the principal came to observe. I wanted students to understand the idea of a function machine. I had one student be the machine (they would tell me their rule) and the other students would file "through" the machine, saying their "input" and receiving the related "output." Students seemed to have fun making up rules and guessing them. I was able to use this lesson to help students appreciate the difference between functions and relations as described in the text.

While I often worked up explanations and illustrations of this kind, we did not have discussions and never strayed far from the text. Students did not even have to listen carefully to each other's questions, though sometimes they did so—not so much to learn from each other, but more often to help a friend get an answer.

As I contrasted my mathematics teaching with my teaching of other subjects, I was concerned that in the mathematics classroom students did less independent thinking and that discourse was more heavily teacher-centered. As has been the case in many mathematics classes (Welch, 1978), students constantly looked to me as the authority to tell them right from wrong; their questions were chiefly about what to do when they were stuck. In other classes, the same students trusted their own judgment and experience and were willing to question my views. In mathematics, when we were focused on the content, we did not have real conversations very often; at most there was a tutorial form of dialogue. In other classes, there were conversations: students talked to the group, not just to me. Ironically, given traditional arguments for the ways in which mathematics improves people's reasoning skills and critical faculties, when contrasted with other classes, my mathematics classes did not seem like a context that would foster such faculties or skills.

I wondered whether the difference in discourse patterns was a simple reflection of the nature of the subject matter. In traditional school instruction, there is a strong dichotomy between matters of opinion or interpretation and knowledge. According to this view, given the nature of the material, it is natural to see differences between classes. Algebra is not about interpretation; algebra is about facts. In mathematics classes, students' statements are either "right" or "wrong." In my other classes, students' interpretation of a text was rarely "wrong"; instead, if it was "off the mark," it was "unlikely" or "unconvincing."

I also wondered whether the differences I was noticing were somehow intrinsically linked to different subject matters and their role in schooling. Acceptance to college would be influenced by students' scores on a multiple-choice mathematics test. Maybe this explained the difference. But neither of these potential explanations made teaching mathematics feel any better.

An Illustration of My Teaching at This Time

To illustrate how I taught mathematics at this time, I'll examine, in some detail, how I taught one lesson in Chapter 10 on page 380 of the Dolciani and Wooton (1970/1973) text, a lesson titled "Determining an Equation of a Line." Though this example may bring back painful memories for some readers, I think it is important to illustrate the kind of teaching I used to do (which is still prevalent in many algebra classrooms). Though I will do my best to explicate the method that I taught, the details of the method are not crucial. It is more important to characterize the kind of teaching that I did at this time and the nature of the tasks students faced.

I am choosing the skill of writing an equation of a line through two points as an illustration of my teaching at this time because of its continued importance in school mathematics; it appears even in algebra textbooks that downplay the manipulation of symbols. (For example, this method appears in the University of Chicago School Mathematics Program's algebra text, McConnell et al., 1990.) Perhaps it continues to appear because, in statistics and in analytic geometry, students are expected to be able to write the equation of a line through two points. But in my early teaching, like many other mathematics teachers, I did not help students learn why this skill is considered important in school mathematics. I did not teach students how this line represents a constant rate of change, let alone help them examine purposes for writing the equations of lines. I just taught the method.

To be more specific, we did not explore how, if one assumes a constant rate of growth, a line can be used to interpolate or extrapolate from two data points—representing the coordinated values of two quantities—and make predictions. We did not discuss, for example, how this kind of extrapolation is routinely used in surveys for predicting some characteristic of a population based on responses of a small sample.

why!

This kind of assumption of linearity to make predictions is made in other situations as well. Perhaps an example will clarify. If we are given two measurements of the length of an infant, one on its 7th day and one on its 21st day, it seems natural to try to compute the rate at which the baby is growing—the average number of inches it is growing per day—by taking the total amount of growth and dividing it by the number of days elapsed. We can use the resulting number to interpolate—to determine likely lengths of the infant on intervening days—and to extrapolate—to predict the likely length of the baby in the future.

In computing this growth rate and using it to make predictions, we have made some important assumptions. Recent research, and much folk wisdom, suggests that infants grow in spurts (a large amount of growth one day and almost no growth another), that this process is not even constant across a week's time. Yet we are deciding to assume that babies' growth in length can be approximated with a constant rate. In doing so, it is as if we are saying "Don't bother me with the day-to-day details." We imagine a situation in which babies grow at a constant rate. We postulate the equal sharing of change in length across equally sized units of time, even though we know this is not true. We hope that the predictions that we make using this strategy will be "close enough." I did not talk about this sort of prediction in my class or debate with students when it might be used profitably, and when it might be inappropriate.

Also, I am struck, in retrospect, by the complexity of the method I taught. The reasons that this complex method works seem quite complicated. It is also striking to me that I taught only one method and had no alternatives.

Background to the Method. Before presenting the complicated method I used to teach, for those who have not been thinking about algebra recently, I'll begin with some background. In traditional algebra instruction, students do most of their work with x's and y's. But there is another mathematical representation that also appears, graphs (straight lines and curves) in the Cartesian, or x-y, plane. Points in the Cartesian plane are located and named with a pair of numbers or coordinates that represent their "signed" horizontal and vertical distance from a point of origin. For the points (5, 2) and (2, −1) in the Cartesian plane, the first numbers represent right/left "signed" distance from the point of origin and the second numbers the up/down distance from that point.

The Cartesian plane and the x's and y's of algebra are linked in the following way: x's stand for the first coordinate (the right/left distance from the origin) and the y's stand for the second coordinate. Thus, an equation in x's and y's can represent a graph. In particular, when a straight line graph is described in the Cartesian plane, students are taught to write its "equation" (commonly, if superficially, defined by its form as a symbol string with one equal sign). In teaching this lesson from Dolciani and Wooton's (1970/1973) text, I taught students how to find the equation in "slope-intercept" form for the line through two points in a Cartesian plane (e.g., Find the equation of the line through the points (5, 2) and (2, −1)).

For the line through the points (5, 2) and (2, −1), the expected equation would be $y = x − 3$. This equation is related to the line in the following sense: All the paired values of x and y that make this equation a true statement are the coordinates of points along this line; if you subtract three from the x-coordinate, you get the y-coordinate. Most important in terms of the goal of the problem, 2 is equal to $5 − 3$ and −1 is equal to $2 − 3$, so both (5, 2) and (2, −1) lie on the line (see Figure 1.1).

The Method. Given the coordinates of two points—I will continue to use (5, 2) and (2, −1) as an example—students were to go through four steps, one of which is downplayed in the text. This four-step procedure (see Figure 1.2) involves other procedures taught in different chapters in the book.

First, in the downplayed step, students were expected to realize that they were being asked to write an equation for a line in the "slope-intercept form," $y = mx + b$. For readers not fluent with this terminology, in this form, m stands for the slope of the line. The word *slope* describes the graph visually in terms of rise and run; a steeper line has more "rise" per unit of "run." But this number also represents the rate of change of y in terms of change in x. Typically, slope is reported as a ratio, rise/run; creating this ratio and carrying out the division allows one to compare different lines by finding the amount of rise for one unit of run. b stands for the value of y-coordinate of the point where the line crosses the y-axis, the "y-intercept" of the line (see Figure 1.3).[3] x and y for their respective coordinates for the points on the line described by the equation. Thus, this form is the "slope intercept form," or more appropriately "the slope y-intercept form." (See Chazan, 1995, for consideration of two other forms for writing linear functions.)

Students were to choose this form, even though the two given points do not automatically provide information on the slope and the y-intercept, because the slope-intercept form had been introduced in the previous section. Earlier in

Figure 1.1. Representing $y = x - 3$.

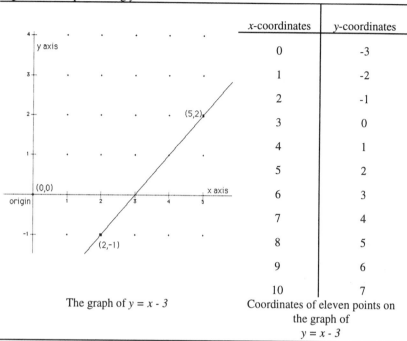

	x-coordinates	y-coordinates
	0	-3
	1	-2
	2	-1
	3	0
	4	1
	5	2
	6	3
	7	4
	8	5
	9	6
	10	7

The graph of $y = x - 3$

Coordinates of eleven points on
the graph of
$y = x - 3$

the chapter a different form of an equation for a line had been given, but that form (which in this case would give the equation $-x + y = -3$) was not to be used here.

Second, students were to compute the slope from the information given about the two points, a task familiar from earlier in the chapter. They were to do this by subtracting the y-coordinates of the two points to get the total rise ($2 - -1 = 3$), subtracting the x-coordinates ($5 - 2 = 3$) to get the total run, and then creating a ratio of rise/run ($3/3 = 1$). So m, the slope, is equal to one; along this line for every one unit of run the graph rises one unit. Since, in my teaching at the time, all of this work to compute the slope was being done without a graph, students did not use visual strategies, like counting over, for determining rise, run, and slope.

The third step, finding the y-intercept, which regularly confused my day-school students, was not justified in the text and is difficult to explain succinctly. At this point in the method, the slope has been determined, but the y-intercept has not been. In the Cartesian plane, the book's strategy is the equivalent of fixing a line through one of the two points with the correct slope and then

Figure 1.2. Finding the equation of a line.

EXAMPLE. **Find an equation of the line which passes through the points whose coordinates are (5, 2) and (2, −1).**

Solution: **1. Slope $= m = \dfrac{-1-2}{2-5} = \dfrac{-3}{-3} = 1$**

2. The slope-intercept form of the equation is $y = mx + b$. Thus:

$$y = 1x + b$$

Choose one point, say (5, 2). Since it lies on the line:

$$2 = 1 \cdot 5 + b, \quad \text{or} \quad 2 = 5 + b$$

$$\therefore \ -3 = b.$$

3. To check, show that the coordinates of the other point (2, −1) satisfy the equation:

$$y = x - 3$$
$$-1 \stackrel{?}{=} 2 - 3$$
$$-1 = -1 \ \checkmark$$

$\therefore$ an equation of the line is $y = x - 3$.   Answer.

Reprinted with permission from Dolciani & Wooton (1970/73)

---

determining where it crosses the *y*-axis (where the *x*-coordinate is 0). In order to determine the *y*-intercept, students were to take the form $y = mx + b$, substitute the value of the slope and the coordinates of one of the points, and create an equation in *b* (e.g., $2 = 1 * 5 + b$). They were then supposed to solve this equation for *b* (in this case, by subtracting five from both sides).[4] Having in this way determined the *y*-intercept, they were supposed to take the final value for *b* (−3) and substitute it into the *y*-intercept slot in the equation, while reintroducing *x* and *y* into their slots, giving the equation $y = 1 * x - 3$.

Finally, students were to check that this equation worked by substituting the coordinates of the second point and verifying that the equation worked. In this case, −1 is indeed equal to $1 * 2 - 3$.

Figure 1.3. Slope and *y*-intercept.

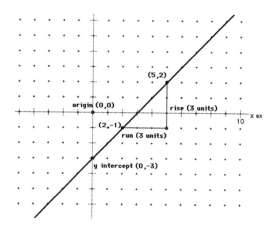

Reflection on This Illustration. What does the long exposition of my teaching of this method tell us about the nature of my dayschool students' experience of algebra? I suggest that teaching this procedure in this way fits with what Richard Skemp (1976) calls an instrumental view of mathematics. In this view, mathematics is a set of procedures (some of which are complicated) that must be mastered (not understood) for solving problems whose origin and purpose are not available to students.

For some of my students there seemed to be a feeling of accomplishment associated with mastering such procedures, but for many, learning this procedure was frustrating. The procedure is long; it is hard to keep the goal in mind as you tackle one of the subtasks. The students had mastered the skills required to solve the subtasks one at a time when we "covered" them, but usually had forgotten each skill just a few short weeks later. Their skills did not accumulate and become linked into the larger routines needed to solve more advanced problems like finding the equation of a line through two points. Furthermore, at each step, there are reasons to wonder why this method works or how anyone ever invented or discovered it.

In class, I would spend a few days helping students gain limited (and I might add short-lived) mastery of this procedure. But I did not engage students in an examination of purposes one might have for determining an equation for a line between two points.

needs to be addressed

We also did not talk about the difference between solving for a coefficient, or parameter (as in the third step), and the solving of equations "for x" that they had done before. In my teaching at that time, this complex procedure was taught divorced from the reasons that it works and consideration of anything but the textbook exercise of generating an equation for points in the Cartesian plane that were not intended as representations of other quantities.[5]

An Opportunity for Change

In my third and final year of teaching at this school, though I still did not know how to change the nature of the rationale for student engagement, I began to see how conversations in the mathematics classroom might be different, how I might be able to create a more student-centered classroom. I heard about a project that was looking for teachers willing to pilot the use of a new piece of software then under development for teaching geometry classes. I had a small class and access to a small number of Apple II computers; I decided to try and was encouraged by what I saw. While algebra class was still the same, we had more interesting conversations in geometry class. This difference was illuminating.

The Geometric Supposer (Schwartz et al., 1985; Schwartz & Yerushalmy, 1990) was developed to facilitate students' development of conjectures (or what George Polya, noted mathematician and mathematics educator, calls "educated guesses") by providing them with opportunities to explore geometrical constructions empirically, with measurement of particular cases. The notion underlying the design of the software is that access to the drawing and measurements provided by the computer helps students evaluate their own ideas. Rather than waiting for a text or a teacher to indicate that an idea is right or wrong, students can use exploration of particular cases to discover counterexamples that support or refute their ideas. If there are no counterexamples, there is good reason to think that the idea is true and to try to understand why by writing a deductive proof. Furthermore, students' opportunity to work with many diagrams on a regular basis can help develop their facility with diagrams. (For an examination of this claim, see Yerushalmy & Chazan, 1990.)

By examining diagrams and at measurements, my students were able to decide what relationships they thought were true for a particular construction. This had a big impact on our conversations in class. For example, I once asked students to draw one median, two medians, and then three medians in a triangle (a median is a segment from a vertex or corner to the midpoint of the opposite side, see Figure 1.4) and record conjectures they had about relationships between elements in the resulting diagrams. I did not hold out great hopes for the part of the problem about one median, but included it since they would have to pass through that stage in making the other medians.

Figure 1.4. Drawing medians in a triangle.

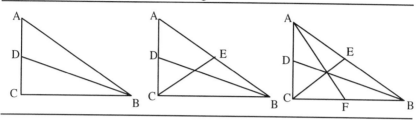

The students developed their own ideas, which we then discussed. Students had different ideas. One student, whom I'll call Rachel, had an idea that I had not seen before. Based on the triangle inequality that we had studied before (that the sum of the lengths of two sides of a triangle is always more than the length of the third side), she developed an argument, different from the proof in our book, that the length of any median to a side in any triangle is less than half the sum of the lengths of the other two sides (in Figure 1.5 the length of AD is less than half the sum of the lengths of AB and AC).

She doubled the median and extended it out past the side of the original triangle. I do not know what made her think to do that. When I asked, she could not really explain. She noticed that if she connected the endpoint of the extension to the vertices of the original triangle, she got a parallelogram (see Figure 1.6). If ABEC is a parallelogram, then its opposite sides (e.g., AC and BE or AB and CE) have equal lengths.

Then she looked at the diagram in a different way. She imagined that the parallelogram was split into two triangles by the segment AE; she focused on

Figure 1.5. One median in a triangle.

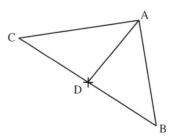

Figure 1.6. Extending the median to draw a parallelogram.

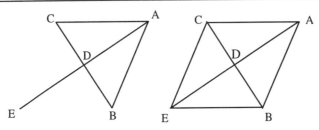

these two triangles that share the segment AE (the median and its extension). Each of these triangles has two sides whose lengths are the same as the two sides of the original triangle; the third side in each of these triangles is AE. So, by the theorem we had studied earlier, the triangle inequality, the length of AE, which is twice the length of the median (AD), has to be less than the sum of the lengths of AB and AC.

Needless to say, it took a lot of explanation on her part for us to follow her. Along the way, other students asked her questions. One asked her how she knew that ABEC had to be a parallelogram. She said that she could tell by measurements that it always was, but she could not prove it (we had not yet studied the diagonals of quadrilaterals).

I was very pleased with this interaction among the students; it felt like there was a real conversation; the students talked to each other, about mathematics, and not just to me. The contrast with my algebra class was stark.

In search of more knowledge about mathematics education, a better personal understanding of the school curriculum, and other ways to change the nature of classroom interaction, the following year I went off to graduate school. In graduate school, among other experiences, I had further opportunities to think about the teaching of Euclidean geometry with the aid of computer technology.

A SHORT STINT IN A NORTHEASTERN
SUBURBAN PUBLIC HIGH SCHOOL

My second opportunity to teach algebra came in the late 1980s, after completing a doctoral program in education, during which I student-taught geometry classes in an urban high school and was certified to teach in public schools. In a suburban high school in an affluent community, I taught two sections of Algebra Two, while holding another half-time job. At this high school, there were three tracks of Algebra Two. I taught one class in the middle track and one class in the lowest track.

While my classes were in two different tracks, regardless of track, almost all of these students, including the African-American students voluntarily bused from the city, were college bound, many to very exclusive private colleges and universities. Most took initiative in academic matters—they volunteered in classroom discussions, did homework regularly, brought in questions about parts of the homework they did not understand, and followed up by coming to see me individually during their "free periods" for extra help.

Just as in the dayschool teaching, the structure of schooling in this community shielded me as a teacher from many of the realities of teaching in many public school settings, particularly from issues of student motivation. Though in this setting I did not know my students as well as I did in the dayschool, there were still ample opportunities to meet them as individuals. Students had free periods; they were trusted with an open-campus policy and could come and go as they pleased. As a result, even though I was only on school grounds for three class periods a day, most of my students were able to find me for individual conversations. In addition, each student had a mailbox for personal communications and was responsible for checking this mailbox regularly.

The expectation in this community was that schooling was vital to students' future opportunities. There was much conversation in the halls among 10th and 11th graders about school applications, PSATs, and the like. Students were interested in learning where I had gone to college and graduate school and what that experience had been like for me. Once again, there were commonalities between me and the students. Even though we did not share as much as I had shared with the students at the dayschool, we nonetheless had much common ground.

As a text for the Algebra Two classes, we used pre-publication versions of what was then the new University of Chicago School Mathematics Program's (UCSMP) *Advanced Algebra* text being piloted at the high school (the published version of this text is Senk et al., 1990). We also trekked down to the business wing of the school about once a week to use two computer programs that had just been published, *Visualizing Algebra: The Function Analyzer* (Schwartz, Yerushalmy, & Educational Development Center, 1988) and *The Function Supposer: Explorations in Algebra* (Schwartz, Yerushalmy, & Educational Development Center, 1989). It was this use of technology, in fact, that had gotten me the job. By hiring me, the school hoped I would bring to their attention new uses of microcomputers in high school mathematics teaching.

My work with technology was part of what made me an attractive candidate to the school, but it also was part of what led me to seek this teaching position. My experience during graduate school made me want to go back into the classroom as a teacher. During graduate school, I had opportunities to observe the development of educational software. In my experience, when developing technology-based educational innovations, developers initially concentrate on software and accompanying print materials; little attention is paid to the developments in teaching and the teacher learning necessary to support the use of these innovations (though not all technological innovations equally require substantive changes in teaching). Once a product is on the market, there is pressure to evaluate its effectiveness. Since innovations are evaluated by their impact on student learning, development is quickly followed by evaluation of student learning.

But the quick move to the evaluation of student learning assumes that the work of development ends with the creation of the tool, that implementing a curricular change supported by a technological tool is an uncomplicated task requiring no further developmental effort. Four years of working with teachers attempting to introduce the use of *The Geometric Supposer* (Schwartz et al., 1985) into their classrooms, once the software and support materials were already in existence, convinced me that there was serious and challenging intellectual work in developing teaching practices to make use of this software. To explain my desire to develop teaching practices by teaching myself, I'll use the example of teaching geometry to illustrate the intellectual challenges that I see in developing teaching practices.

An Intellectual Challenge for the Teacher: Measuring Diagrams in Geometry Class

What developmental work remained once *The Geometric Supposer* (Schwartz et al., 1985) and support materials had been written? For one thing, we had to conceptualize the role of student exploration within the context of a high school Euclidean geometry course. Traditional deductive geometry teaching practice is focused on justification of results and has no conceptualization of the role of measurement of diagrams in teaching and learning. According to a rationalist philosophy of mathematics, mathematics is not about the objects of everyday experience and is independent of nature (Nagel, 1956, takes this position, while Tymoczko, 1986, is a collection that critiques this philosophical position). Thus, geometry teachers teach that diagrams are illustrations, not evidence for or against a theorem. This view is widespread. For example, Israel Scheffler (1965), a noted philosopher of science and philosopher of education, takes this view for granted in an introductory text on knowledge in teaching:

> Should precise measurement of the diagram show that it failed to embody the relations asserted by the theorem, the latter would not be falsified. We should rather say that the physical diagram was only an approximation or a suggestion of the truth embodied in the theorem. (p. 3)

Following along with this point of view, geometry texts have limited numbers of diagrams and only in texts written for courses that deemphasize deductive proof (usually known by the title Informal Geometry) are students ever asked to measure a diagram.[6]

This sort of teaching practice, however, overlooks the value that measuring diagrams may have in the discovery or creation of conjectures, rather than in their justification. Yet simply including the measurement of examples as a technique to help students derive their own ideas is not sufficient. There are different schools of thought on the importance of the particular in mathematical practice and on the relationship of the particular to the general in the development of new ideas, which is sometimes known as the problem of induction (see Frank, 1957; Goodman, 1978). How does a teacher help students develop their own conjectures from the examination and measurement of diagrams? Do people create ideas by collecting reams of data and then discerning patterns in this data or does the very decision to collect certain data stem from an underlying hunch? (For two discussions of this issue, see Frank, 1957, and Lakatos, 1976, especially pp. 73–74.) Conceptualizing the role of measurement of examples in geometry classrooms involves one in thorny issues related to the nature of mathematical creativity.

The presence of such thorny issues in the development of teaching interested me. By definition, the sort of developmental work that responds to such questions must be undertaken in the midst of teaching, in the classroom, in the interaction between students, teachers, and the curriculum of schooling. Influenced by Magdalene Lampert's pioneering work on mathematics teaching (1985, 1990) and her desire to find ways to do research on one's own evolving teaching practice (1998), I was looking for an opportunity to teach and to reflect on that teaching. I wanted an opportunity to be back in the classroom and not merely working with others who were teaching.

The work with *The Geometric Supposer* (Schwartz et al., 1985) added another aspect to the mix: It influenced my preferences for the type of class I would teach. Some teachers teaching with *The Geometric Supposer* in "lower-track classrooms" insisted that innovations involving exploration and conjecturing were not appropriate for their classes because of their students' "ability." They claimed that their students did not have the "skills" to work independently and to come up with their own conjectures. I wanted to understand this issue, and their perspective, by placing myself in their circumstances, by working with students who had been less successful in school mathematics. I was curious about the notion of "ability" in mathematics.

However, I was eager to teach algebra and not geometry. For 4 years I had concentrated on geometry, one of the classes that I taught at the dayschool. I remembered my frustrations with the lack of conversation in my algebra class and with the feeling that I did not know what algebra was about, that I did not truly have a conceptual understanding of the subject. I had long discussions with Michal Yerushalmy and Judah Schwartz, the creators of *The Geometric Supposer* (Schwartz et al., 1985), about ideas for reworking the algebra curriculum. Though Michal and Judah have a particular perspective, the ideas we discussed are often referred to as "a functions-based approach to algebra." Ideas of this sort have been around in some senses for many years (see, for example, discussions in Fehr, 1951; Hamley, 1934; van Barneveld & Krabbendam, 1982); they have recently been explored at the secondary and tertiary levels by many researchers, particularly by researchers interested in the use of technology in mathematics education. (Here are a small number of key references: Confrey & Smith, 1995; Demana & and Waits, 1990; Goldenberg, 1988; Heid, 1996; Kieran, Boileau, & Garancon, 1996; Moschkovich, Schoenfeld, & Arcavi, 1993; Nemirovsky, 1996; Schwartz & Yerushalmy, 1992; Sfard & Linchevski, 1994; Thompson, 1994; Yerushalmy & Gilead, 1997.) They have also been critiqued as driven by a focus on the capacities of technology and not the needs of instruction (Pimm, 1995). I wanted to explore these ideas in my teaching of the two sections of Algebra Two in the northeastern suburban public high school.

My First Attempt to Teach Algebra Differently

Though this opportunity to teach algebra did not last as many years as my opportunity at the dayschool, my initial attempts to explore a "functions-based" approach to algebra suggested that these ideas had potential. This potential was most evident in the roles students played in classroom discussions after they used the *Visualizing Algebra* and *The Function Supposer* software that Yerushalmy and Schwartz had developed to support their ideas (Schwartz et al., 1988, 1989). I'll illustrate with an example of a conclusion a student developed one day in class.

We had been studying linear expressions, like the ones described in my teaching at the dayschool. This class of expressions—when an implicit output variable (the classic y) is added and when x is interpreted as a variable that can take on a range of values—can be represented as a straight line in the Cartesian plane. For example, $2x + 10$ is the symbolic representation of the procedure "Take an input number (whatever it might be, x for example), multiply it by 2, and then add 10 to the result." When you make a graph of the relationship between the numbers used as inputs (x) and the numbers that result as outputs (y), one gets a straight line in the Cartesian input-by-output plane (see Figure 1.7). For this example, 2, the number the input is multiplied by, is known as the slope, the ratio of rise (change in outputs) over run (change in inputs). It describes a feature of the input-output relationship that can be seen in the graphed line. If one starts from any particular input-output pair along this line and moves

Figure 1.7. The Cartesian graph of $y = 2x + 10$.

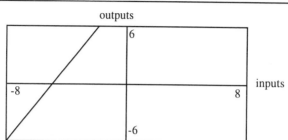

along the line to another point whose input is one unit larger, the output value for this new point will have increased by 2. For other linear expressions in this form—where you have some number times x and then add another number ($ax + b$)— the number that multiplies x, the coefficient of x, a, is the slope.

We moved on to study nonlinear expressions, among them $4x^2$, which as a procedure means "Start with an input number and multiply it times itself, then multiply the result by 4." I took the students to the computer laboratory and students created tables of values and graphs for each expression on a list of 23 expressions. To learn what the students saw in the graphs the computer generated, I had the students group the expressions by the kinds of graphs they created. The students noted that some were straight lines and others were curves. For example, the shape of the graph of $4x^2$ (see Figure 1.8) was curved; $4x^2$ is not a linear expression. I asked them to work on explaining why this expression does not give a straight line.

As the session was ending and I was assigning homework from the text, one of the students asked me if expressions like $4x^2$ have a slope. Since the graph was not a straight line, he was not sure whether it had a slope or not. The question warmed my heart. He was taking slope as a property of a class of expressions and, now that he was investigating a new class of expressions, he wondered whether this new class would have a similar property.

In some ways, there is a straightforward answer to his question. Slope as a single number is a property of straight lines, not curves; having a "slope" could be one way to define what it means for a "line" to be straight as opposed to curved. On the other hand, mathematicians have generalized what one might mean by slope to talk more generally of rates of change. For a curved line, like the graph of x^2, they define the slope at a point (the rate of change at that point) to be the slope of the straight line that is just tangent to the curve at that point.

Figure 1.8. A graph of $y = 4x^2$.

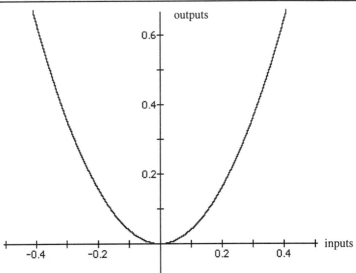

By their definition, a curved line has slope, but the slope changes as one moves along the curve. But that is calculus, and this was Algebra Two.

I decided that the students could benefit by thinking about this question of what the slope of a curved line is or could be. I suggested they give it some thought. Some of the students thought maybe the slope of $4x^2$ should be 4; after all, the 4 seems to be in the same sort of place as the 2 had been in the linear expressions—it is in front of the x.

The next day, I came back to this question and used x^2, "Take a number and multiply it times itself," as the example for discussion. A student whom I'll call Alexander said he had an answer. He explained that he thought that the slope of x^2 was x. After trying to explain his reasoning verbally, he came to the board and argued that he was going to put x^2 into the same form as a linear expression, some number times x plus some other number; for x^2 he argued this was $x * x + 0$, with the first x as the coefficient of the second x. So x was now the slope. He said this made sense to him because in a curved line, the slope is always changing—again, a comment that warms the heart of a mathematics teacher. For Alexander, the form of an expression had some meaning; he used this form to make an argument. I had never heard anything like his explanation. In a purely technical sense, he is wrong,[7] but that misses the boat. He has an extremely important insight. Besides, in class, a student had raised a good mathematical question and another student thought about it overnight, used what we had learned in class, and came back with a response. This was especially gratifying since Alexander, though he often did well on tests, was not someone who did his homework. He had been interested in this problem; later he told me that he had been thinking about it on and off all day.

Still, I was dissatisfied. As this anecdote illustrates, I made some progress in having students' play a central role in conversations around students' explorations with *Visualizing Algebra* series (Schwartz et al., 1988, 1989). But there was little conversation when we discussed problems from the textbook. As a result of a formative experience in graduate school, a seminar called Teaching and Learning, I was not content with the nature of the discourse around textbook problems.

A Graduate School Experience and Its Classroom Ramifications

When I took a course named Teaching and Learning, Eleanor Duckworth illustrated how difficult it is to understand the thoughts of others—a key part of the ongoing assessment of student learning with which teachers are always engaged—and how rewarding this attempt can be. To illustrate, she carried out model interviews of young people in front of the class. (For a description of this use of a clinical interview, see Duckworth, 1987, especially "Understanding Children's Understanding.") In these often hour-long interviews, she modeled "giving children reason" by using carefully crafted tasks and questions to elicit their thinking (p. 86, this phrase is attributed to a teacher). Following up on children's responses to the tasks, over the course of the interview, she uncovered the underlying conceptions they held. When I took this course, I was amazed to see phenomena described by Piaget in his research (e.g., Inhelder & Piaget, 1958) take place in front of my eyes, with American children. I was struck by the coherence that lay behind what were often incorrect first answers and the time that it took to elicit these responses. I later had the opportunity to do interviews myself and to practice eliciting people's thinking, as opposed to helping them reach "correct" answers, a difficult task for one, like me, used to teacher-centered "teaching."

Duckworth's seminar also shook the faith I had, as a teacher, in language. It helped me focus on ways language does not communicate meaning with perfect fidelity. She asked us, as a class, to work on understanding the motion of the moon—a complex phenomenon to which few have ever given serious thought (Duckworth, 1987; the chapter titled "Learning with Breadth and Depth" describes her use of the study of the moon). Furthermore, she insisted that we not use complicated technical vocabulary. This sort of vocabulary might intimidate some and might substitute for clear communication and deep understanding. I was impressed by the numerous "aha" experiences that seemed to result from the avoidance of technical terminology.

My faith in language as a tool for communication was particularly shaken by an experience interviewing some friends about the poem "Ozymandius" by Shelley. In this poem, a traveler describes a scene viewed on a journey in the desert. Before dinner, I interviewed a close friend about the poem and I thought I understood the scene in the poem as she described it. It matched my reading of the poem. I imagined pieces of a large sculpture fallen in the desert, half-covered by sand.

I then interviewed two other friends and they described in great detail the large abandoned pieces of the sculpture and what they looked like. I was amazed by the similarities between their description and that of the first interviewee. I was astounded, and a bit disappointed, that all of us should understand the poem so similarly.

During their description, the first interviewee walked by. After listening for a moment, she said that she had been thinking of a completely different scene.

> *First I*: See I guess that basically one of the things that I differed on was my perception of what the scope of the statue was, its size, its magnitude. I thought "two vast and trunkless legs of stone" that those weren't necessarily legs. They were pillars. Not necessarily legs of the statue. Just pillars of the area of where the statue is. And that it's not like there is this huge thing of these huge enormous legs. And this huge head lying in the sand. . . . I thought that it was just a much smaller scale. It's a statue that he happened to come upon.
>
> *Second I*: But it says vast.
>
> *First I*: Well, I tend to think of pillars being vast, as opposed to legs. I took it much more figuratively "legs of stone." The legs I thought were pillars. . . .

To her, the sculpture was small. It was inside a structure whose pillars remained standing. I was shocked by how badly I had misunderstood her.

This experience shook me. I wondered how well I understood what my students said to me in my mathematics classes. In class, students have much less time to speak, much shorter conversation turns. They have to express themselves in a small number of words and use mathematical terms that are unfamiliar to them. Here I had spent over an hour interviewing a close friend about a poem, without using any technical language. The interviewee had ample time to express her thoughts. Yet I completely misunderstood her.

My experiences in this seminar convinced me that it is much harder to understand what a speaker really has in mind than standard teaching practice would lead one to think. I was astounded by the diversity of thought revealed beneath the surface of seemingly transparent conversations about agreed-upon notions. The experience left me wondering how to find out what my students were really thinking about in class.

So when I began the Algebra Two teaching, I had ideas about the kinds of conversations I wanted to have in the classroom. I wanted to teach classes in which student thinking was central and the norm was that everyone in the class tried to understand each other's thoughts and the material. (I have in mind the work that Duckworth calls teaching/extended clinical interviewing; see, for example, the chapter "Teaching as Research" in Duckworth, 1987, and see Duckworth, 1991.) Such a class includes contexts that allow students to discuss their understandings of the material and of other students' understandings of the material. The communication is careful enough to allow members of the class to appreciate ways in which classmates have diverse ideas, understand the same concept or term differently, and have conflicting ideas. In order to have this level of communication, everyone needs the opportunity for extended turns. Students need to be able to come to the board to draw or to make reference to objects that can be used to clarify their intent. They also need to be able to ask for clarification and elaboration when they have not understood a speaker. In order to have such conversations, it is necessary to develop different dynamics in the math classroom. Everyone must be seen as a participant in the unfolding understanding of the whole class and as a resource for learning. "They [students] should be the audience for one another's comments—that is, they should speak to each other, aiming to convince or to question their peers" (National Council of Teachers of Mathematics [NCTM], 1991, p. 45).

But these were not the sorts of conversations I had in the late 1980s with my students when we discussed homework from the textbook. In the Algebra Two classes, the sessions that did not involve technology remained similar to my classes at the dayschool. Students wanted help with homework problems they found difficult. Even when they could decide whether an answer was correct or not, they looked to me, or to the answer key, as the arbiter of truth; they did not value their own opinions.

Continued Frustration with the Curriculum

There were other ways in which I was not happy with my teaching of Algebra Two in the northeastern suburban high school. I began to see strong tensions between a functions-based approach, on the one hand, and traditional texts—and even the new UCSMP text (Senk et al., 1990)—a tension that cuts to the core of the algebra curriculum. (For a detailed examination of this subtlety, see the section "How Is a Relationships-Between-Quantities View Different from a Traditional View? Focusing on x's and y's" in Chapter 3 of this volume.) This tension is caused by a subtle difference in the treatment of x's and y's, a key component of students' experience of high school algebra. If x sometimes can be seen as a variable that takes on many possible values, or as an unknown, particular number, a functions-based approach makes the first, variable view of x central and the second, particular unknown view of x background, while traditionally the roles of these views are reversed.

The tensions between these two views of x caused some difficulty in class. My students in this school came into Algebra Two having learned about x in Algebra One. They were familiar with x as a particular unknown when they solved equations. In the UCSMP (Senk et al., 1990) text, x remained the particular unknown until Chapter 7, and then was treated as a variable in a cursory manner. In trying to foreground x as a variable and in asking students to think of x in equations as a variable (for details, see Chazan, 1993), I felt that I was asking a lot of students. They had already taken on a particular view of x; it had worked for them and was consonant with the textbook. They were reluctant to investigate another perspective. I decided that in my next chance to teach algebra, I would work with Algebra One students and introduce them to x as variable from the start of their work in algebra.

Also, I was still concerned that students might want to know what algebra is all about—why study algebra—and that I still did not have a reasonable response. Highlighting a "variable" view of x suggests one perspective on the objects of study in algebra, on what algebra is about: It is about expressions where x is viewed as a variable (some might identify such expressions as one representation of the mathematical objects called functions). But that does not explain why one should study algebra. Although in many ways the UCSMP text seemed a great improvement over the texts I had used before, to my mind, its response was not sufficient either. The implicit answer of the textbook was that, if one knows algebra, one can solve problems that come up in different professional pursuits. However, in many cases, the problems that were supposed to help students see the "utility" of algebra in "the real world" (the world outside of school) seemed forced, especially if x's and y's stood for unknown particular numbers. For example, in the problem below, there was a certain human element missing; I could not reconstruct how these questions would actually come up for someone who actually mixed solutions.

A chemist mixes x ounces of a 20% alcohol solution with y ounces of a 30% alcohol solution. The final mixture contains 9 ounces of alcohol.

   A. Write an equation relating x, y, and the total number of ounces of alcohol.

   B. How many ounces of the 30% alcohol solution must be added to 2.7 ounces of the 20% alcohol solution to get 9 ounces of alcohol? (Senk et al., 1987, p. 121)

If x and y are particular unknown numbers, part A of the problem almost seems as if the chemist has simply forgotten how much of each fluid was used. A student asked how the chemist would know that the mixture contained 9 ounces of alcohol unless he or she already knew how much of each solution had been used. Do chemists have instruments that would allow them to measure the total alcohol content of a solution at any concentration? In part B, I could not understand why a chemist would be interested in creating a solution that had 9 ounces of alcohol in an unknown concentration. (For further critique of this problem and others from a functions-based perspective, see Chazan, 1993.) Problems of this type lacked a certain kind of face validity. I could not reconstruct the situations that would give rise to such questions (for an in-depth examination of such difficulties, see Gerofsky, 1996), but luckily, in this teaching situation, the students did not often ask.

In sum, this short experience teaching Algebra Two was useful. I appreciated the opportunity to try to develop a teaching practice by doing the teaching myself. My interest in the problematic aspects of teaching school algebra was strengthened. I also wanted to work more intensively on creating conversations in secondary school math classrooms. Though I was happy to be back in a classroom, with the combination of teaching two sections and holding down a separate job, I did not feel that I had enough time to do the serious reflection required to do the development work I had in mind. In thinking about my next opportunity to teach algebra, I wanted a structure that would allow me more time to develop my teaching.

LOWER-TRACK ALGEBRA ONE IN A RURAL MIDWESTERN PROFESSIONAL DEVELOPMENT SCHOOL

While I was teaching Algebra Two at the suburban high school in the Northeast, I began looking for university-based positions. I had been intrigued by Magdalene Lampert's (1991b, 1991c) descriptions of a clinical faculty position, where a university subsidized research on teaching by providing a faculty member with a reduced teaching load at the university in exchange for carrying out research on one's own teaching at the K–12 level. Such a position would allow me to do the sort of research and development work that I was imagining.

Earlier, when discussing technology-based innovations like *The Geometric Supposer* (Schwartz et al., 1985), I suggested that developers tend to concentrate on software and print materials, to the neglect of development in teaching and teacher learning. There is a similar phenomenon in mathematics education print-based curricular work; there is usually greater focus on the development of curricular materials themselves than on the development of teaching practices that use these materials. Attempts to focus on the development of reform-minded mathematics teaching practices (as opposed to curriculum materials) have been carried out primarily at the elementary or middle-school levels, before adolescence and when high-stakes standardized tests are less ubiquitous. (The following studies of this kind are all situated in elementary school classrooms: Ball, 1993a, 1993b; Lampert, 1990; Peterson, Fenema, & Carpenter, 1991; Wood, Cobb, Yackel, & Dillon, 1993.) Having worked with high school teachers who were developing alternative teaching practices, I now wanted to understand—from the inside, from the position of the teacher—what it is like to attempt to reform secondary school mathematics teaching practice. (Others doing such work outside the field of mathematics education include Hammer, 1995; Lensmire, 1994; Roth, 1992; Wilson, in press; Wong, 1995.) In accepting a clinical faculty position at Michigan State University (MSU), I was eager to take advantage of the opportunity to design an alternative to traditional algebra teaching by teaching on a daily basis.

I continued to be particularly interested in working with students who had not been successful with mathematics, the kind of students who some teachers suggested could not make conjectures or lacked the ability to handle an unstructured, National Council of Teachers of Mathematics (NCTM) standards vision of teaching and learning. I had not seen many difficulties of this kind in my suburban teaching and I wanted to understand the dimensions of these students' difficulties with mathematics and to explore the challenges of reform-minded teaching.

In sum, I wanted to use this teaching opportunity:

- to develop a deeper understanding of school algebra by emphasizing x as a variable;
- to develop a way of teaching algebra that involved students in meaningful mathematical conversations;
- to grapple with the experience of teaching a lower-track high school class;
- to explore the role of microcomputer technology in teaching algebra; and
- to enrich and develop my skills at orchestrating mathematical discussions.

During the 1990–1991, 1991–1992, and 1992–1993 academic years, I team-taught a lower-track Algebra One class at Holt High School, a Professional Development School,[8] for one period a day. The first year I worked with a student teacher first semester and with the chair of the math department during the second semester. Over the following two years I worked with Sandra Callis Bethell, who, at the time, split her instructional responsibilities between the mathematics department and the foreign language department.

I found these three years of teaching challenging, humbling, illuminating, occasionally exhilarating, and often difficult. I learned much from my colleagues. The students also taught me a lot—about algebra, about American society, and about themselves. At the same time, they reminded me what it is like to be "the teacher" in a compulsory setting, the one responsible for discipline and for imposing a course of study. Often, students did not appreciate my efforts to "reform" my teaching of algebra. On other occasions, I received backhanded compliments that only underscored the problematic nature of traditional instruction.

Initial Impressions, Questions, and Attempts to Understand

My first year was a rude awakening. The previous year, my lower-track suburban students were almost all college-intending, including those voluntarily bused from the city. Holt was similarly described as a suburban setting with many affluent parents who commute to the state capital or to the university. I was again going to be teaching a lower-track class, this time for tenth grade Algebra One students. As a result, for the 1990–1991 school year, I was planning a course for students who were not doing well in math (I still wanted to understand the notion of "low ability"), but who were college bound.

I was used to teaching students who took initiative in academic matters, to an open campus and student mailboxes. I was planning to use the textbook for guidance about the topics to be covered, but to prepare my own materials and to require students to collect and organize these papers in notebooks that would be their central record of class work. I was also contemplating asking students to purchase a calculator for use in the class. But "suburban" and "lower-track" do not mean the same thing everywhere; they are not well-defined terms with widely shared meanings. "Lower-track" and "college-intending" may describe a class of students who have some particular difficulty with mathematics, but many students are not going to pursue postsecondary education. Students in a lower-track mathematics classroom may not have particular issues with the learning of mathematics; their issues may concern the larger enterprise of schooling. I had stumbled into a different sort of teaching problem.

My first impressions of my students at Holt was that some were "unhappy about school and [said] that loud and clear with body language."[9] All the students were White; English was everyone's native tongue. On the surface, the students and I seemed similar, but we differed. I felt much less connection to these students than to my students the previous year; there was some sort of gulf. On the fourth day of class, I introduced the notebook requirement. A student whom I'll call Faith objected strenuously. She was so angry it seemed that she would shake. She said, throwing down a challenge, that she would not spend $1.59 for a notebook for a math class. She would only be willing to spend 29¢ on a folder. Inwardly, I was taken aback both by the stance and by the anger that she expressed. I was clearly not in the same sort of suburban setting I had taught in the year before. I was not exactly sure who my students were.

The year got off to a rocky start. Day in and day out the teaching was often disheartening. When explaining why they try to avoid lower-track class assignments, teachers often indicate that teaching such classes is difficult because students are not "motivated" (Page, 1990). I had not experienced motivation as an overt problem the year before, but, at Holt, this description fit my lower-track Algebra One class perfectly. It was a rare day when a large number of students were investing their all in the academic pursuit I was offering. Invariably, some students would be distracted, sleepy, or actively disruptive. Students would write each other notes, have side conversations, put their heads down on their desks, or retreat inside themselves. I had "discipline" problems and was given advice by teachers about how to be "tougher." Only a few students volunteered to speak in class. Work that I assigned out of class came back in dribs and drabs. To substitute for student mailboxes, I instituted a weekly note to students in which I gave them feedback, both positive and negative, on their class participation and homework. Since there was not an open-campus policy and students did not have unscheduled periods in which to consult with me, I also wrote specific comments in which I assessed their progress in understanding the material covered in class.

I began to understand that I would need to think hard about student motivation. There was a teaching problem here (as in many schools) that had existed in the two other schools, but perhaps less saliently. Some students in those schools also wondered why algebra was part of their compulsory schooling, but did not act out a need for some justification. An alternative conceptualization is that, in the two other schools, the structure of the school and the community had "solved," or obscured, issues of student motivation. Perhaps the students in these schools did not think to ask such questions, or, if they did, perhaps what I perceived as thin and utilitarian justifications were sufficient for them.

Because my circumstances were so different from those of my previous teaching, I was learning at a fast pace. There was much that I did not understand initially. For example, when thinking in terms of the diversity of the citizenry of the United States, my class and the school as a whole were quite homogenous, but there were tensions between students. On the second day of class, three of my female students had received suspensions ranging from 5 to 10 days for fighting. During the first 3 weeks, each day at least two students were not in class because they were serving suspensions. A colleague suggested that I read Penelope Eckert's (1989) description of student peer groups; her field work had been done in a similar high school in Michigan. *Jocks and Burnouts* helped me begin to see diversity underneath the seeming homogeneity.

Holt High School is a grade 10–12 building; ninth graders study at the junior high school. I began to learn how students arrive in a tenth grade Algebra

One class, or perhaps more accurately in a high school Algebra One class; some of my students were eleventh and twelfth graders. Since my first year at Holt, there have been changes in the course offerings, but that year there were three common paths—students came from a preparatory course at the junior high school (Pre-Algebra or Math 9), a preparatory course at the high school (Practical Math or Pre-Algebra), or a failure in Algebra One at either the high school or junior high school.

These different paths led to other tensions among the students. During my first week at Holt, Darlene explained to me that she expected little from her classmate Sam. Indeed, if he said something, she assumed that he was wrong because he was a senior coming from Practical Math class at the high school. Similarly, some students had low expectations of students labeled "special ed." or even "voc ed." Correspondingly, they expected more of a sophomore who had taken Pre-Algebra the year before at the junior high school.

I had expected to work with college-intending students who had not done well in mathematics, but it turned out that most of the students in my class were not college-intending, had failed mathematics before, and needed to pass Algebra One in order to complete their mathematics requirement and graduate high school. Most had failed the mathematics portion of the state certification test, given at the beginning of tenth grade, which was required to receive a state-certified diploma. At Holt, at that time, typically 35 to 40% of such lower-tracked students dropped their Algebra One course during the year or failed. (This figure is high, but probably common in most settings where non-college-intending students take algebra.)

Students' experience with this kind of failure seemed to play a role in classroom behaviors that I often found perplexing. For example, Joe was an extremely articulate student, though confrontational. He often came into class very angry and was frequently violently upset when he felt someone else was disturbing a class activity in which he wished to participate. On the other hand, he often carried on side conversations himself and made it difficult for others to concentrate on schoolwork. However, when he participated he often had keen mathematical insights.

I expected him to do very well on the tests I gave, but invariably he would do poorly. His test sheets would come in mostly blank. When I asked why his pages were blank, he said that he did not understand what the instructions said. For a quiz in mid-November, I offered to stand nearby and provide clarifications if necessary. Whenever I was in his part of the room, he worked, but whenever I went to talk with another student, he would stop. He never asked for any clarification, nor did I offer encouragement of any kind; I simply stood in that part of the room. Even though he had not worked for the full time and had not asked me for any clarifications, he turned in an outstanding paper. Indeed, on the following exams, as long as I was in his general vicinity he did quite well.

If I spent time in other parts of the room, his sheet would come back partially empty. It seemed as if he needed a certain kind of reassurance and structure in order to concentrate on attempting the test.

Another day, his frustration boiled over. I had asked students to work on a task and many were not doing so. I went around and spoke with individuals and got them working, which took some time. When much of the time for working on the problem had elapsed, he still had not started. When I asked why, he said that he did not understand the instructions. Linda spoke up; she seemed to want to get a rise out of him. She chided him for not asking sooner and did not let up until I reprimanded her. When I turned to him to help him get started, he was in a frustrated rage and unable to speak. He took his books, stomped out of the room, slammed the door, and ended up in the counseling center. After class, in the counseling center, he attributed his anger to a fight with his father before school. Later in the discussion, he told us that school was just "a waste" anyway and that he did not see any purpose to any of what he learned in school. He also despaired of passing the Algebra One class.

There were other phenomena to which I was unaccustomed. My Holt students did not seem to be either interested in or very good at diagnosing the state of their own knowledge. While students in the other schools regularly brought homework problems into class when they felt they did not understand—even, on occasion, when they had been able to get the correct answer, but somehow felt dissatisfied—often my students in Holt did not even seem to know whether they were working correctly. This led us into conflicts about "covering" the curriculum.

I'll illustrate by referring to their work with one type of symbol manipulation problem that appears early in Algebra One textbooks. The problems are sometimes known as "simplification" problems. They involve rewriting an expression in a different form, while preserving a certain kind of sameness, the kind of sameness that $2(x + 5)$ and $2x + 10$ have. For particular values of x, these two expressions produce the same number. (For more background on this problem type and how it is addressed in a function-based approach, see Chapter 3, "Meaning for Symbol Manipulation.")

Early in the year I realized that most of the students had already met x and y and these sorts of simplification problems in junior high school or in Pre-Algebra. As a result of their lack of success in those encounters with x and y, they brought a hodgepodge of faulty algebraic rules to Algebra One, not an uncommon phenomenon. What was striking was that they seemed not to have ways to check their work, even when I pressed them.

For example, during the first year at Holt, I had a student who came into class in early November and needed credit only for the first semester of Algebra One. I'll call her Danielle; she was the explosive Joe's cousin. The previous year, Danielle had failed the first semester of Algebra One, but had passed the second. School policy dictated that she must pass the first semester of Algebra One. Her teacher from the previous year was concerned that even though she had passed the second semester of the course she had not mastered the basics of algebra and would, as a result, not pass the first semester of my class.

Based on this information, I was not surprised when she said she was frustrated by what we were doing in class and found it too easy. We were doing simple problems of the "simplifying" type. I was exploring ways of explaining what such problems are asking, of checking one's work, and of understanding the purpose of being able to write different, but equivalent, expressions. I wanted to show her that we would progress and do more difficult problems of that type. After class, I showed her one of the problems we would do in a week or 10 days. To show me that she "knew" everything we were going to "cover" in the class, she filled the board with seven steps, introducing a new error at each step along the way, and triumphantly producing a solution at the end. According to her calculation, which used up the whole board, $(x - 4)(x + 3)$ was equivalent to x^2.

While Danielle knew that with such problems she had been taught to proceed step-by-step, writing a new expression at each step, she had no sense of the equivalence that is supposed to be preserved from step to step and no way of determining, when I asked, whether her answer was correct. This demonstration drove home to me how deeply, for her, such tasks were embedded in the doing of school, in the production of answers, and how completely disconnected they were from the consensual meanings ascribed to such tasks by the mathematics community.

And Danielle was not the only student who, in my view, misdiagnosed his or her own learning. After the first 3 weeks of school, students' participation, effort, and achievement were diminishing. The students who had participated at first stopped participating. Students were not being successful when they worked on problems, but they were not then working to understand why. I thought it might have to do with the ways in which this class was different from their previous math classes. We were not yet using a book. We were talking a lot about functions and using a representation of functions with two parallel (rather than perpendicular) axes that the students had never seen before. (This representation has been instantiated on computer, for example, Nachmias & Arcavi, 1990.) Perhaps they were finding the material too difficult.

So one day I asked them to talk with me about the class. It turned out that, based on their prior experience of mathematics classes, and because there were students from a range of different previous classes, the students were assuming that in September I was reviewing material that had been covered in previous years in order to create "a common foundation" for all. For that reason, they were bored; they assumed that the work was too easy and to some degree irrelevant to the course. Though I knew that what we were doing was different from what they had done before, they were not able to identify how it differed. I also thought that many students were having difficulties with much of the material. But that was not their view. It was the beginning of the year and there were Practical Math students in the class, so they assumed the material was review material that could not cause them difficulty. They wanted to move on! Either they did not notice the difficulties they were having, or they had different standards and were not particularly perturbed by feeling that they did not have complete control of the subject. I had a different standard telling me when it was time to "move on."

REFLECTION AND LOOKING AHEAD

Rather than continue with a chronological description of my 3 years of teaching at Holt High School, I'd like to emphasize three dynamics, or questions, central to my teaching of algebra, ones that have surfaced already and that will structure the remainder of this book.

In stark terms, my first year at Holt raised the question of students' motivation and engagement with algebra. For the first time, I was working with students most of whom were not college-intending. Rather than viewing the issue of student motivation in this school as a new and unfamiliar dynamic, even though some of the behaviors I encountered at Holt were new to me, I view this classroom dynamic as one that existed in my previous teaching, but was masked. Unlike students intending to attend college, for my Holt students, there were fewer motivations, external to the mathematics itself, for learning algebra. As a result, from teaching at Holt, I was able to see more clearly my lack of intrinsic arguments for the importance of learning algebra. As a teacher that year, I kept asking myself questions that torment many algebra teachers:

- How do I help students—with diverse interests and talents; learning in a tracked, compulsory setting; many of whom are planning to work and are not college-intending—see value in a shared exploration of algebra?
- On what grounds can I appeal, implicitly or explicitly, for their energies and effort?[10]

But these questions of student motivation do not exist in a vacuum; they are intimately linked with curricular questions. What is school algebra? Here is a copy of a page of homework from the first chapter of the algebra text that was given to me for my first year of teaching at Holt (see Figure 1.9). Homework exercises like these make me wonder what it is that we really want high school students to learn when we think of "algebra" and why. As educators, do we believe that mastering the manipulative skills assessed by such exercises

Figure 1.9. An early Algebra One assignment.

1-5 EXERCISES

A

Use the distributive property to write an equivalent expression.

1. $2(b + 5)$ 2. $4(x + 3)$ 3. $(1 + t)7$

4. $6(v + 4)$ 5. $3(x + 1)$ 6. $(x + 8)7$

7. $4(1 + y)$ 8. $9(s + 1)$ 9. $6(5x + 2)$

10. $9(6m + 7)$ 11. $7(x + 4 + 6y)$ 12. $(5x + 8 + 3p)4$

Factor.

13. $2x + 4$ 14. $5y + 20$ 15. $30 + 5y$

16. $7x + 28$ 17. $14x + 21y$ 18. $18a + 24b$

19. $5x + 10 + 15y$ 20. $9a + 27b + 81$ 21. $14c + 63d + 7$

22. $4y + 10 + 8x$ 23. $9r + 27s + 18$ 24. $24x + 72y + 8$

Factor and check by multiplying.

25. $9x + 27$ $9(x + 3)$ 26. $6x + 24$ $6(x + 4)$

27. $9x + 3y$ $3(3x + y)$ 28. $15x + 5y$ $5(3x + y)$

29. $8a + 16b + 64$ $8(a + 2b + 8)$ 30. $5 + 20x + 35y$ $5(1 + 4x + 7y)$

31. $11x + 44y + 121$ $11(x + 4y + 11)$ 32. $7 + 14b + 56w$ $7(1 + 2b + 8w)$

33. $5x + 10y + 45z$ 34. $9p + 3q + 27r$

Collect like terms.

35. $9a + 10a$ 36. $12x + 2x$

37. $10a + a$ 38. $16x + x$

39. $2x + 9z + 6x$ 40. $3a + 5b + 7a$

41. $7x + 6y^2 + 9y^2$ 42. $12m^2 + 6q + 9m^2$

43. $41a + 90 + 60a \div 2$ 44. $42x + 6 + 4x + 2$

45. $8a + 8b + 3a + 3b$ 46. $100y + 200z + 190y + 400z$

47. $8u^2 + 3t + 10t + 6u^2 + 2$ 48. $5 + 6b + t + t + 8 + 9h$

49. $23 + 5t + 7y + t + y + 27$ 50. $45 + 90d + 87 + 9d + 3 + 7d$

51. $\frac{1}{2}b + \frac{1}{2}b$ 52. $\frac{2}{3}x + \frac{1}{3}x$

53. $2y + \frac{1}{4}y + y$ 54. $\frac{1}{2}a + a + 5a$

B

Extension

55. The money you deposit in a bank is called the principal. When you deposit money in a bank and earn interest, the new principal is given by the expression $P + Prt$, where P is the principal, r is the rate of interest, and t is the time. Factor the expression $P + Prt$. $P(1 + rt)$

56. a. Factor $17x + 34$. Then evaluate both expressions when $x = 10$. $17 \cdot 10 + 34 = 204$; $17(x + 2) = 17(12) = 204$
    b. Will you get the same answer for both expressions? Why? Yes; distributive property

57. Find a simpler expression equivalent to $\frac{3a + 6}{2a + 4} \cdot \frac{3}{2}$

58. Find a simpler expression equivalent to $\frac{4x + 12y}{3x + 9y} \cdot \frac{4}{3}$

C

Challenge

Collect like terms, if possible, and factor the result.

59. $x + 2x^2 + 3x^3 + 4x^2 + 5x$ $6x + 6x^2 + 3x^3 = 3x(2 + 2x + x^2)$

60. $q + qr + qrs + qrst$ $q(1 + r + rs + rst)$

61. $21x + 44xy + 15y - 16x - 8y - 38xy + 2x + xy$

62. Simplify $a\{1 + b[1 + c(1 + d)]\}$. (Hint: Begin with $c(1 + d)$ and work outwards.)

Source: Smith, Charles, Keedy, Bittinger, & Orfan (1988). Reprinted with permission from Addison-Wesley.

gives students a new perspective on, and insight into, our world? If not, what does such mastery provide and why is it important? How does it relate to questions or problems with which students might become intellectually engaged? If it does not relate, are there alternative ways to structure algebra instruction?

These sorts of questions, with which I had already begun to struggle when first teaching algebra, have become much sharper for me as technology has evolved over the last 15 years. The graphing calculators and computers of today can accomplish all of the manipulations traditionally taught in high school and early college. The effect is similar to the effect of arithmetic calculators on the elementary school curriculum. Do we want students to spend a substantial amount of their time in secondary school classrooms learning to solve problems that relatively inexpensive calculators can solve? If so, for what reason?

Finally, from my very first algebra teaching experience, I have been concerned about the nature of conversations in mathematics classrooms. I have been concerned that I do not ask my students to reason more independently and to develop greater intellectual autonomy. I have also been concerned that the mathematics classroom is overly teacher-centered rather than focusing on students and their ideas. These concerns lead me to wonder: How does one create a more student-centered secondary school mathematics classroom? In the secondary school mathematics classroom, how can we have free and wide-ranging conversations? What is it about the mathematics classroom that discourages such conversation? To explore these questions in greater depth, in the remainder of this book, I will examine my experiences teaching at Holt, particularly those from 1992–1993, my second year of team-teaching Algebra One with Sandra Callis Bethell.

SANDRA CALLIS BETHELL:
A BRIEF TEACHING BIOGRAPHY

The remainder of the teaching that I examine in this book was done together with Sandy Callis Bethell. Sandy is a member of the Holt faculty whom I sought out because of her reputation for being particularly committed to helping students in lower-track classes find meaning in the academic content of the high school curriculum. She is an important part of the rest of the story and has influenced me considerably.

Sandy came to teaching mathematics in a different way than I did. However, it turned out that we had somewhat similar frustrations with our teaching and compatible desires to change algebra teaching. Based on her own presentations about her teaching, here, in brief, I give the reader an introduction to her teaching biography and her reasons for joining me in my attempts to create a different algebra teaching practice.

Sandy describes herself as having grown up in a town quite like Holt. She graduated Michigan State University as a mathematics major and Spanish minor—with certification to teach at the high school level and after student teaching in an urban setting. When she first started to teach, she expected that her life experiences had prepared her for teaching working-class students in a suburban setting. She thought that she would be able to transmit her excitement about mathematics to her students. She was a core participant in a project on teaching General Mathematics at the junior high school level.

Sandy's first 3 years of teaching at Holt Junior High School disabused her of such notions.

> Every year, only about 50% of my students in the lower level courses chose to pursue further mathematical study. Up to one third of my students failed the classes I taught. While this seemed to be acceptable in my school and in many other schools, I found it unacceptable. I also found that because of my role as a mathematics teacher, my students did not identify with me as an adult version of themselves, even though I came from a culture very much like theirs.

When I came to work at Holt High School, Sandy described herself as being in the midst of a "professional transition." A hiatus of 3 years from teaching, during which she began and discontinued a Ph.D. in Teacher Education at Michigan State University, had provided Sandy with opportunities to visit many schools, to see alternative methods of mathematics teaching at the elementary school level, and to think hard about the purposes of education. When she was hired back into the Holt district, at the high school this time, she decided initially to concentrate on Spanish. However, with a continued commitment to students who did poorly in math, she took on one Practical Math class as part of her load and participated in research on that class (Kirsner & Bethell, 1992). Teaching Spanish seemed much more comfortable than teaching mathematics; in the Spanish classroom, Sandy felt that she could have the sort of relationship with students that she wanted.

> Teaching language fit with my idea of what school should be about. In a Spanish class, every day was a celebration as students learned to express themselves, to find information, to make jokes and all the other things people learn as they become immersed in a new language.

In Spanish, the atmosphere of the class was relaxed. Sandy felt she could enjoy the students and they could enjoy her, all the while feeling that the class was productive and that the students were learning and growing. Mathematics teaching felt quite different. In Practical Math, there were opportunities to create comfortable relationships with students, but it seemed that it often was at the expense of teaching academic content.

After watching me struggle in my first year of teaching at Holt, Sandy was interested in my attempts to teach algebra. She had never taught Algebra One or more advanced mathematics courses at the high school in a conceptual way and thought I was working in that direction. On a pragmatic level, she was also looking for ways to provide her Practical Math students opportunities for further, and richer, mathematical study. She was reasonably certain that they would not succeed in the standard Algebra One course taught at Holt. Together, she thought we might be able to design a course that challenged them to learn the academic content of Algebra One, but one in which they could be successful. However, like me, she was concerned that her own knowledge of algebra was not sufficient to help her teach conceptually:

> I knew how to do a lot of things [algebra problems], given specific directions, but I didn't know what it was all about. I had the sense that I had amassed a lot of tools, but I didn't know what those tools were for.

Starting in August 1991, we took on the shared responsibility for one section of lower-track Algebra One in a tracked school system. Together, we explored who our students were, what we wanted them to learn and why, and how to have more comfortable classroom interactions while maintaining our commitment to teaching academic content. The following three chapters represent my understandings of some of what we learned.

Curricular Engagement and Personal Trajectories: "Motivation" in High School Mathematics

High school teachers teaching academic content to students in lower-track classes face important challenges that give this sort of teaching its unique character. Thinking about teaching the subject matter can be daunting; students have been unsuccessful in the past—their performance has not met evaluation standards of some kind. Especially in mathematics teaching, this part of the challenge is discussed in terms of "students' ability," or lack thereof. In combination with these challenges around student performance, teachers in this sort of setting often must come to grips with students' skepticism about schooling and anger at being compelled to study material they believe to be of little or no value. This skepticism and anger are often directed at the teacher, as a representative of the larger educational system; they are expressed both through interactions between teacher and student and in the intensity of students' involvement with successful completion of assignments. Colloquially, this challenge is known as the problem of "student motivation," or, more descriptively, as issues of student disengagement from schooling.

Though issues of student performance are a challenge, student disengagement is extremely hard on teachers. In explaining the nature of this difficulty, Mary Metz (1993), a sociologist of education, suggests that there is a paradoxical dynamic—which she labels "Teachers' Ultimate Dependence on Their Students"—at the heart of teaching and similar practices:

> As the results of teaching reside in the minds and characters of students, students have ultimate control over the fruit of teachers' labors. Teachers cannot obtain the satisfaction of a job well done through their own efforts alone; they can obtain them [sic] only through the cooperation of their students—the very students they are supposed to discipline, lead, transform or even reform. . . . Both as adults relating to children and as professionals relating to clients, teachers are expected to be in control and in charge. . . . To be dependent on clients who are children for the accomplishment of one's own success is both technologically paradoxical and so-

37

cially demeaning. But in teaching—or in any other kind of work in which professionals try to change the inner states of people of lower status than themselves—it is inescapable. (pp. 104–105)

While many teachers develop repertoires of strategies to manage these challenges to learning and create meaningful, cooperative relationships with their students, this uncomfortable feeling of dependence on students is a familiar one to teachers in lower-track classes. In such classes where placement, at least theoretically (see DeLany, 1991, for other influences on placement), represents an evaluation by the school of insufficient prior academic achievement, students are often unconnected with schools. Students may experience their placement as a critical comment on their abilities, as discrimination against the community of which they are a part, as a devaluation of the knowledge they bring to school, and more. There is a host of reasons that students in lower-track classes can use cogently to defend a retreat from schooling and lack of engagement with classroom activity (see Page, 1990). Critics, and reformers, of high schools suggest that, as a result of teachers' dependence on students and student disengagement, lower-track classes are rife with tacit treaties, or bargains, according to which students do not disrupt class while teachers do not make heavy intellectual demands. (This argument was made in a series of books published in the 1980s. See, for example, Cusick, 1983; McNeil, 1985; Powell, Farrar, & Cohen, 1985; Sedlak, Wheeler, Pullin, & Cusick, 1986.) Teachers who violate such treaties by making heavier intellectual demands on lower-track students risk having their students do so as well, by disrupting class and causing problems of "discipline."

At Holt, as a teacher of a lower-track math class in a high school, I found issues of "student motivation" an important part of my subjective experience of teaching. Students' engagement in class varied dramatically, and it was hard to predict. Sometimes, students were quite engaged. When students were disengaged, on some occasions, they made their views known loudly and forcefully, and, at other times, disengagement was expressed in quiet and sullen ways. However, on a regular basis, the students that Sandy and I taught were not "motivated"; they did not come to class ready to work on the academic tasks we had so carefully designed or chosen. Sometimes we were able to overcome initial disengagement. At other times, there were serious issues that occupied students' minds and made doing mathematics relatively unimportant: Someone had stolen property from their locker, or a classmate was pregnant and planning to get married and drop out of school. We then had to decide how to respond. And, sometimes, we did not find out what was on their minds or why they did not want to invest their all in our studies.

By the time I began teaching with Sandy, I did not expect our students to be motivated every single day to work hard for a full class period. Our students were primarily intent on graduating high school, receiving a diploma, and getting on with life, not school. We were attempting to teach algebra—a subject with which they had already had difficulty, one that folk culture suggests is particularly difficult, that can be academic in the worst sense of the word, and that can focus narrowly on a series of arcane skills—in a compulsory, tracked setting. Furthermore, we were breaking our part of the bargain: We were not content to have them do the minimum to pass a watered-down course; rather, we sought to create an intellectually rigorous course. We expected a certain kind of friction. On the other hand, we were doing our best to change the nature of the course, to acknowledge their skepticism about schooling, to rethink both the subject matter and the nature of classroom interaction, to make the course academic in the best sense of the word. We hoped that our intentions would be recognized and appreciated.

Instead, while Sandy and I were struggling to rework the algebra curriculum and create an experience that was meaningful, connected, and educative for our students, they often did not engage with the material. Sometimes students were actively not engaged and acted out; other times they simply disengaged passively and retreated inside themselves. (For reflection on a similar phenomenon in the same school in science, see Anderson, 1995.) Sometimes it felt that our very efforts to improve the course only made us more dependent on our students for their engagement and participation than the teachers in Metz's (1993) sociological analysis of classroom instruction.

MOTIVATION AND TASK-CENTERED INSTRUCTION

To illustrate this dynamic in our teaching, I will describe the format of our instruction (which was quite different from that of my dayschool instruction) and focus for the moment on the role of the mathematical tasks we posed to students. We modeled the design of our classroom sessions on descriptions of instruction published by Lampert (1990) and Ball (1993b), then colleagues at Michigan State University (MSU).[1] We would begin class sessions with the presentation of a mathematical task. Students would then explore the task on their own or in pairs or small groups, sometimes with the aid of technology. We would then reconvene as a whole group to have students share the results of their explorations and to develop shared notions of the mathematics related to the task. Tasks for such teaching clearly need to be chosen carefully. Such tasks do not sound like the "30-seconds apiece" exercises that fill pages of textbooks.

This sort of task-centered design of teaching is advocated by the current mathematics education reform movement for two reasons (see NCTM, 1991). On the one hand, this sort of design is predicated on the notion that students' ideas play a central role in learning and are a key resource in the process of teaching. *student ideas* In the instructional design built on these ideas, mathematical tasks play an important role in eliciting student thinking. As a result, not just any task will do. Students must be able to understand the task. The task must create contexts within which students express their thinking. There must be important mathematics that can come to light from students' exploration of the task.

But, separate from eliciting students' mathematical ideas, there is another reason for centering instruction around tasks. There are particular kinds of tasks that are thought to be helpful in terms of student motivation. One way that teachers argue implicitly that mathematics is *not* an esoteric subject and that there *are* important reasons to study mathematics is by their choice of tasks. A genre of tasks designed with this goal in mind is what mathematics educators call "real-world" problems. (For discussion of dynamics related to the use of such problems, see the section in this chapter title "Real-world" Problems and Student "Trajectories.")[2] Inherent in the notion of a real-world problem is a dichotomy between school and the "real world" and a theory of student motivation. Many problems traditionally given in a mathematics class are found only in school. (This observation is made forcefully by Victor Katz (1993) in his examination of algebra texts throughout history.) A real-world problem is one that someone, perhaps even the student, might encounter outside of school. The notion is that students will be attracted to problems that implicitly suggest that mathematics is a useful body of knowledge that allows people to solve problems they face in their lives.[3]

Though these two rationales for task-centered instruction seem plausible, this sort of design for instruction has a risk: It heightens the teacher's dependence on the student. With this instructional design, not only were Sandy and I ultimately dependent on our students for the success of our efforts as assessed through student learning, but we were also dependent on our students for the success of individual sessions. We could not lecture to a quiet, but disengaged, class. We were dependent on students' willingness to explore problems, share their ideas, and engage with the ideas of others. If students were not willing to explore the problems, then there was nothing to discuss. If students were not willing to share their ideas with the whole group, then their peers could not learn from their explorations. Finally, if students were not willing to examine each other's ideas, there were successive dialogues with Sandy and me, but no discussion with other students. Thus, we could not successfully educate our students in the way we wished without coming to grips with student disengagement from school. For this reason, we felt the problem of "student motivation" acutely.

Our students' engagement was quite variable. Task-centered instruction suggests one important course of action. If students are not engaging with certain tasks, then there must be something wrong with the tasks and they should be changed. As a result, Sandy and I spent much time designing and redesigning tasks. But this strategy seemed limited; it seemed there must be other important factors to explain the variation in classroom sessions, even though students' engagement, from our perspective, often seemed to fluctuate without rhyme or reason.

To illustrate this variability, I'll focus on the behavior of one student who played a key role in setting the tone in the classroom during two successive sessions. On a Tuesday, when we walked into class, Bob, who was wearing shorts, had drawn faces on his knees. Before the bell rang and we began class, his "knees" began to carry on a conversation that acknowledged the start of class only by lowering to a loud stage whisper. Later, he spent a good part of the period getting students throughout the class to imitate his ability to clap one hand and thus disrupt class. Primarily as a result of his efforts, we expended much effort (with only partial success) in creating and sustaining a focus on the mathematical task we had prepared. Yet, during the next class session, we had one of the best sessions of the year. Students were actively engaged with a relatively abstract task. We asked them to correct a set of solved problems that I had collected from the work of my students from the previous year. The solutions included many standard simplification errors. (These errors are like those Danielle made, which were alluded to in Chapter 1. An example is to say that $2(x - 3) + 5$ is the same as $2x + 2$—and not $2x - 1$. For an extended discussion of simplification tasks, see Chapter 3, the section titled "Meaning for Symbol Manipulation.") Our students' task was to find the errors, to explain what the error was, and then to create a hypothesis about what the student had done in creating this error. On this day, Bob played an important role in having his group persevere on a self-imposed extension of the task. His group used trial and error and their experience with tables and graphs to tackle a simplification problem with a nonlinear expression—Is $2(x - 3)(x - 1)$ the same as $3x - 7$? Why or why not?—a problem for which they had none of the typically prerequisite mathematical tools. But this sort of student engagement was not an every other day occurrence.

As Sandy and I experienced this sort of variability in our students' engagement, we began to feel that we would not come to grips with it solely by changing the nature of the tasks we posed. We thought we needed to develop resources that might eventually help us change the tasks we were posing and/or how students viewed them. In particular, we began to think that we needed to learn more about our students.

For me, this desire had a different dimension than for Sandy. As I came to know the students at Holt, I felt keenly the importance of differences between my life experiences and theirs. For example, many of the students Sandy and I were teaching regularly had encounters with law enforcement agencies and the courts. In my childhood, these societal institutions were not salient for me. It seemed to me that this sort of difference and others might play crucial roles in my students' disengagement from schooling, and more particularly from algebra class. It was more difficult for me to see a younger version of myself in these students than it had been when I taught in the dayschool, and I assumed that it was harder for these students to see their future selves in me. I did not feel that I had a deep enough understanding of my students to be able to take informed action.

Earlier and less explicitly, this sort of desire was part of what led me to team-teach with Sandy Bethell. Sandy had a reputation for not compromising on the academic agenda of her lower-track mathematics courses, while maintaining important connections to her students. Though she had been moving away from mathematics teaching, she had a reputation for using innovative methods to help students in lower-track classes become involved in mathematical explorations.

When Sandy and I began teaching together, we sought out information about our students; we read the folders in the counseling department that tracked our students' performance and documented their interactions with schools, psychologists, and the court system. In class, we gave our students' writing assignments about their views of some of our classroom practices. But we began to feel, and then gradually to be convinced, that we still needed more information.

Donald Dryden, then a Michigan State graduate student, convinced us. Donald came to Michigan State straight from his first teaching experience, a difficult experience teaching science in a junior high school in inner-city Chicago. In his teaching, he had harbored many questions about his students' experiences of schooling. At Donald's instigation, we began to read literature about students' experience of the curriculum and psychological theories of motivation. (Some of the pieces we read include: Lee & Anderson, 1993; McClelland, Koestner, & Weinberger, 1989; Newmann, 1992; Nicholls, 1989.) Finally, during our second year of shared teaching, Sandy and I helped Donald arrange to hire four of our students as research assistants to design and carry out an investigation of students' experience of our class. As a result of this project, Sandy and I gained insights into our students and their perceptions of schooling.

COMPLEXITIES IN DESIGNING A RESEARCH PROJECT ON STUDENTS' EXPERIENCE

Though Sandy and I became convinced that we needed more information on students' experience of our class, the very organization of high schools made it hard for us to learn enough about our students to have any chance of coming to grips with student disengagement. (This point is made forcefully in Sizer, 1984, 1996.) As high school math teachers, we did not have opportunities to see students in a range of activities and studying a variety of subjects during the course of a day. Our experiences with students were limited to the one hour a day during which we were charged with the responsibility of teaching a subject matter curriculum that was already overpacked. Furthermore, unlike school counselors, we could rarely meet students one on one. At Holt, students do not have study halls or free periods; our opportunities to meet with students were limited to before or after school. In this respect, as only a part-time teacher, my situation was worse than that of most full-time teachers; I had university responsibilities before and after school.[4]

Yet even if the organization of high schools were different, arguably, it would still be difficult for teachers to collect information useful for understanding and tackling student disengagement. While making an eloquent plea for the consideration of the subjective experience of students as they are engaged in learning, in "Students' Experience of the Curriculum," educational researchers Fred Erickson and Jeffrey Shultz (1991) also argue that adults have difficulty collecting useful information because:

- when students are visible they are viewed from the adult educator's goal-directed perspective—as failing or succeeding, motivated or unmotivated, or having a misconception,
- as a real time phenomenon in a social context, student engagement in classroom tasks cannot be studied directly—observation is limited and interviewing solicits retrospective accounts,
- students may initially find it difficult to cope with the unfamiliar task of articulating their experience. (pp. 466–482)

All of these difficulties would be exacerbated for the teacher interested in learning more about students' experience of the curriculum in a class they themselves are teaching. Students might understandably be reluctant to share their views with a person who is responsible for evaluating them.

Thus, in designing this research project, Donald was concerned that students be able to say what they thought and that they not feel that participation might jeopardize their grades in class. He was also concerned about whether students would view him as a "teacher" and thus not share their thoughts freely. Finally, he was concerned about having students participate in a regular and serious manner.

As a result, we introduced him to our students as a graduate student at the university. He hired students and paid them $5 per hour for meeting with him. The students met regularly throughout the year with Donald at the school building, but outside of school time. They carried out a survey that, they felt, other students did not take seriously. They also practiced interviewing and then interviewed members of our class. Sandy and I were not privy to their conversations and data until we were no longer their teachers, no longer in the position of evaluating them. During the summer of 1993, we met regularly over lunch to talk about their year's work and to plan a research project that they would carry out the following school year.

The evolution of Donald's project was interesting in and of itself. Though many students expressed an interest in the project, only four female students completed applications (Susie, Lynn, Angela, and Victoria). Each of these students was a strong-minded individual who in some ways felt that she was more mature than her peers. Susie moved out of state after attending the first few sessions. Two of the remaining three students, Lynn and Angela, who happened to be friends, later convinced their friend Bob that he would enjoy participating. The last student, Victoria, was not part of this peer group and her attendance dwindled during the year. She did not attend any of the summer meetings. So, later, when we understood more about students' social groups, we came to understand that the three students we came to know best were all "smokers," one student-labeled social group. We did not have any student-researchers who could shed light on the perspectives of other groups they identified, like the "preppies."

By the end of the summer, the students had developed a series of hypotheses and had designed a research project. Their experiences with questionnaires and interviews in school led them to design a structured interview, which they planned to carry out with a range of students after school at Bob's house. They were interested in looking at the relationship between student peer group affiliation and thoughts about homework. They wanted to see if other smokers shared their views about homework. They also felt that they would be able to solicit the participation of preppies and see if the views of students in this group were different. They also had constructed a method of checking their judgment of student affiliation by having students use the high school yearbook to identify the social circles in which they traveled and indicate the members of the groups with which they affiliated. We were very excited about the possibilities of this research project.

Yet, as in other research that depends on students as informants (Farrell, Peguero, Lindsey, & White, 1988; Phelan, Davidson, & Cao, 1992; Phelan, Cao, Yu, & Davidson, 1994; Stinson, 1993), we ran into obstacles in carrying out the project. All along, students had been spotty in their attendance at the meetings with Donald. If something else "came up," even though they had spoken with him just the day before, they would miss the meetings. They did not seem to feel that this indicated a lack of commitment to the project.

More serious barriers intervened at the end of the summer. One of the three students had gotten pregnant and then married. She was no longer going to be in school and, though interested, could not participate in the project. She was working at a fast-food restaurant. Another student left the high school because of fear for her physical safety and enrolled in a GED program offered within the district. She was concerned about interviewing students enrolled in the high school. The third remaining student violated agreements with his stepfather and was sent to live with his mother, too far away to participate in the project. At that point, the project ended before the students had been able to do any of the planned interviews.

PEER GROUPS AND EXPERIENCE OF SCHOOLING

Though the student-researchers never carried out their final research project, we learned much from our conversations with them. They told us about their peer groups and the interactions between peer-group affiliation and schooling. The stories they told match what others have found in studying adolescence and schooling.

As students move to high school, they are also entering adolescence, becoming increasingly aware of social class (Brantlinger, 1993b) and beginning to associate with adult roles in society. According to Eckert (1989), within schools, student social groups that are roughly aligned with social class begin to develop. Whether these groups are the jocks and burnouts, which she notes, the punks, stoneheads, grits, and trendies noted by others (like Brantlinger, 1993a), or the smokers, preppies, nerds, and hard people, which our students used as labels, affiliation and group association are important markers of students' experience of schooling.

To illustrate the categories our students used to describe their peers and the makeup of a typical Algebra One class at Holt High School, Sandy and I have created composite portraits of students from the different groups. During the 1992–1993 school year, there were 19 students who were in our class all year long. Two students were in the class only for the first semester; 2 were in the class for second semester only; and 2 dropped out of school just before the end of school. While there were 7 other students who were members of the class for a very short time, we will concentrate on the 25 students who spent a significant amount of time in the class. Based on our conversations with the student-researchers, in 1992–1993, our students' affiliation with social groups are tallied in Figure 2.1.

Stoners are students whom other students describe as seeking a "hard"

Figure 2.1. Group affiliation in our 1992–1993 class.

1 "stoners"/hard people

7 "preppies"

15 "smokers" (9 strongly affiliated; 6 less so)

2 "nerds"

reputation. They are involved in gang activity in the area, as well as use of illegal drugs. Drawing on different students Sandy and I taught together, we have created a composite portrait of a stoner we will call Matt. During the first half of the year, Matt was a leader in our class. Outside of school, Matt was involved extensively with gang activity.

Matt came to school from jail. He had been convicted of breaking and entering and had received a sentence of six months jail time and further time in a halfway house. Matt had permission from the court to attend two classes at school, Algebra One and American Studies. He could not take books or other materials back and forth to school. However, while in jail, Matt had few distractions; he completed all out-of-school assignments and excelled. He often participated in, or led, class discussions. However, when he entered the halfway house at approximately the time of the change in semesters, his engagement and performance dropped off significantly.

Often other students relied on Matt for legal advice, since in their eyes he was an expert on the court system. During the second semester, they used group work time to confer with him. Matt began to sleep during class or react defiantly to suggestions that he participate. He began to show signs of, perhaps, substance use or serious depression.

Preppies are students who are strongly affiliated with school. Many are involved in school sports and are thus also called "jocks" by the smokers. We will call our composite preppie Steve. Steve is a tall young man who is quiet and polite. He feels that he is well connected to the school. For example, both he and his father in their senior years starred as Sir Lancelot in the school play (*Camelot*).

In our class, he saw himself above other students. He felt that somehow at the junior high school he had been misplaced in a low math class. As a result, he had worked very hard the previous year in Pre-Algebra with a teacher who emphasized the absolute necessity of daily homework. He felt he had made substantial progress in "catching up." Now, he was concerned that the other students in the class and our teaching style were holding him back.

These feelings were expressed through sarcastic remarks to other students as the year progressed. He wanted us to split the class into two parts, one for those who wanted to learn and one for those who did not. He was frustrated when we recognized and valued other students' comments and participation, particularly Matt's.

As the year progressed, Steve retreated further into himself. At the beginning of the year, he made interesting comments during mathematics discussions. Later, he did not participate as actively and often did not pay attention when others spoke. He stopped making use of opportunities to ask questions that went beyond what was being done in class. He began reading novels in class.

However, during the following year, his view of the class and what was taught and learned began to change, seemingly as a result of his success in Algebra Two. When his girlfriend had difficulty with Algebra One, he suggested that she switch into Sandy's class. She did so and felt successful.

Smokers tended to be the majority of the students in our classes. Affiliation with this group was signaled by spending time before and after school or at lunch at the loading dock behind the cafeteria. At the time, this was informally known as a place where students could smoke cigarettes. Some students who did not smoke cigarettes nonetheless chose this affiliation and gathering place. Teri referred to herself as a smoker, somewhere in between a preppie and a stoner. She was social and popular in our class, although she missed class often—she had asthma, which sometimes caused her to miss class; other times she chose to spend school time with her boyfriend, who did not attend school. Teri often participated eagerly in discussions but never completed a homework assignment. When she missed a class, she very rarely made up in-class assignments. Thus, her grade was very low. However, this was not problematic to her; on the contrary, she seemed to enjoy her classmates and class activities. The class and the grade were simply not a high priority. Teri did not foresee attending college.

Because of Teri's intelligence and strong social skills, other students enjoyed working with her. Often, though, their conversations would turn to social issues or gossip. Again, receiving a low grade was not a problem for her, so these lapses from the class activity were not problematic from her perspective. Teri failed the course, but indicated that she enjoyed the class.

Nerds were not usually self-identified. These were students whom others saw as being separate from the other three social groups and were looked down upon. In this context, there did not seem to be a particular association with academic pursuits. Instead, nerds were seen as unadventurous. Our composite student to represent this social group is Carla, a very tall girl who was a little heavy-set. She had difficulty reading. She was especially close to her father, who sold farm equipment. She would often accompany him on his work after school.

Carla was very quiet. As a student, she was initially extremely shy. Her arithmetic skills were weak at the beginning of the year. We were told by her special education teacher that she benefited tremendously from our practice of reading problems out loud before having students work on them individually.

Often Carla complained of a headache during class discussions or while working on a difficult problem. However, she became our resident expert on combining like terms and using the distributive rule. Whenever a question of this kind came up, she uncharacteristically would raise her hand and volunteer an answer, which was usually correct. We had the sense, though, that often students disregarded her comments.

With this analysis of social groups as background, in discussing our class,

Bob indicated that he thought it was very difficult for teachers to manage the tensions created by having students from different peer groups in the same class. When we talked about our grouping practices, Bob indicated that he could learn from someone he did not "hang out with" and gave an example of learning from a student named Joe, whom he classified as a nerd. By contrast, he thought that you could not learn from people who were your enemy. He gave the example of one "cooperative" group in our class in which two girls, unbeknownst to us, were sworn enemies.

When asked more generally about relationships between members of different social groups, he suggested that people who were preppies and people who were smokers were by definition enemies (this was one occasion on which I wished we had the perspective of a preppie):

> The preppies they don't agree with smoking so anybody who smokes they're against them because it's against what they do so they're thinking why should we be friends with somebody who does something that is against our morals.[5]

We then moved on to discuss relationships between peer groups and the degree of student engagement with curricular tasks. Bob argued:

> Different people have different things they want, to do I mean. That's the only way I think about it. Like the preppies, they'll go off and they'll like, most of the preppies they do their homework and they get really good grades and they'll go off they'll go to college and they'll get a good job. Some of the smokers they don't really care about their grades they don't really care about homework so they'll go off and they'll like, they won't go to college but they'll try and get a good job with what they can. And the smokers you know how smokers they don't really care about what they're doing so they figure why should I go to college and waste my time with school because I didn't really want to do it in high school so why do it again, you know. So the preppies they'll go "Well, homework I was pretty good at that and I like that." So they'll go off and they'll go to college and they'll do good and the preppies they'll get good jobs and some of the smokers seeing how they didn't care they won't get as good of a job.[6]

Bob's comments suggest important relationships between peer-group affiliation and classroom engagement. Strikingly, he seems to find such correlations and their ramifications natural (and perhaps inevitable), as opposed to unfair or discriminatory. In addition, his comments emphasize student choice and agency.

As a consequence, Bob seemingly disregards the role of schooling in the development of relationships between student peer groups and classroom engagement. For me, this aspect needs to be emphasized in addition to students' choices. As our student-researchers noted, student peer groups began to form during junior high school; the development of students' peer groups and their associated views of schooling coincides with changes in the organization of schooling and tracking. In the movement from the younger grades in elementary school to high school, in most public education in the United States, there is a movement from a school day organized within a self-contained classroom and taught by one teacher to a school day characterized by movement from room to room, from subject to subject, and from teacher to teacher on a schedule marked by periods and bells. Conventional wisdom suggests that this transition can be a difficult one for students to effect and that it results in markedly different student experience of schooling. Rather than having one teacher, students now have many teachers. These teachers are "subject matter experts"; they spend smaller amounts of time with students, and know their students in much narrower and more circumscribed ways.

Concurrent with this change is another—movement from tracking within a self-contained class to tracking by class assignment. In mathematics, rather than the groups often found within the elementary classroom, students are now grouped into tracked classes with a differentiated curriculum (Page, 1990). The language for describing the differences between groups takes on different layers and nuances. Where groups before might have been called ability groups, now classes are labeled according to the futures with which they are aligned. In particular, some students are in the college-intending track and are taking mathematics that will prepare them for college, while others are not.[7]

A METAPHOR FOR THINKING ABOUT SOCIAL CLASS AND CURRICULAR ENGAGEMENT

Learning about students' peer groups and students' perceptions of relations between these groups and schooling gave Sandy and me much to contemplate. With Donald's help, over time, I came to appreciate ways in which Erickson and Shultz's (1991) and Berryman's (1987) use of the metaphor of "trajectories" helps capture what we learned; Berryman uses trajectories to describe the "futures that they [students] expect for themselves—their visions of their adult 'places' in the world" (p. 6). Both Bob's comments about preppies and smokers and the tracking descriptors highlight students' futures. Berryman, like Bob, argues that this is no accident, that students' engagement with curricular tasks is directly related to students' views of their future:

I suggest that all children develop an image of their niche in the adult world—in the ecological sense of niche. Their ideas about the ecology of adult "places" may be distorted and are usually pitifully and pathetically partial.[8] However, they seem to work out notions of their basic futures and of the trajectories relevant to them, even if they cannot state these explicitly. *And they act on these ideas*, such as electing into or out of advanced mathematics. . . . The child who scrapes by to high school graduation, or who drops out, or behaves so intolerably that he or she is pushed out, may not be able to envision and emotionally claim an adult future that requires the core curriculum of high school. (1987, pp. 6–7, emphasis in original)

I have found this analysis and the metaphor of trajectories compelling and illuminating. The word *trajectory* suggests an orientation toward the future; when an object is "on a trajectory," we envision the way its movement will continue from the past to the future; we are able to predict its location in the future. Similarly, my students' lives are on a trajectory. Their pasts may lead them, and us, to expect or hypothesize a certain future. Yet there is paradox as well. As Bob's comments remind us, students, unlike inanimate objects, have consciousness and will. Thus, students make decisions that help them keep on a particular trajectory or change their trajectory. Alternatively, students may not feel that they are able to exert their will and are not able to change the trajectories on which they find themselves. (For Donald's more elaborate use of the metaphor of trajectories, see Dryden, 1995.)

The metaphor has other dimensions. Students who arrive in the same class with seemingly similar superficial characteristics (same race and ethnic background, from the same previous class, similar grades, etc.) may be at the same point, but may be traveling on very different trajectories. In addition, this metaphor suggests the unique nature of individual experience. Rather than traversing the well-worn paths of the terrestrial world, I imagine students' trajectories traveling through space, without necessarily needing to follow paths that are labeled or marked.

Thus, one way to conceptualize an adolescent's lack of curricular engagement (an alternative to student "laziness" or "lack of ability") is to suggest there is a mismatch between the students' sense of their trajectory and the curricular content of the course. This conceptualization helps explain the seemingly limited utility of the arguments teachers often make for studying mathematics. Many of the timeworn rationales that mathematics teachers offer for studying mathematics are future-directed; we suggest that mathematics provides access to further educational or career opportunities. But many of the students Sandy and I taught at Holt did not see themselves as headed toward college. They had questions of the "what are we ever going to use this for?" variety. They did not see algebra in the world around them. Nonetheless, as argued by Sedlak et al. (1986), they did view the high school diploma as a necessary credential on their trajectory. So, to avoid failure and its ramifications for graduation, many of our students would do the minimum amount of work required to pass.

STUDENT "TRAJECTORIES" AND THE SITUATION OF THE LOWER-TRACK MATHEMATICS TEACHER

I find the student-researchers' comments and the metaphor of trajectories useful when thinking about the situation of the lower-track mathematics teacher and ways in which it is complicated by the particular position of mathematical knowledge in our culture. In the United States, and elsewhere as well, success in mathematics and opportunities for further education are tightly linked. Indeed, for many, this link, rather than any intrinsic interest in the subject, is the primary reason to study mathematics. And, as I illustrated earlier in describing my day-school teaching, many of the traditional justifications to students for investment of their energies in school mathematics are future directed: "This material is important because it provides you with skills that will help you solve next year's problems."

In many teaching situations, these features of the position of mathematical knowledge in our culture are not experienced as creating difficulty; indeed the rationales the textbook and I provided to my dayschool students did the trick. However, in other teaching contexts, this is not the case. Differences between the trajectories that teachers have traveled and the trajectories that students are traveling cause friction; there are structural dynamics that make it difficult for teachers and students in lower-track mathematics classes to identify with each other. As a result, for many high school mathematics teachers, even in settings, like Holt, where there is little ethnic or racial diversity among students and teachers, students in lower-track classes are experienced as "other." Alternatively, perhaps the word *even* is not quite right. Maybe, in settings with greater diversity, social class would not be such a strong category. If there were other affiliations between students and teachers who differed in social class, the sense of "otherness" might be less. Regardless, at Holt, the distance between lower-track Algebra One students and their teachers loomed large.

Why? I'll begin with a thought experiment. Imagine for a moment a school, like Holt High School, where there is a strong correlation between academic track and social class. Students in the school are aware of this tracking and belong to social groups correlated both with social class and their track in school (Eckert, 1989). Now imagine the trajectory of a high school student who will go to college, study mathematics, perhaps even be a mathematics major, become a teacher, and return to teach in this school.

If the future teacher is not of a working-class or poor background, but is instead from a middle- or upper-class background, this future teacher may not have the opportunity as a high school student to learn much about the sort of students he or she may end up teaching in a lower-track mathematics class and those students' trajectories. He or she may not share many classes with students outside of the college-intending track. He or she may even be a member of a social group that is in conflict or tension with the members of the cohort most like the students he or she will eventually teach in lower-track classes. Some of this tension may be related to different attitudes toward school, the value of school knowledge in the world of work, and the importance of success in school.

If, however, this future teacher is working-class or poor, the picture is quite different. This future teacher may actually know quite well members of his or her own cohort most like the lower-track students he or she will teach. This future teacher may live in the same neighborhood and may even socialize with such members of his or her own cohort. However, the difference in his or her own experiences of school in a college-intending mathematics class means that he or she has not experienced a lower-track mathematics class. Furthermore, as experience of school differs, these differences cry out for explanation; placement in the college-intending track can begin to strain relations with peers in non-academic tracks.

This thought experiment suggests that high school mathematics teachers and students in lower-track classes have different experiences of schooling. Few mathematics teachers were themselves ever students in lower-track high school mathematics classes. In order to receive secondary mathematics teaching certificates, most high school mathematics teachers were themselves in college-intending mathematics tracks and were successful in school.[9] Few mathematics teachers have ever failed a high school mathematics class; yet, failure rates in lower-track, non-college-intending courses are often quite high. Furthermore, because of relationships between social class and schooling, differential experiences of schooling and attitudes toward schooling can make it difficult for working-class or poor students to identify with middle-class mathematics teachers and the value they place on achievement in mathematics.

This can happen even if a teacher identifies strongly with students from working-class backgrounds. As Sandy has helped me appreciate, mathematics itself may come between teacher and student. She argues that her experiences of mathematics and Spanish teaching are not idiosyncratic, but indeed symptomatic of a more general predicament of mathematics teaching. To explain, she juxtaposes Bertrand Russell's (1910) rhetoric about mathematics—for example, that it possesses not only truth, but a cold and austere otherworldly beauty—and her sense of the despair of many students, students rooted in the particulars of difficult situations who see no possibility of escaping "the dreary exile of the natural world" (p. 73). Though Russell's view of the beauty of mathematics was part of what drew Sandy to teaching mathematics, she argues that much of the rhetoric about mathematics may alienate the very students she seeks to teach.

Finally, the organization of high schools does not help. Even if a teacher acknowledges differences of school experience and/or social class and decides he or she would like to learn more about students in lower-track classes, there may simply be little or no time. Most high school teachers teach between 120 and 180 students. Disaffected students do not usually come to meet with their mathematics teacher before or after school. Passing time between classes is much too short. Students and teacher rarely have a shared free hour during school time and there are myriad responsibilities for "covering" material during the time of instruction.

HOMEWORK, STUDENT MOTIVATION, AND STUDENT "TRAJECTORIES"

I also find the student-researchers' comments and the metaphor of trajectories useful when thinking about particular classroom practices. The classroom institution called "homework" is a prime example. When assessing students' motivation, teachers often use a student's attitude toward homework as a yardstick. Students' homework effort is one of the characteristics that distinguishes higher-track, particularly college-intending, and lower-track classes. On the whole, in higher-track classrooms, students who see themselves continuing their academic studies take school and their homework assignments seriously. In classrooms where students do not envision themselves continuing in academic settings, homework becomes a major struggle between teachers and students. Homework is assigned and graded. Systems are devised to reward completion of homework and to punish missing homework, or compromises are made and homework is not given or is deemphasized.

Over lunch one June day, once school was out, we discussed homework with Bob and Lynn. Sandy and I pointed out that we gave less and less homework as the year progressed and explained that one reason was that few students would hand in the homework, even when this had a detrimental effect on their grades.[10] Lynn suggested that the lack of homework was related to the way we organized our class:

> Every day the class had discussions so every day people wanted to learn *in* the class instead of *out* of the class having to do homework—so they'd rather have you guys give them a ditto and do it *in* class, *with* groups, rather than having to do it by themselves.[11]

Sandy did not think Lynn's explanation worked and followed up by asking whether they did their homework in other classes. Both Lynn and Bob indicated they did not. I followed up:

DC: So then, if a class is really based on that you have to do your homework in order to be successful, then just count you out?

Lynn: Exactly. I cannot. When I go home I don't like to spend my time,
at home, doing school work. I have a really hard time with that. I
got places to go, and . . . [12]

Sandy asked what their priorities were after school. Lynn spent her time
talking on the phone with friends who had moved away or whose parents would
not let her visit. Bob spent his time playing basketball. Our conversation moved
away from the topic of homework.

At our next meeting, we talked in more detail with Bob about his feelings
about homework. His way of thinking about homework seemed rooted in a
larger view of life. In previous conversations, he had indicated that in his experience there is a sharp dichotomy between work and leisure time. He and his
stepfather shared a love for astronomy, yet this interest was something to pursue
during leisure time and not as a career. He used this dichotomy in discussing
what school should require of students.

A lot of the smokers, a lot of people, actually, not just smokers, they
don't really care about homework. They don't do it because they figure
you know it's just *"home" "work."* We shouldn't. If it's going to be
school, then it should be *"school" "work" in school* and we shouldn't
have to do anything *at home*, since it's not "school" "homework." It
should be anything that we are going to learn we should learn at school
not at home. [italics and quotation marks added to capture emphasis][13]

Sandy picked up on a similarity between this view and how she had viewed
some of the jobs she had held previously.

SB: It reminds me kind of like a job. When I was a secretary I worked 8
to 5 and that was it and if I worked to 5:15 they paid me extra.

Bob: That's exactly how it is. I mean why should we spend our own
time doing stuff that we should be doing at school? Like you're supposed to learn at school so why don't they just teach us everything
in school instead of sending stuff home with us, so we have to waste
our own time. So we have waste our own time, you know, doing
homework, when we could hang out with our friends. A lot of people they don't really care about homework too much. Like me, I
don't really like homework all that much.

Rather than interpret Bob's disdain for homework as laziness, Sandy was sensitive to other dimensions of his remarks:

SB: You know, I never saw the connection before. When I used to work as a waitress or a secretary that's how I saw my job I think that's the way you're talking about school.

Bob: That's exactly how I'm talking about it.[14]

This conversation gave us much food for thought. Is the very concept of homework biased toward certain conceptions of the relationship between work and leisure, toward white-collar unpaid overtime rather than blue-collar over-time? Is homework one of the school practices that acts to sort by social class? Are the usual categories of motivation appropriate for talking about Bob's views about homework? When a mathematics course is not devoted solely to mastery of skills, is daily homework a necessity? Does reduction or elimination of home-work indicate that standards have been compromised and that students are not being taken seriously? If so, are there alternative ways to indicate that course-work is serious work? Or is it that the nature of homework must change as one attempts to actualize reform rhetoric about mathematics for all students? If so, how?

"REAL-WORLD" PROBLEMS AND STUDENT "TRAJECTORIES"

Knowledge about students' peer groups and their relationships to views of schooling is also helpful background for appreciating difficulties of task design in task-centered classroom. For the mathematics teacher, this background helps foreground some of the complexities in the use of real-world problems to in-crease student engagement. What does "real world" mean? Whose world do I use? Real-world problems designed to suggest implicitly the utility of mathe-matics in pursuits that students judge completely foreign to them and their possi-ble life trajectories may not convince students to engage with the material; in-deed, they may have the opposite effect. On the other hand, deciding what students' trajectories are and what will, as a result, interest them, when one does not know them well, when one knows only their superficial characteristics, can unfairly limit and pigeonhole students.[15] Moreover, finding problem contexts that are "real" for a class full of students on a range of different trajectories seems unrealistic.

In critiquing extant work in mathematics education, Ricardo Nemirovsky (1996) makes related points. He suggests that the adjective *real*, as in real-world problems or real problems, is not appropriately attached to the nouns *problem* or *world*. In other words, he believes that *real* should be thought of, for example, not as an objective description of the text of a problem, but rather as a descrip-tion of a relationship between a problem and the experience of the person solv-ing the problem. Rather than assuming "that the context belongs to the formulation of the problem," he suggests that "*real* contexts are to be found in the experience of problem solvers" (p. 211). Thus, he argues that it is wrongheaded to label seemingly "abstract" problems as not "real-world." He suggests that students' experiences in school with number are an important part of their world and may offer a valuable context and set of resources for student engagement with seemingly abstract problems.

Though Nemirovsky's (1996) point could be taken as support for not re-thinking the algebra curriculum and continuing the sort of teaching I did at the dayschool, I do not believe this is his intention. I think instead that his point is to call our attention to students' worlds of experience. As I contemplate and interpret relationships between types of problems I have given my students and their classroom engagement, Nemirovsky's point about the importance of the learner's relationship to a problem context has been useful. Taking his point seriously makes it clear how difficult it is to design mathematics instruction that engages students and that is "real" for them by his standards. One way to think about this challenge as a teacher is to take on this challenge oneself, to conclude that in order to design effective problems one needs to know one's students well enough to know what is real for them. This was an early conclusion of mine.

During my first year of teaching at Holt, I began to attempt to use the problems I posed to address student motivation. For example, on one occasion (as a prelude to the type of abstract simplification problems alluded to earlier in Chapter 1 and discussed in detail in Chapter 3) I was trying to design problems in which students would come up against different ways of computing the same quantity. One, perhaps trivial, example of this phenomenon is the following two ways of computing the sales price of an item during a 25%-off sale given its original asking price:

- Take 25% of the original price to figure out the discount given by the sale and subtract this discount from the original price to get the sale price.
- Take 75% percent of the original price. This is the final sale price.

I wanted students to appreciate that, as in this example, two seemingly different calculations can reliably give the same results.

When teaching at the dayschool, I had become interested in strategies dif-ferent people had for computing a 15% tip in a restaurant. Many junior high school students in one of my classes had been taught different "rules of thumb" by their parents for computing such tips. I thought this might be a "context" for students to share strategies and to be able to evaluate whether different strategies gave the same results.

When I gave this problem at Holt, however, it turned out that none of the students had ever left a tip in a restaurant. Victoria had just started a job waitressing in a restaurant where customers regularly left tips, but she had no idea how they decided how much of a tip to leave, or how to interpret the sums they left. As a result of social class differences, this context, which had been "real" to my dayschool classes, was not real for these students.

While this example suggests the importance of teachers' local adaptation of produced curriculum to meet the experiences, and trajectories, of their students, such adaptations still face important difficulties. As the earlier discussion of peer groups and trajectories suggests, the students in my Holt classes did not all share the same experiences or orientations toward the future. Such variation among the students made it hard to design problems situated in contexts familiar to all of our students. For example, in a discussion with Bob and Lynn, we discussed an investigation that Sandy and I had designed to capture student interest. The investigation explored how the cost of cigarettes would change under a new tax plan that was being promoted by the governor and debated in the state legislature.

In discussing this investigation, Bob suggested that it was impossible to find contexts that would be real to different groups of students. He and his friends had found the activity informative and of interest; in fact he thought that, as a result of the activity, some people were contemplating quitting smoking if the new tax plan went into effect. However, given tension between preppies and smokers about smoking, he did not think others found the activity as compelling. From his perspective, our class was so heterogeneous that it might even be impossible to teach with a single problem.

While Bob perhaps overstated the differences among our students—after all they do have much in common: growing up in the same town, going to the same school, being in the same non-college-intending track—I believe there is an important point to be made. If one wants problems to be real for students by virtue of their context, classes in which peer groups are in conflict are a challenge. For example, in the context of tensions between preppies and smokers around identification with school, commonly utilized strategies—like designing problems around school activities (e.g., planning for a school dance or play)—may be problematic. Thus, "real-world problems," "applications," or "contextualized problems" are not a panacea and have limitations in helping a teacher address issues of motivation.

REFLECTION AND LOOKING AHEAD

While the discussions with Donald's student-researchers about student peer groups, homework, problems contexts, and their own lives taught us a great deal, they were more helpful in indicating limitations of strategies typically used in mathematics education than in concretely suggesting alternative approaches.

While we felt these discussions helped us understand our predicament, they did not help us, as mathematics teachers, identify specific grounds on which we could argue explicitly that our students should invest their energies in studying algebra. However, the student-researchers' comments, Mary Metz's (1993) emphasis on teachers' dependence on their students, and the notion of student trajectories emphasized the importance of engaging students in the task of making their own individual connections to the mathematics we studied. These influences pushed us to involve students in the task of making algebra meaningful, rather than to take on the sole responsibility for that task. Sandy and I tried to design ways to have students tell us about algebra they saw in their lives, rather than for us to invent problems we hoped would be real for them.

Yet, if students were to tell us about algebra in their lives, we needed to be able to help them see algebra in the world around them. As I suggested when discussing my initial dayschool algebra teaching, my old understandings of algebra were not sufficient to this task. Our students at Holt would not see the x's and y's of my dayschool algebra course in widespread use by adults they knew. Sandy and I needed a different understanding of algebra, one that would allow students to recognize algebraic thinking and activity in the world around them.

In the next chapter, I turn to the attempts Sandy and I have made to develop our subject matter knowledge, to come to a conceptual understanding of algebra, one that could be used to help students find their own connections to the subject. This exploration will require an in-depth examination of the subject matter, of algebra, and will initially take us far from the students. It will also include exploration of just what might be meant by the adjective *conceptual*.

Chapter 3

Toward a "Conceptual Understanding" of School Algebra

Like many other teachers, algebra teachers, particularly those who teach students in lower-track classes, are currently under pressure to reform their teaching. There are three dynamics associated with such desires for reform that are particular to school algebra.

In an effort to make a college education more equitably accessible to all students, many states and districts have adopted "algebra-for-all" policies. In some cases, these policies mandate that in order to graduate every student must pass an algebra class. But, while states and districts have adopted such policies, students in lower-track classes are not necessarily convinced that school algebra is an important set of skills and knowledge for them to learn.

At the same time that teachers are supposed to help all students pass algebra, the traditional algebra course has been roundly criticized by reformers who are part of the NCTM Standards movement. The traditional course is seen as emphasizing "meaningless manipulation." Teachers are supposed to change the course and emphasize "conceptual understanding." Yet most algebra teachers have taught traditional courses for years and took such algebra courses as high school students. Most high school teachers have no images of what a different course might look like and few resources from which to begin to construct such alternatives. Few would argue that they themselves have a "conceptual" understanding of the subject.

Finally, advances in symbol-manipulation technology have supported the creation of hand-held calculators that can do all of the symbol manipulation traditionally taught in high school algebra. As this sort of technology becomes more widely available, the mathematics education community is debating the importance of having students learn to carry out symbolic manipulations by hand. The debate is quite fierce (part of what is known in some circles as "the Math wars"; see Jackson, 1997a, 1997b), with some continuing to emphasize the enduring importance of the development of symbol-manipulation skill and others arguing that these skills are completely unnecessary (e.g., Ralston, 1999).

Earlier, I described my frustrations when teaching algebra at the dayschool.

I felt that my students had no idea what algebra was about, beyond the skills we "covered" each day in class. Worse, I did not feel that I personally had a *conceptual* understanding of the subject; certainly I did not have an understanding of the subject that would have helped me cope with the type of disengagement I later found when teaching at Holt High School. When teaching at the dayschool, I could not have helped my students "see" algebra in the world around them. And I do not think I was alone in this feeling. It is difficult for many teachers of high school algebra, mathematics educators, and mathematicians to say what school algebra is about; as a result, rather than describe school algebra as a particular field of mathematical study, many describe it as the language in which much of mathematics is written. For example, in the proceedings of the Algebra Initiative Colloquium, Usiskin (Lacampagne, Blair, & Kaput, 1995, Vol. II, p. 89) describes algebra as a language, while, in her summary (Vol. I, p. 6), Lacampagne argues that participants had difficulty articulating a "story line" for algebra.

Faced with this difficulty, some reform efforts have changed the high school curriculum in dramatic ways, in the process doing away with courses titled "Algebra One." But such curricular changes were not what I sought when teaching at Holt. I was not convinced that simply changing the material would address the issues of student motivation, conceptual understanding, and classroom discourse that I have described.

I took on a different task. I arranged to teach Algebra One. The principal at the time made it quite clear that I *could* change what I did in the Algebra One classroom as long as my teaching could be legitimately regarded as an approach to high school algebra; I would have to teach the "skills" commonly taught in that class. Thus, the work I undertook at Holt was a reinterpretation of an existing course. I sought a way of thinking about algebra that would help my students—be they smokers, preppies, stoners, or nerds—see algebraic thinking in the world of their experience.

This chapter continues the story of attempts to engage Holt lower-track Algebra One students in the study of algebra. Now, the story widens to include both the students and the subject matter. It examines the curricular choices that Sandy and I made in our class and our assessment that this particular approach to algebra provided us with resources that we had not had before. But, by looking at the predicaments we faced in our instruction, this chapter is also an attempt to understand more general issues of teaching. It investigates such questions as: What is a conceptual understanding of a subject? In what ways does having such a conceptual understanding provide resources for teachers to change the nature of their instruction (Chazan, 1999)? What does it mean to look to the "discipline" to fashion instruction in school? These questions are sometimes explored in general, sometimes vis-à-vis mathematics instruction, and sometimes in the context of school algebra and the choices that Sandy and I made.

Thus, in this chapter, the particular task of reinterpreting the algebra curriculum and the more general desire to understand what could be meant by the term *conceptual* will at first take me far from the students I taught. In the first half of the chapter, I visit John Dewey's and Joseph Schwab's theoretical work on the nature of curriculum, explore a key time period in the history of algebra, and then examine the varieties of algebra now part of the mathematical land-scape. Having gone far afield, in the second half of the chapter I return to the students I taught and the question of helping them see school algebra in the world around them. I describe and examine the choices that Sandy and I made. Since the chapter investigates curricular questions in mathematics, the subject matter itself must be taken seriously. So, when addressing mathematical topics, I have tried to provide material to support readers not as well-versed in mathe-matics, while not losing the thread of more general issues about teaching. The notes contain both further clarification for some readers and pointers to more elaborate discussions of mathematical points for others.

"CONCEPTUAL" UNDERSTANDING

In describing my frustration when teaching at the dayschool, I have described the understanding I felt I lacked as "conceptual," for want of a better word. My exploration of this term will begin with mathematics teaching, but will then range further afield.

A Helpful Initial Comparison

The limitations in my understanding of school algebra were especially apparent to me once I had begun to give serious thought to high school geometry. While traditional high school geometry instruction is routinely criticized for the way in which it caricatures mathematical proof (for a telling critique, see Schoenfeld, 1988), the traditional course at least identifies particular mathematical objects as the focus of instruction, as intangible as those objects may be. In the United States, the course has focused on the study of figures in the Euclidean plane (for a description of alternative choices and a defense of this choice, see Chazan & Yerushalmy, 1998). The high school geometry curriculum is devoted to, in the words of the Russian mathematician Aleksandrov (1956/1963), "the spatial forms and relations of actual bodies, removed from their other properties" (p. 22). So chapters in one traditional textbook (Jurgensen, Brown, & King, 1980) include the following titles: "Parallel Lines and Planes," "Congruent Triangles," "Similar Polygons," "Right Triangles," and "Circles." When teaching from this textbook, I knew what the objects of study in the geometry course were; I could help students learn to "see" these "objects" of study, even though we did not think of them as physical objects, in the world around us.

    It is useful to note that this curricular focus represents a choice, which is sometimes controversial, to attend both to the child and to the curriculum, and not simply to represent the discipline authentically. Geometry has become a much more abstract affair than what is represented in the traditional high school Euclidean geometry course. Since the discovery of non-Euclidean geometries, many modern mathematicians no longer conceive of geometry as the literal science of space and would object to Aleksandrov's (1956/1963) description. The school curriculum tries to mediate between these developments in the discipline and the experience of students.[1] The traditional course regularly appeals to students' intuitive understandings of the geometry of objects they see.

By way of contrast to the situation in geometry, where the objects of study are clear, some of the chapters in the traditional Algebra One text I used when teaching at the dayschool (Dolciani & Wooten, 1970/1973) are: "Solving Equations and Problems," "Solving Inequalities," "Working with Polynomials," "Special Products and Factoring," and "Operations with Fractions." When I taught at the dayschool, these titles did not really help me understand what material was going to appear in the chapter; I would have to page through the chapter to know which skills were "covered." Furthermore, some of the mathematical objects that are mentioned in these titles are already quite familiar to students; *fractions* and *equations* are terms students usually meet in elementary school. The titles of the chapters do not indicate what new territory is going to be examined.[2] Finally, the prevalence of gerunds in the titles, and the choice of vague ones at that ("solving" or "working"), indicates that the course is organized in terms of actions to be taken, rather than particular mathematical objects of study. In short, the algebra textbooks I knew did not seem to be useful resources for learning to see algebra in the world around me, for developing the type of understanding of algebra I felt I lacked.

Conceptual Understanding and Psychologizing the Subject Matter

In mathematics education, when discussing student understanding, *conceptual* is not a well-clarified term (for attempts to remedy this situation, see Hiebert, 1986). Rather than being defined in its own right, it tends be contrasted with a caricature of the term *procedural*, where procedural is equated with a certain limited kind of knowledge that traditional teaching fosters. In the current climate of mathematics education reform, there is a desire to have students develop conceptual knowledge; there is pressure on teachers to "teach for conceptual understanding" or to "teach adventurously" (Cohen, McLaughlin, & Talbert, 1993). In the words of the NCTM Standards (1989):

> The 9–12 standards call for a shift in emphasis from a curriculum dominated by memorization of isolated facts and procedures, by proficiency with paper-and-pencil skills, to one that emphasizes conceptual understandings, multiple representa-

tions and connections, mathematical modeling, and mathematical problem solving. (p. 125)

Yet it is hard to specify just what "conceptual understanding" means in such rhetoric, other than indicating that it is deeper or more connected than what is labeled procedural understanding.

There is a similar difficulty in characterizing teaching that aspires to help students construct such understandings. Acknowledging this difficulty in a tongue-in-cheek fashion, researchers at the National Center for Research on Teacher Learning have labeled teaching that has such aspirations TKOT—This Kind of Teaching—as opposed to a different TKOT—That Kind of Teaching— the sort of teaching I did at the dayschool, which intends to produce skilled performance by carefully planned focus on student mastery of prerequisite skills (National Center for Research on Teacher Learning, 1992). Though these phrases are meant humorously, they capture the sense in which educators do not have well-elaborated ways to talk about teaching that evidences a conceptual understanding of subject matter; it is easier to caricature what conceptual understanding is not than to describe what it is.

At the same time, the desire to teach students so that they come to construct conceptual understandings of subject matter is not a new one. One step toward "teaching for understanding" is described in John Dewey's "The Child and the Curriculum" (1902/1990) as "psychologizing subject matter" or viewing subject matter "as an outgrowth of [the child's] present tendencies and activities" (p. 203). Dewey conceptualizes psychologizing the subject matter in the following two ways.

> From the side of the child, it is a question of seeing how his experience already contains within itself elements—facts and truths—of just the same sort as those entering into the formal study; and, what is of more importance, of how it contains within itself the attitudes, the motives, and the interests which have operated in developing and organizing the subject-matter to the plane which it now occupies. From the side of the studies, it is a question of interpreting them as outgrowths of forces operating in the child's life, and of discovering the steps that intervene between the child's present experience and their richer maturity. (p. 189)[3]

To psychologize the subject matter, I would therefore need an understanding of algebra and of my students' experience, which would help me see how my students' experience can be viewed as having "algebra" in it.

Since Dewey's words were penned, mathematics and algebra have stubbornly resisted this type of psychologizing. By exploring some of the historical unfolding that led to modern views of algebra, I would like to explore a reason for this resistance—one that is, perhaps, unique to the discipline of mathematics.

Mathematics and "Meaning"

The discipline of mathematics in the Western world has developed a profound philosophical ambivalence about meaning and experience that makes it difficult to psychologize mathematics. Traditionally, philosophers of mathematics of different stripes have denied relationships between the experience of people, whether adults or children, and the formal study of mathematics. For example, mathematics is often taken as the paradigmatic example of knowledge that is *a priori*, independent of sensory experience. In the modern age, in reaction both to standard mathematical practice that seems to ignore problems of the infinite and minority views that argue for limiting mathematics to procedures that can be accomplished in finitely many steps, this ambivalence has risen to a fever pitch. For example, formalist philosophers of mathematics, in the words of computer scientist and mathematician Johann von Neumann (1983), have come to "regard classical mathematics as a combinatorial game played with [the] primitive symbols" (p. 62). For Abraham Robinson (1969), the developer of Non-Standard Analysis, such views are attractive philosophically because they do not require that one "comprehend the incomprehensible" (p. 49)—by that he means the existence of infinite totalities; while they do not restrict mathematical activity, they allow one to use infinitary concepts freely.

Yet such views are not a strong foundation for psychologizing the school curriculum. While games are often of great importance to those who play them, the implication is that in mathematics, as in other games, it is not fruitful to pursue questions of meaning or of the connections between the game and other pursuits.[4] In its (admittedly) most extreme form, this perspective rules out the possibility of developing an explanation of how the experience of a child contains the seeds of formal mathematical study; children learning mathematics must leave behind their experiences and learn the rules of the "games" that others have designed. Adherents of an extreme view of this sort would label my search for a conceptual understanding of algebra misguided, or at least quixotic. But even in less extreme forms, I would argue that this view is part of what makes "psychologizing" mathematics a difficult task for teachers. To give a flavor for this difficulty, I would like to examine cursorily some 19th-century developments in British mathematics.

Toward Modern Algebra. The roots of modern, foundational philosophies of mathematics, like the formalist one, are often traced to the central role of Euclidean geometry in the philosophy of mathematics (e.g., Kline, 1980). In this telling of the story, the foundations movement in the philosophy of mathematics is a result of the traumatic development of non-Euclidean geometries, geometries as internally consistent as that of Euclid, though seemingly unlike Euclidean views of the world of experience. But this movement has other sources as well. More directly relevant to my quest, modern mathematical ambivalence toward meaning also arose among 19th-century British mathematicians seeking foundations for algebra. During the 19th century, conflicts developed between British mathematicians who insisted on "meaning" as a grounding for mathematics and others who proposed what historian Helena Pycior (1976) labels "the principle of mathematical freedom," an important precursor of formalist views of mathematics (for her description of these developments, see 1976, 1981, 1982). As a result of this conflict, the term *algebra* began to have its modern connotations.

By the 19th century, algebra—the name commonly thought to derive from the title of a book by the ninth-century Islamic mathematician al-Khowarizmi, *Al-jabr wa'al Muqabalah . . .* [5]—was an established body of techniques that could be expressed in a symbolic notation—school algebra's familiar x's and y's (the choice of letters, due to René Descartes, overturning the earlier practice of Franciose Viete; see Boyer, 1968/1985, p. 634). Mathematicians used these techniques to solve problems about unknown or missing quantities. But in the context of such problems, in some cases, when the standard techniques were used, "negative" and "imaginary" numbers appeared and were used in reasoning. Over time, a certain comfort developed around the use of these numbers in calculations and a field, later called the theory of equations, developed.

However, to Maseres and Frend—two vocal English 19th-century Cambridge-educated mathematicians schooled in Euclidean geometry—this comfort was a delusion; algebra and its techniques suffered by comparison with Euclidean geometry. While geometry was presented by Euclid in a deductive, synthetic manner, algebra had no similar deductive foundations that could justify the subtraction of the greater from the lesser or the resulting quantities less than nothing (their description of the use of negative numbers). In the words of Frend,

> To attempt to take it [a number] away from a number less than itself is ridiculous. Yet this is attempted by Algebraists, who talk of a number less than nothing. (quoted in Kenner, 1994, p. 683)

While other mathematicians were sensitive to this criticism, they often justified the use of negative numbers by recourse to images and metaphors still used in today's textbooks: direction along a line segment, payment and debt, or loss and reclamation of land from the sea. Frend dismissed such justifications as sloppy thinking that is irrelevant to a discussion of the principles of algebra:

> When a person cannot explain the principles of a science without reference to metaphor, the probability is, that he has never thought accurately upon the subject. (quoted in Pycior, 1981, p. 28)

Frend and Maseres championed the restriction of algebra to the positive rational numbers and were willing to suffer the consequential losses in the theory of equations.

In the 1830s, George Peacock, another Cambridge-educated English mathematician, responded to the concerns raised by Frend and Maseres in a different way, by distinguishing between two species of algebra: arithmetical and symbolical (see Pycior, 1981). In his distinction, he laid the groundwork for modern views of mathematics. In Peacock's view, arithmetical algebra is a generalized arithmetic in the strictest sense; it is arithmetic written with algebraic symbols. Subtraction in arithmetical algebra is limited to the subtraction of the lesser from the greater; the definitions of the operations, which come from the world of experience, determine the rules for operating on the algebraic symbols. On the other hand, symbolical algebra is an independent science in which "the rules [for operating with the symbols "+" and "−"] determine the meaning of the operations, or more properly speaking, they furnish the means of interpreting them" (Pycior, 1981, p. 36). Thus, for Peacock, the world of experience no longer provided the meaning for the operation of subtraction, though one can interpret subtraction by making analogies to experience. In symbolical algebra, mathematicians may define operations according to their own purposes. Thus, in order to preserve the results of the theory of equations, in symbolical algebra, the greater may be subtracted from the lesser.

As Peacock's innovation was debated and digested, much attention centered on the notion of what was then called "meaning." Are the symbols of mathematics abstract descriptions of everyday activity in the world around us? If so, does their meaning derive from these activities and must they conform to the activities they are designed to describe? Or do mathematical symbols have a completely autonomous existence? Can mathematicians write down rules that the symbols must obey and that indicate how to interpret the symbols? Can mathematicians write down any rules they desire or must they write down rules that conform with experience?

Mathematicians differed in their responses to these questions (Pycior, 1982). Though he married Frend's daughter, Sophie, August De Morgan, in his algebra text, wrote that "with one exception (the equals sign), no word or sign of Arithmetic or Algebra has one atom of meaning through this chapter" (quoted in Boyer, 1968/1985, p. 623). On the other hand, Sir William Rowan Hamilton, an Irish physicist and mathematician, often described as the first to make use of the mathematical freedom proposed by Peacock, had an initially negative reaction:

> When I first read that work . . . and indeed for a long time afterwards, it seemed to me . . . that the author [Peacock] designed to reduce Algebra to a mere system of

symbols, and nothing more; *an affair of pothooks and hangers*, of black strokes upon white paper, . . . and I refused, in my own mind, to give the high name of Science to the results of such a system. (quoted in Pycior, 1981, pp. 40–41; emphasis added)

But the freedom of mathematicians to lay down rules for operating with symbols subsequently won the day and led to further developments in algebra. Hamilton developed a generalization of the complex numbers, the quaternions, and George Boole, an English logician, developed his logic and a system of symbols to capture his insights. Algebras proliferated and, subsequently, the mathematical subdisciplines of abstract algebra and linear algebra developed. In the development of these subdisciplines, the mathematical freedom first proposed in 19th-century England was assumed. Mathematicians were allowed to create whatever systems they liked, without concern for whether these systems represented the world of experience. In this sense, the formalist description of mathematics as a combinatorial game with symbols became accurate (see Goodman, 1986, especially pp. 83–84, for a discussion of the insights afforded by formalist philosophies of mathematics).

Formalist Views and Psychologizing the Subject Matter. Formalist views of mathematics are a part of the intellectual landscape of mathematics—part of the challenge of reconceptualizing the teaching of mathematics, in general, and the school algebra curriculum, in particular. While this cursory examination of debates about "meaning" and mathematics in the 19th century helps one understand how formalist views developed, it does not seem helpful to me as a teacher of school algebra with my task of psychologizing the subject matter. If mathematics is only a meaningless game played with symbols, then do I introduce my students to algebra by having them make up rules that determine games? How would I justify the particular game that is played in school algebra? How is this particular game to be found in the world of their experience? With a formalist view, I do not feel that I would have resources for addressing the difficulties of student motivation that faced me in my teaching at Holt. This view of the nature of mathematics and the rejection of "meaning" (alluded to in the quotations from von Neumann and DeMorgan above) seems only to complicate the task of psychologizing the curriculum.

However, luckily, formalism is not the only view of mathematics available to those constructing school curricula. Formalist views have been criticized strongly as an example of what Goodman (1986) calls "surfacism"; these views do not adequately explain the public and social aspects of mathematical activity (see Tymoczko, 1986, for a collection of papers aimed at exactly that task). For example, mathematicians Philip Davis and Reuben Hersh (1981) remind us that the formalist view of mathematics, while prominent in philosophical discussions of mathematics, is not the unambivalent view of the majority of mathematicians and, in particular, does not describe how mathematicians usually work:

> The typical mathematician is a Platonist on weekdays and a formalist on Sundays. That is, when he is doing mathematics he is convinced that he is dealing with an objective reality whose properties he is attempting to determine. But then, when challenged to give a philosophical account of this reality, he finds it easiest to pretend that he does not believe in it after all. (p. 321)

While Platonist views on the foundations of mathematics are problematic to me for other reasons (I prefer recent developments in the philosophy of mathematics that emphasize the role of meaning, intuition, and the particular in mathematical practice—see the discussion in Chapter 4), in the next section I will use the notion of mathematical "objects" to make progress on the task of psychologizing the algebra curriculum.

Identifying "Objects of Study": An Essential Question[6]

If formalist views represent an obstacle to psychologizing the discipline of mathematics as school subject matter, what might help overcome this obstacle? The differences between the high school geometry and algebra texts that I described earlier and what Joseph Schwab (1978) infelicitously calls a "substantive" (as opposed to "syntactic") approach to disciplines suggest a potentially fruitful path. When seeking to find continuity between students' experience and a discipline, I have found it is useful to address this question: *What are the fundamental objects of study in this discipline?*[7] If one's own understanding of the discipline allows one to describe its objects of study, perhaps one would then be able to appreciate how they manifest themselves in students' experience. Thus, for me, a conceptual understanding of a discipline identifies its central objects of study.

What do I mean by "objects of study?" This seems like an easy question in those branches of the sciences where one studies physical phenomena. One can study primates, ferns, light, or magnetism; yet, in my view, objects of study need not be physical objects, physical phenomena, or time periods. Thus, a teacher planning a unit on the history of the U.S. Civil War might suggest that the objects of study in this unit are not the events that transpired, but the processes by which legalized slavery was abolished in the United States.

However, this is not the only approach to a study of the Civil War; there is room for interpretation and for controversy. Another teacher might construct instruction about the Civil War whose focus is on the structures for negotiation between the state and federal governments about conflicting mores and values.

A third approach would be to study the ideologies that supported both slavery and abolition.[8] Thus, as Schwab's work on curriculum (1978) suggests, Dewey's (1902/1990) "side of the studies" is not a unique and well-defined perspective. In Schwab's curriculum-driven pursuit of the structure of the academic disciplines, he suggests that many disciplines have a multitude of such structures.[9] There are different potential takes on the objects of study in a particular discipline.

Finally, when I suggest that identifying objects of study is a step toward psychologizing subject matter, I am not suggesting that the answer to this question must necessarily be easily shared with students on the first day of class. Students may not be comfortable thinking of some things as objects (Perkins, 1986, is coping with a similar issue when he gently helps readers appreciate ways in which knowledge has design, just as material objects do); they may not think of the objects of study that organize the teachers' view of the subject as objects at all. It may turn out that students can appreciate what was studied only at the end of the experience or on reflection on the experience.

A Perhaps Surprising Difficulty Conceptualizing School Algebra

One might think that it would be easy to identify the objects of study in school mathematics, but this turns out not to be a simple task. My pursuit of a conceptual understanding of school algebra began with my use of a functions-based approach to teaching Algebra Two in the northeastern suburban school and developed through my attempts to help students at Holt see school algebra in the world around them. It has drawn me to a range of experiences, including participation in the electronic mail Algebra Working Group sponsored by the National Center for Research on Mathematical Sciences Education (NCRMSE, 1993), the Office of Educational Research and Improvement's Algebra Initiative Colloquium (Lacampagne et al., 1995), and the Institute for the History of Mathematics and Its Use in Teaching sponsored by the Mathematics Association of America. These experiences have made it clear that, surprisingly, there is no one single clear answer to this question: What mathematical objects do the symbols of school algebra represent? In contrast to common conceptions of mathematics (Joseph Schwab's [1978] included), there is a range of views about what school algebra is; there is no consensus. As a teacher, I have choices to make and to justify, if seemingly only to myself.

And the debate is, understandably, a contentious one within the mathematics education community. There are pressures for stability and consensus, as well as for change. On the side of stability, algebra is a central component of the high school mathematics curriculum. It is easier to change it than to abandon it. But, because of the use of secondary mathematics in the testing processes that certify high school diplomas and allocate opportunities for further study, changes to the curriculum are a high-stakes endeavor and extremely threatening. The use of mathematics in testing also generates pressure to define and to implement a single vision, rather than to have alternative visions of school algebra.[10] As a result, there will be "winners" and "losers" in this increasingly politicized debate.

At the same time, there are the pressures for change that I have alluded to before: Student achievement is poor, school algebra's gatekeeping role has been criticized, and technology is now available that can do the manipulations that are the traditional focus of the course.[11] While the availability of such technological tools certainly does not dictate that students should no longer learn to manipulate symbols for themselves, it does force the mathematics education community to have a well-elaborated justification for the manipulation of x's and y's that is taught. What kind of experiences should students have in manipulating symbols (Pimm, 1995, takes this issue very seriously)? What *could* school algebra be about?[12]

So, What Are the Fundamental Objects of Study in Algebra? A Survey

Capturing the debate on this question is a daunting task. Distinctions among different positions are often subtle. Some of the debate assumes understanding, not commonly found among teachers or the general public and not well articulated by mathematicians, of similarities and differences among the essential natures of abstract fields of mathematics.[13] The subject deserves a fuller treatment for the specialist than I am able to attempt here. For the nonspecialist, my main goal is to illustrate the claim that there are conflicting conceptualizations of relationships between what Schwab (1978) calls the discipline and the school subject matter, in this case, between arenas of mathematical exploration (subdisciplines like Linear Algebra, Abstract Algebra, Applied Mathematics, the Theory of Equations, and Real Analysis) and school algebra. I hope this attempt will capture the flavor of the debate and, at the same time, illustrate how the notion "central mathematical object of study" organizes the conceptualization of curriculum.

Debates about the future of school algebra can be conceptualized as conflict over how to represent to students the nature of the x's and y's of school algebra. These sorts of symbols appear throughout mathematics and have quite different senses and roles in a variety of contexts. Which mathematical points of view should be represented in school algebra and in what order? How should students be taught to think about strings of literal symbols and numbers with an equal sign (e.g., $x(30 - 2x)^2 = 0$, or when it is written with literal coefficients in the places of numerical ones, $x(a - bx)^2 = 0$)? The mathematical fields of inquiry that I will survey disagree about what such equations are, whether they are the central focus of study, and what the literal symbols (e.g., x) in such equations represent.

Taking a point of view based in arithmetic suggests that numbers are central, that the x's and y's of school algebra represent numbers, and that algebraic equations are general statements about the numbers with which students have been gaining experience in school (Lee, 1996, portrays her work as an example of this sort of approach, see also Mason, 1989). The notion of "algebra as a generalization of arithmetic" is the point of view of what Peacock called Arithmetical Algebra. It builds nicely on the experiences students have had in school with numbers.

Alternatively, one can look to the theory of equations—historically an important strand in the development of algebra, but now not an active field of mathematical research—for guidance. For this theory, types of polynomial equations (e.g., linear equations, quadratics, cubics, quartics, quintics, etc.) are the fundamental objects of study. This theory concentrates on finding general solutions for types of polynomial equations. For example, the 9th-century mathematician al-Khowarizmi presented six types of problems (which would now be described as resulting in quadratic equations in different forms) for which he had developed solution procedures.[14] When algebraic symbols and conventions for distinguishing known and unknown quantities were introduced, it was possible to describe the general solution of a class of polynomial equations, rather than to exemplify the solution strategy by use of a particular example. (Rojano's [1996] problem-solving-based approach to algebra, which utilizes spreadsheets, is based on her analysis of these historical developments.) The quadratic formula of the high school curriculum is one vestige of this type of exploration; as a result of the acceptance of negative numbers as coefficients, it condenses al-Khowarizmi's six types of solutions into one. For an unknown x, it describes symbolically how to solve any quadratic equation of the "standard" form $ax^2 + bx + c = 0$, in terms of known coefficients symbolized by a, b, and c:

$$x = \frac{-b \pm \sqrt{b^2 - 4ac}}{2a}$$

Of course, in order to use this formula, one must first transform whatever equation one wants to solve into this "standard" form.

Applied mathematicians might instead suggest that school algebra is fundamentally about mathematical models for nonmathematical situations. A traditional modeling problem is to ask students to create a mathematical model for the volume of liquid held by a rectangular box made by cutting four same-sized squares, of any reasonable size, out of the corners of a 30-inch by 30-inch piece of sheet metal (see Figure 3.1). If one uses x to represent the lengths of the sides of the removed squares, taking into account that two sides of the box are of length $30 - 2x$ inches, one mathematical model is: $volume(x) = x(30 - 2x)^2$.

Figure 3.1. A traditional modeling problem.

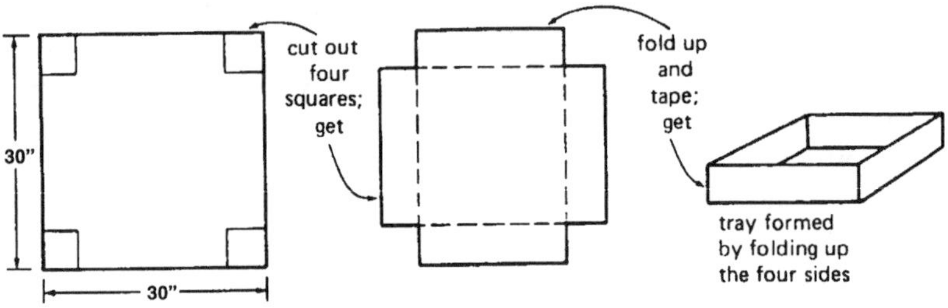

Reprinted with permission from Stein & Crabill (1970/84)

Students can then be asked to determine what size box will hold the maximum amount of liquid and what size squares must be cut out in order to create this box. In this use, the literal symbols of school algebra represent quantities, numbers and an associated unit of measure, in the world around us. Since Galileo began emphasizing the role of mathematical models in science (Kline, 1953, discusses these developments on pp. 182–195), such modeling has come to play an increasingly important role in the mathematics curriculum.

One the other hand, one can choose to look to Real Analysis (as opposed to other varieties of analysis, like Abstract, Complex, Fourier, or Harmonic Analysis) for guidance.[15] While Real Analysis is not one of the fields that grew from what Peacock called symbolical algebra, it is a mathematical field in which the x's and y's of school algebra are prominent.[16] Historically, analysis, as a subdiscipline of mathematics, was originally associated with the study of functions, then loosely defined as curves that could be drawn without lifting up a pencil (continuous in that sense) and whose coordinates were easily expressed as a relationship written with algebraic symbols. Those studying these curves became interested in questions now considered central to calculus: What is the area contained between these curves and the axes of the coordinate systems used to display them? What is the rate at which the values of the function are changing at each point along the curve? However, over time, the definition of function developed; mathematicians defined multitudes of new functions, some of which could not be easily drawn. The focus of the field shifted to an examination of the assumptions about the relationship between the continuity of curves and the nature of the real numbers used to describe coordinates of points on curves (Kline, 1980).

Thus, in Real Analysis, equations are not the central object of study. Functions—some of which can be represented as expressions, the strings of symbols found on one side of the equal sign in an equation (e.g., $x(30 - 2x)^2$ from the equation $x(30 - 2x)^2 = 0$)—are the central object of study. For analysts, the literal symbols in school algebra are variables, not unknowns; the x in an expression is a variable whose domain typically is the real numbers. Thus, expressions, rather than being names for numbers, are calculation procedures that generate output numbers from input numbers (which can be graphed or can generate a table, as in Figure 3.2). Together, these numbers produce a function, a set of input/output ordered pairs (e.g., the input of 0 to $x(30 - 2x)^2$, after calculation, gives the output 0; an input of 10 gives an output of 1,000). Analysts would want to ask about the shape of the graph of $x(30 - 2x)^2$, the numbers of maxima and minima it has, and how to categorize the graphs of such expressions into families of functions according to the shapes of their graphs and the rates at which the outputs change as the inputs are varied (to this point, these ideas are some of what is meant by a functions-based approach to algebra).

But an approach to school algebra based on Real Analysis might want to do more. Analysts might also want to use a precise modern set-theoretic definition of function (by way of contrast, see the next section for a discussion of the

Figure 3.2. A graph and table of f(x) = x(30 - 2x)²

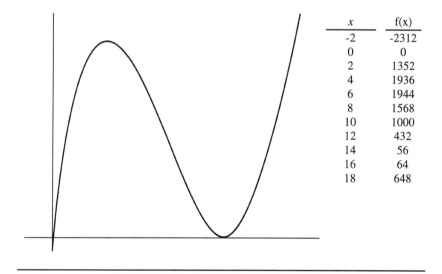

x	f(x)
-2	-2312
0	0
2	1352
4	1936
6	1944
8	1568
10	1000
12	432
14	56
16	64
18	648

type of definition Sandy and I used in a function-based approach). They might also want to examine functions that cannot be graphed, explore the structure of the real number system in detail, and be rigorous in defining a wide range of functions (like the exponential function, various trigonometric functions, or the logarithm) typically introduced into the high school mathematics curriculum in quite informal ways.

If, instead, one looks to the fields that developed out of British symbolical algebra, one might similarly emphasize the importance of expressions, viewed as calculation procedures built up out of additions and multiplications, and not equations; x, once again, is viewed as a variable. But in this view, expressions and the operations that are used to create them, like chameleons, cannot be understood without reference to their environment—to the number system from which the possible replacements for x are chosen. In order to appreciate the nature of expressions, rather than take the real number system for granted as the replacement set for the variable, students could explore the ramifications of taking different number systems as the replacement set for the variable. Thus, for this approach, the fundamental objects of study in algebra are expression-number system dyads (Cuoco, 1990, describes the use of programming in LOGO to teach a course based on this point of view).[17]

Finally, those grounded in the mathematical field called Abstract Algebra might suggest that the true objects of study in school algebra are not the calculation procedures built up out of additions and multiplications operating on number systems. This is too narrow a perspective. Algebra is about binary operations in general—of which commonly used addition and multiplication are but two examples, which operate on sets—number systems being one type of set. This is the point of view that lay behind many of the innovations of the New Math (for a critique of this use of Abstract Algebra, see Thom, 1986).

Approaches based in Abstract Algebra might suggest that the level of abstraction with which students work with symbols could be raised in three directions. In the first direction, approaches based in Abstract Algebra might suggest that students study the properties of addition and multiplication on different number systems. Properties of operations, like addition and multiplication, might be such things as: commutativity—does the order of the elements being operated on matter[18]—or closure on a set—for all members of the set, when I do an operation like addition or multiplication on two elements of the set is the result a member of the set or does it fall outside of the set? This sort of study leads students to appreciate how different combinations of sets and operations have different sorts of structure. Then this sort of view might suggest that students study the properties of other binary operations—operations that take two inputs and output one. For example, for real numbers, two such operations are the binary arithmetic mean, $\frac{1}{2}(a + b)$—which for a equal to 5 and b equal to 20 produces 12.5—or the binary harmonic mean, $\frac{1}{2}(1/a + 1/b)$—which produces

0.125 for a equal to 5 and b equal to 20. Finally, students might be asked to move beyond number systems. While students might work with equations with coefficients (like $x(a - bx)^2 = 0$), the literal symbols might stand for other mathematical objects, such as matrices (something that is sometimes done now in high schools), polynomials, or sets, rather than numbers. Eventually, students might even be asked to work with equations in which the symbol x is indeterminate—one does not specify what it represents and does not concern oneself with such questions.

In my presentation, the details of each mathematical field's perspective may not be perfectly clear, and what I have outlined oversimplifies the picture in many ways. But at least it should be evident that "What are the fundamental objects of study in school algebra?" does not have a single, simple answer.

While most approaches to school algebra merge views that I have presented separately and have associated with different mathematical fields of study, mathematics educators tend to have a special allegiance to some combination of these fields of study. Some mathematics educators, under the banner of "ontogeny recapitulates phylogeny," suggest that historical developments guide curriculum design and that school algebra be approached through arithmetic and the Theory of Equations (e.g., Pimm, 1995; Sfard, 1995). Others are more focused on modern ideas; they are concerned that students do not have opportunities to learn about the mathematics that modern mathematicians create (with regard to school algebra, see Cuoco, 1990). Some look to the recent developments in the philosophy of mathematics and focus on a curriculum's representation of how mathematics is done, more than on its particular content. I would probably fall into this camp. In the context of school geometry, in Chazan and Yerushalmy (1998), I have made that sort of argument. Those who champion a functions-based approach think that the capacity of current technology to link algebraic symbols, Cartesian graphs, and tables of values makes functions a more accessible mathematical object than in the past.

For high school teachers, however, these discussions are not an everyday concern. School algebra is a large part of daily experience; it is a central and enduring part of the curriculum. While there are pressures to reconceptualize algebra courses, the task is a difficult one. For teachers accustomed to teaching the traditional course, the course may simply be the material that is in the textbook, rather than a representation of a particular field of mathematical study. Thus, prior experience may not provide many resources to bring to bear on the problem. While mathematics educators debate the future direction of the course, they have not arrived at a consensus and it is unclear whether many teachers are informed about this debate. Then there is the matter of abstraction. There are tensions between authentically representing the abstraction of algebra as a mathematical subdiscipline, authentically representing current views of the ways in which mathematics is done, and being responsive to learners' needs.

A CHOICE: A "RELATIONSHIP-BETWEEN-QUANTITIES" APPROACH

Against the background of different potential views of the school algebra curriculum, I hope that the choices I made in my teaching at Holt will be clearer. I personally do not know how to base a beginning school algebra course on some of the more abstract views of algebra that I have described, particularly for students who are not engaged with school (which does not mean that it could not be done). I was most concerned with being able to convince my students to engage with their studies; I thought that it would help if they could "see" school algebra in the world around them.

Thus, in my teaching at Holt, I continued to explore a position on the objects of study in school algebra that is close to that of analysts. Based on ideas I initially learned from Michal Yerushalmy and Judah Schwartz (Schwartz & Yerushalmy, 1992; Yerushalmy & Schwartz, 1993, but see also: Confrey & Smith, 1995; Demana & Waits, 1990; Fey et al., 1995; Fehr, 1951; Hamley, 1934; Kieran et al., 1996; Leitzel, 1989; Moschkovich et al., 1993; Nemirovsky, 1996; Romberg, Fennema, & Carpenter, 1993; Shell Centre, 1985; Thompson, 1994; van Barneveld & Krabbendam, 1982), Sandy and I thought of the literal symbols of school algebra as variables and of expressions as calculation procedures that express relationships between input and output quantities ("quantifiable" qualities of experience involving a quality, a value or potential value, and a unit of measure). We took relationships between quantities where output variables depend unambiguously on input variables, which some might want to view more abstractly and call functions, as the central objects of study to structure our classes. While these relationships between quantities are not tangible or directly accessible to one's senses, the focus on relationships between *quantities*, as opposed to relationships between numbers, grounded the course in descriptions of the world around us. To study or describe these relationships, they can be represented in canonical ways—tables of values for the quantities in question, symbolic expressions, Cartesian graphs (Moschkovich et al., 1993; Schoenfeld, Smith, & Arcavi, 1990)—and informal ways—diagrams, mechanical devices, gestures, and written or spoken language (Hall, 1990; Hall, Kibler, Wenger, & Truxaw, 1989; Koendinger & Tabachneck, 1994; Nemirovsky, 1994; Schwartz & Yerushalmy, 1995).

I am keenly aware that this approach is but one from a large range of conflicting possibilities for teaching a school algebra course. Further, I recognize that "function" is an abstract, complex, and subtle mathematical construct, which has been in explicit use only for the last 200 years and which has taken its modern form only recently. Indeed, not all functions can be represented by all three types of representations to be described below! We limited our study to graphs that could be described analytically or to sketches that could be made out of piece-wise smooth sections.

For some mathematics educators, taking functions as the central object of study in beginning algebra may seem to fly in the face of lessons learned from New Math and its ill-fated focus on sets, an abstract modern mathematical object then in vogue. Others might argue that this choice reveals a historical contempt for how algebra developed and turns the curriculum away from modern understandings of algebra. Yet others might suggest that this choice is insufficiently abstract in its approach to algebraic symbols and does not authentically represent 20th-century mathematics. While I am cognizant of these objections, nonetheless, I have found this approach particularly useful in teaching lower-track Algebra One.

Still, as I outline this view of the objects of study in algebra and indicate how it has assisted me in developing the kind of understanding of algebra I felt I was lacking, I am not suggesting that a "relationship-between-quantities" view is the only one that leads to a conceptual understanding of school algebra. I can imagine that other views of the objects of study in school algebra might be similarly useful to teachers who wish to develop a conceptual understanding of school algebra. Rather than arguing for a particular view, my main interest here is in the relationship between teachers' understanding of school subject matter, the nature of the teaching they do, and their preparation to tackle questions of student motivation.

Thus, in the remainder of the chapter, I will clarify what I mean by a functions-based approach to school algebra by contrasting it with the way in which I used to teach and by outlining how Sandy and I began our Algebra One course. Then I will outline two ways in which this sort of approach has helped me argue, both implicitly and explicitly, to the Holt students for their commitment of energy and effort to our exploration of algebra. Finally, I will indicate two ways in which I would like to learn to develop this approach further.

How Is a Relationships-Between-Quantities View Different from a Traditional View? Focusing on x's and y's

To examine the impact that a relationships-between-quantities view of school algebra had on my teaching, I will start by clarifying some of the subtle differences between this sort of approach to the fundamental objects of study in beginning algebra and the traditional approach, which I originally used in my day-school teaching. These subtleties became evident to me before I came to Holt, when I was teaching Algebra Two with the University of Chicago School Mathematics Program (UCSMP) text in the northeastern suburban public school (Senk et al., 1987; for descriptions of that teaching, see Chapter 1). I'll illustrate how literal symbols are viewed differently in these two approaches by exploring what some would call an ambiguity or complementarity at the center of school algebra. I use the term *complementarity* in the same sense as it is used in describing light. Light is viewed at one and the same time as both particle and wave. Our understanding of light as a phenomenon is complete only when we can integrate these two seemingly contradictory views. Similarly, in school algebra, the literal symbol x is at one and the same time both particular unknown and variable quantity. In taking a relationship-between-quantities or functions-based approach, one chooses to make the second, variable view of x central and the first, particular unknown view of x background, while traditionally the roles of these views are reversed.

I'll analyze the dual nature of x by describing and examining a "correct" solution to an archetypal algebra distance/rate/time problem from the text I used when teaching at the dayschool. This problem is as problematic as the "mixture" problem that I described in Chapter 1.

> A submarine left a surface ship and cruised due south at a constant rate of 28 knots (nautical miles per hour). If the surface ship started off at the same time on a course due north at a constant rate of 22 knots, in how many hours will the ships be 125 nautical miles apart? (Dolciani & Wooten, 1970/1973, p. 188. Reprinted with permission)

The "realism" of this problem can be critiqued and lampooned— clearly there are myriad practical concerns that would complicate the computations of someone who really needed to determine such a time (How long does it take for the ships to get to their cruising speeds? Is there a current and if so how strong?). But for now let us take the problem on its own terms.

One view of algebra as the quintessential analytic art suggests that it is about reasoning with the unknown (or the as yet unknown) to make it known (Euclidean geometry by comparison is a synthetic arena where reasoning proceeds from the known "givens" to the heretofore unknown "to prove"). In this analytic art, the fundamental step is to begin by naming the unknown. When doing this sort of algebra, one then reasons with this unknown until its identity is revealed. In this case, we are asked to find the number of hours from the starting time at which the two ships will be 125 nautical miles apart. Let us call this particular unknown number x, a traditional approach.

In solving the problem, we begin to build a web of statements that will allow us to determine the value of x. Using an understanding of the relationship between distance, rate, and time when vehicles are traveling at a constant rate (specifically, distance covered is equal to constant rate times elapsed time), we can write that the distance covered by the submarine in this particular number of unknown hours is $28 * x$, while the distance covered by the surface ship is $22 * x$. While many students can solve such problems without the aid of algebraic symbols, in algebra classes, they are often taught to figure out such rela-

Figure 3.3. A DeRT table.

Distance =	*Rate*	*	*Time*
28*x nautical miles	28 knots		x hrs
22*x nautical miles	22 knots		x hrs

tionships using a DeRT table (for a discussion of the use of DeRT tables in problem solving by college students, see Hall, 1990), like the one in Figure 3.3: Already, the complementarity of *x* has surfaced. On the one hand, in the traditional view, 28*x* represents the distance covered by the submarine at the point in time at which the two ships are 125 nautical miles apart; we could take a "snapshot" of the ships at that instant and include 28*x*. 28*x* is a description of a frozen moment, of stasis (see Figure 3.4).

But if *x* is viewed as a variable, and not an unknown, time, this very same 28*x* represents something else as well; we get extra information. If *x* stands for the time elapsed since the ships parted ways (and not just the particular unknown value for which the ships are 125 nautical miles apart), 28*x* represents how the distance the submarine travels from the starting point varies with the time elapsed since the ships parted ways. For any positive numerical value in-

Figure 3.4. When the ships are 125 nautical miles apart.

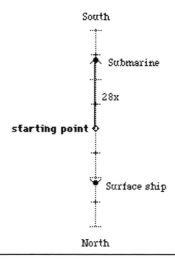

serted into the expression 28x (see Figure 3.5), we can ascertain the amount of distance covered by the submarine in that elapsed time. For $x = 2$, two hours after the ships started, the submarine is 56 nautical miles from the starting point.

Now x is no longer just a particular unknown number. It also can be viewed as a variable in an expression that represents the relationship between two quantities—elapsed time and the distance covered by the submarine. 28x is now a description of duration and motion.

Let us continue with the solution to the problem. The ships are headed in completely opposite directions. Therefore, to find the total distance between them, we add, not subtract, the distance that each ship covers from the starting point. So we add 28x and 22x and say that the total distance between the two ships as a function of elapsed time is 50x, or we can say that the total distance between the two ships at the time at which they are 125 nautical miles apart is 50x.

Taking the latter, particularistic (traditional) interpretation, it is clear that 50x should equal 125 nautical miles; they are both names for the same number. So we write 50$x = 125$. Taking the former, dynamic interpretation, 50x describes the distance between the two ships as a function of elapsed time. We are interested in knowing when this distance is equal to 125. So we ask ourselves: When is 50x equal to 125? To emphasize the conditional nature of this equation—that it is true for some values of x and not true for others—Hans Freudenthal (1973) a Dutch mathematician and noted mathematics educator, encourages teachers of algebra to write such an equation as (?x) 50$x = 125$.

Regardless of which interpretation we take, the solution is that after 2.5 hours the distance between the ships will be 125 nautical miles. The unknown particular number of hours x has been found, even though along the way it may have transmogrified and become the varying quantity, elapsed time x. Thus, the fundamental nature and meaning of x is uncertain and open to interpretation, even if the "solution" to the problem is not. In such cases, I have decided to

Figure 3.5. A table with x as a variable.

elapsed time	distance of submarine from start
0	0
.5	14
1	28
1.5	42
2	56
x	28x

give a greater weight to the view of x as a varying quantity than is traditionally the norm.

This ambiguity in a situated problem also persists into purely symbolic realms and forces one to choose in order to determine the "correct" answer to seemingly simple mathematics problems. For example, how might one create a visual display for the equation $50x = 125$ or the equation $x = 2.5$? One's response is different depending on how one views x; this was part of my problem during my Algebra Two teaching experience when I was trying to use Schwartz and Yerushalmy's (e.g., 1992) ideas and the new UCSMP textbook (Senk et al., 1987), which held a different view.

The particularistic (traditional) answer is to interpret the question about creating a visual display as a request to display the solution sets, the numbers that make these equations ($50x = 125$ and $x = 2.5$) true sentences (see Figure 3.6). This view argues that these two equations have the same display, because these equations have the same solution set. Along the number line, which represents the possible solutions to these equations, 2.5 should be filled in. It is the value of x for which these two statements are true.

Figure 3.6. Representation of the solution to $50x = 125$ and $x = 2.5$.

The dynamic answer, one gaining support as technology (such as graphing calculators) becomes widely available, is to suggest that each of these equations is a question about comparing two quantities. So, in this case, each side of each equation would be represented by a straight line. In the equation $50x = 125$, $50x$ is a quantity. We can graph how it changes as a function of x (see Figure 3.7). 125 is a quantity that does not change as a function of x; it does not depend on x. It is a constant as a function of x. Therefore, its graph is a horizontal line on the Cartesian plane (see Figure 3.8).

The graph of $50x = 125$ is the superimposition of the previous two graphs (see Figure 3.9). The intersection at the point (2.5, 125) indicates that for the value of 2.5, each of these quantities has the value of 125. But, from this graph, we can also read the values of each of these quantities for other values of x. To return to the example of the two ships, we can see when the total distance between the ships is less than 125 nautical miles and when it is greater. The graph of $x = 2.5$ will be different, but will have similar geometric characteristics (see Figure 3.10). The two lines will intersect at a point whose x value is 2.5, but whose other (y) value is 2.5 as well.

Personally, I find the dynamic interpretation of the ship problem attractive.

Figure 3.7. A graph of f(*x*) = 50*x*.

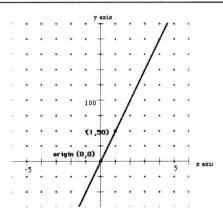

Figure 3.8. A graph of g(*x*) = 125.

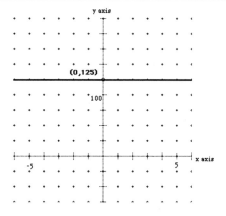

Figure 3.9. A dynamic representation of the solution to $50x = 125$.

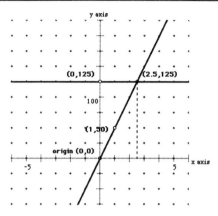

It fits better for me with my sense of what it is that people look for when solving questions about relationships between quantities. This view emphasizes motion and generality. The unknown particular number view seems artificial to me in such contexts. It requires that we freeze the action and consider a particular moment in time, instead of analyzing the dynamics of a situation (Chazan, 1993).

Figure 3.10. A dynamic representation of the solution to $x = 2.5$.

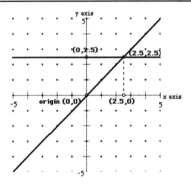

Leaving aside my reasons for preferring this particular view of the x's and y's of school algebra, how does a relationships-between-quantities or functions-based approach change the nature of the algebra curriculum? To explain, I'll delineate what I mean when using the word *function*. There are many ways in which functions can be defined and conceptualized, some of which would not have suited my purposes. Perhaps it is such views of functions that others conjure up when a functions-based approach is mentioned.

I chose to use a conceptualization of function that emphasizes that functions are relationships between quantities where output variables depend unambiguously on input variables. While this view does not capture all the subtlety of the exacting modern mathematical definition of a function, it is a useful starting point. This view, though not always explicitly named by the term *function*, is an ancient one. It may be present even in early Babylonian tablets and Egyptian papyri when they solve problems, which we would solve with systems of equations, by the method of double false position. (For a description of these methods, see Katz, 1993. Smith & Confrey, 1994, argue that covariation is an ancient focus of mathematical activity.)

By this definition, functions are the mathematization of our theories about the relationships of dependence, causation, interaction, and correlation between quantities. Auguste Comte, in his early study of the nature of different sorts of knowledge, sees such theories as methods for determining the values of quantities inaccessible to measurement. When discussing the parable of Thales, the ancient mathematician, and the pyramids, he suggests that the need for the determination of such quantities is the origin of all mathematics:

> In the light of previous experience, we must acknowledge the impossibility of determining, by direct measurement, most of the heights and distances we should like to know. It is this general fact which makes the science of mathematics necessary. For in renouncing the hope, in almost every case, of measuring great heights or distances directly, the human mind has had to attempt to determine them indirectly, and it is thus that philosophers were led to invent mathematics. (quoted in Serres, 1982, p. 85; also examined in Wheeler, 1993)

Functional dependencies conceived of in this way can be found everywhere in the cultural world around us; we use them as tools for making predictions and describing regularities. Traveling along the highway, we are using a function when we estimate the length of time it will take to reach our destination by calculating with our speed and the distance to our exit. When we use a mercury thermometer to "measure" the temperature of our environment, we are measuring *in*directly. We are using a linear function—Galileo's theory about the seemingly linear relationship between the volume of mercury and temperature. Similarly, we may be describing causal theories when we sketch graphs representing

how our mood varies over the course of a typical day in response to the str
of our day.

Outline of an Introductory Relationships-Between-Quantities Algebra Course

Concentrating on these sorts of relationships between quantities led me to change my approach to Algebra One. At the dayschool, I began Algebra One with expressions as representations of unknown numbers and immediately dove into simplification problems using the distributive law (for a description of what this meant, see the section "How Are Students Taught to Write Equivalent Expressions?" below). At Holt, Sandy and I began Algebra One by concentrating on the relationships between quantities we were going to study and the ways in which they can be represented, before approaching even the simplest of symbolic manipulations. Rather than introducing x as a variable, Cartesian graphs, and functions late in the course, we made these focal early in the course. The course began by exploring what the subject was about, by having students learn what the course's objects of study were. I'll outline this part of the course. (For more detail and descriptive vignettes of activities from this part of the course, see Bethell, Chazan, Hodges, & Schnepp, 1995.)

Because mathematicians have a particular way of thinking about quantities, after my first year of teaching at Holt, I realized that we needed to start first with the notion of quantities before we could begin to look at relationships between quantities. In common parlance, there is a view of quantity as amount, a static view, whereas mathematicians think of quantity as something whose value can change. Here is a mathematician's definition of quantity:

> Quantities are conceptual entities that exist in people's conceptions of situations. A person is thinking of a quantity when he or she conceives a quality of an object or event in such a way that this quality is measurable or countable. A quantity is composed of an object, a quality of the object, an appropriate unit or dimension, and a process by which to assign a numerical value to the quality. (Kaput, 1995, p. 45)

So, in my second and third years of teaching, when I taught with Sandy Bethell, we began our course by having the students create lists of qualities of experience that can be measured or counted, as opposed to those that cannot be measured or counted directly but are computed. Students described the quantities to be found in their hobbies—from skeet shooting to talking on the telephone. They also challenged our directions and frequently raised nonquantitative uses of numbers (such as the use of numbers in codes like locker combinations). On occasion, students wondered about the distinction between measuring and counting: Is measuring length really just counting off against a unit measure? Does measuring require a tool while counting does not?

Based on the examples they brought to class, we then discussed situations in which one might think that the value of one quantity depends on (is a function of) the values of others (or perhaps just one other); one such example is the way the cost of a long-distance phone call depends on the length of the phone call. We then examined examples students located in which the value of one quantity can be computed from the values of other quantities—a favorite example of mine is an average. Averages are computed, not measured or counted directly. These discussions set a tone for the course. We were asking students to look around them and to find the mathematics we were going to study.

Although we did not use the word *functions* often in our conversations, once we had looked at series of examples of relationships between quantities, we began to examine how such relationships (functions) are represented by the mathematics community. There are three canonical types of representation. There are representations that focus on the procedural aspect of getting from a particular input(s) to the associated output(s); others focus on the values of the inputs and outputs and less on how one gets from input to output; and finally there are others that are meant to capture the dynamics of the relationship—the way the values of the outputs change as the inputs change. In a similar vein, Smith and Confrey (1994) differentiate between covariational and correspondence views of functions. We tried to become comfortable with all three types of representation.

We first worked on reading sketches of relationships between quantities, rather than the traditional introduction to graphing, which emphasizes that each point has exact coordinates. We used a computer program called *Interpreting Graphs* (Dugdale & Kibbey, 1986), which asks which graph best suits the provided written description. The sketch in Figure 3.11 is taken from Marie's paper. She made this sketch because she had chosen graph 1 and the computer thought graph 3 was the best answer (Sandy and I examine this phenomenon in Chazan & Bethell, 1994, and describe some of the difficulties students had initially with a mathematician's definition of quantity). She wanted an explanation for why graph 1 was not a good description of the speed of the bicycle as the cyclist went up the hill and down the other side. Exploration of this sort of graph created a context in which students began using the words *increasing* and *decreasing* and notions of "steepness." Even though, at this point, they could not create their own coordinate graphs, they could make sketches; they were able to read and interpret some of the information conveyed by a graph.[19]

Next we looked at number recipes such as:

> Start with an input number, add three, and save this result. Start again with your original input, add two, and then multiply this number times the result you saved.

Figure 3.11. A speed-time graph from *Interpreting Graphs* (Dugdale & Kibbey, 1986).

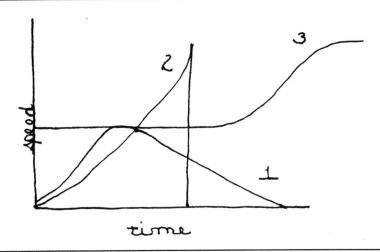

Such procedures are rarely presented in words in a textbook. Instead, right from the start, instructions are presented with literal symbols (in this case $(x + 3)$ $(x + 2)$). Using calculators, students made input/output tables to display the results of carrying out these recipes with calculators (see Figure 3.12). Again, such tables are not typical for early Algebra One instruction. When x is an unknown number, it does not take on a range of values. Only later did we introduce algebraic symbols as shortcut notations for these recipes. We started with I, for input; for this case, that choice leads to the string $(I + 3) \star (I + 2)$. Eventually, we introduced the conventional x, which led to the symbol string $(x + 3) (x + 2)$.

Finally, we practiced making traditional coordinate graphs from tables of values and became versed enough with coordinate graphs for students to read computer displays like the one in Figure 3.13 from *The Function Supposer* (Schwartz et al., 1989).

Figure 3.12. A table of values for the recipe that can be written as $(x + 3)(x + 2)$.

input	0	1	2	3	4	5	6	7	8
output	6	12	20	30	42	56	72	90	110

By this time, students were familiar with terms like *input* and *output, increasing* and *decreasing, variable, parentheses, curved* versus *straight, minimum* and *maximum, steepness, quadrants,* and *intercepts.* They learned to use the software's options to rescale a graph like the one in Figure 3.13 to see its continuation into the first quadrant.

Figure 3.13. $(x + 3)(x + 2)$ on *The Function Supposer* (Schwartz et al., 1989).

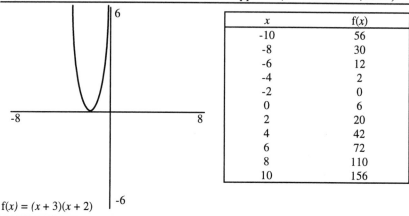

x	$f(x)$
-10	56
-8	30
-6	12
-4	2
-2	0
0	6
2	20
4	42
6	72
8	110
10	156

$f(x) = (x + 3)(x + 2)$

Once students seemed to have developed facility with all of these representations, we could then turn to "family resemblances" among different number recipes (or relationships between quantities). We made posters of different recipes and relationships, looked at similarities and differences between the posters, and began to classify them. Because of the centrality, in the traditional curriculum, of recipes and relationships whose graph is a straight (as opposed to a curved) line in the Cartesian plane, we spent most of the rest of the year in an extended examination of what are called linear functions by the mathematical community. Later in the year, students learned the standard algebraic manipulations. For example, they learned about equivalent expressions for linear functions and, later, how to solve a linear equation by considering it as the comparison of two linear functions.

Meaning for Symbol Manipulation

What initially attracted me to a functions-based approach was the alternative perspective it provides on the meaning of problems involving the manipulation of symbols. I'll illustrate my point by focusing on one type of problem involving the manipulation of symbols (for a similar argument for a different type of problem, see Chazan, 1999).

One central problem type in school algebra asks students to write an expression in different but equivalent forms. This is the type of problem for which Danielle, from my first year teaching at Holt, had no strategies to check her work. In traditional approaches, this problem type is introduced early in Algebra One. It is usually posed as an abstract task about symbols and is rarely connected to geometric contexts (an exception to this general rule is Picciotto & Wah, 1994) or to reasoning about relationships between quantities in the world around us. It is the kind of problem that seems to beg students to ask "Why is this important?" I'll indicate the way a functions-based approach to algebra treats equivalent expressions by contrasting it with the sort of approach I used when I taught in the dayschool.

What Is an Expression? The word *expression* is typically used in school algebra to describe a symbol string made up of numbers, literal symbols, parentheses, and implicit and explicit arithmetic operations, but without the equal sign that comes in an equation. $2(x + 5)$ is an expression and so is $2x + 10$, as are $(x + 5)^2$, $x^2 + 25$, and $(x - 4)(x + 3)$. What kind of mathematical object is an expression? As articulated earlier, the traditional view that I taught when teaching in the dayschool, and which my Holt students learned in Pre-Algebra, is based on a view of x as an unknown particular number; an expression is "a name" for an unknown particular number. When someone tells you the value of x, then you can know the value of the expression; if you are working with $2x + 10$ and someone says that x is 5, then $2x + 10$ is another name for 20, because 2 times 5 is 10 and 10 plus 10 is 20.

By contrast, in a functions-based approach to algebra, expressions represent arithmetic procedures, not names of numbers. According to this point of view, $2(x + 5)$ indicates to the enculturated reader a procedure that starts with some number x (for now, I will not worry about specifying what kinds of numbers can be used), adds 5 to that number, and then multiplies the result by 2. $2x + 10$ is a procedure that starts with some number, multiplies the number by 2, and then adds 10. $(x + 5)^2$ "says" take the starting number and add 5 to it. Then take your result and square it, that is, multiply it by itself. These procedures can also be represented with tables of values or Cartesian graphs.

What Is a Problem of This Sort Asking? Problems in Dolciani and Wooton's (1970/1973) textbook involving the writing of equivalent expressions—usually indicated by the instructions "Simplify," "Expand," or "Multiply" and the presence of an expression—are "answered" by writing an expression that is equivalent to the given expression. Thus, when given the problem "Multiply $2(x$

Figure 3.14. Graphs of $f(x) = 2(x + 5)$ and $g(x) = (x + 5)^2$.

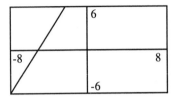 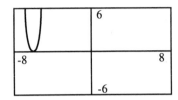

+ 5)," $2x + 10$ is an appropriate answer, because for any particular value of x (used in both expressions), each expression results in the same number; $2(x + 5)$ and $2x + 10$ are different names for the same number, no matter what value x takes on.

In a functions-based point of view, there is a subtle difference. Equivalent expressions represent equivalent (not identical) procedures, that is, procedures that if given the same starting number will always produce the same resultant number. If we choose to let x be 5, then the expression/procedure $2(x + 5)$ gives the result of 20 and $2x + 10$ does as well. By way of contrast, $(x + 5)^2$ gives 100. The two graphs in Figure 3.14 reinforce that $2(x + 5)$ and $(x + 5)^2$ are not equivalent procedures, even though they are strings of symbols that include the same numbers and give the same result for the input of −5.

By way of contrast, $2(x + 5)$ and $2x + 10$ will produce the same number no matter what number we choose, in place of −5, as our starting number. They are equivalent and will produce identical Cartesian graphs. Reading across the table in Figure 3.15 provides this information for a series of numbers in the role of x. Thus, a problem of this kind is asking a very different question than the

Figure 3.15. The equivalence of $2(x + 5)$ and $2x + 10$.

graph of $2(x + 5)$ or $2x + 10$	value of x	result of $2(x + 5)$	result of $2x + 10$
	-3	4	4
	-2	6	6
	-1	8	8
	0	10	10
	1	12	12
	2	14	14
	3	16	16

problem about solving equations that was explored earlier in this chapter in the context of the ship and the submarine.

How Are Students Taught to Write Equivalent Expressions? When I taught at the dayschool out of Dolciani and Wooton's (1970/1973) text, I taught students to be able to complete such problems by recognizing patterns—by having them learn laws to apply to particular types of expressions. I also encouraged my students to check their work by substituting a value for x to see if the two expressions were names for the same number.

So, for example, I taught students to use the distributive law to multiply $2(x+5)$; there is a "hidden" multiplication sign between the 2 and the $(x+5)$. I would say that the distributive law "tells us" how to "remove parentheses" from an expression when whatever is being added in the parentheses—x and 5—is then being multiplied by something outside of the parentheses—2. We remove the parentheses (see Figure 3.16) by "distributing" the multiplication over the addition—multiplying x and 5 each by 2 before adding them.

More formally, the distributive law is a description of a property of our number system. As such, it describes a pattern in a symbol string that indicates that an alternative, equivalent symbol string can be substituted. In order to know that they can apply this law, students need to recognize a pattern in the symbol string, multiplication outside of parentheses surrounding addition. Such pattern recognition is sometimes misapplied by students (like Danielle) who, for example, will also write that $(x+5)^2$ is equivalent to $x^2 + 25$ (Davis, 1984, pp. 331–334),[20] even though in this case "squaring" is outside of the parentheses and not multiplication, and as a result a certain kind of equivalence is not being preserved.[21]

With this sort of pattern-recognition approach, it wasn't possible to assign a "simplify" problem to students before teaching them the algorithm to use and the pattern they had to recognize in order to know that a particular algorithm was required. By contrast, I was regularly able to give my students at Holt simplify problems for which they did not have an algorithm; I became practiced at describing the properties of a solution, rather than giving an example of a solution of a problem of a given type. Simplify problems became problems that asked for a different symbolic representation (expression) for a given function.

Figure 3.16. Distributing multiplication over addition.

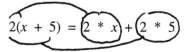

Since expressions were but one representation of a relationship between variables (or function), and the relationship could also be represented with a table or a graph, students could look for expressions that would generate the same table and graph as the given expression. They could use the table and graph to understand what was being held invariant when an expression was replaced by an equivalent expression.

Furthermore, even in "decontextualized" problems, equivalent expressions of the same function that are written in different forms make available by inspection different information about the graphical and tabular representations of the function. For example, when a linear expression is written in the y-intercept, or $mx + b$, form—some number times x plus some other number—the coefficient of the x gives information about the slope of the line in the graph and the rate of change in the table, while the lone number indicates the output for an input of 0, or the point at which the graph will cross the y-axis. By contrast, when a linear expression is written in a factored x-intercept, or $m(x - r)$ form—x minus some number times some other number—the numerical coefficient inside the parentheses gives information about the input for which the output is 0, or the point at which the graph will cross the x axis while the numerical coefficient outside the parentheses indicates the slope of the line in the graph and the rate of change in the table.

Thus, students could understand the goal of simplification problems and they also had resources with which to tackle such problems. After students understood the goal of this sort of problem and had successfully solved some examples, we could then tackle the articulation of general methods of solution for classes of problems (in fact, this is the sort of problem that Bob and his group were working on in Chapter 1) and justification of these general methods. If they became confused, students could always test their answers by creating a table and a graph.

Seeing School Algebra Around Us

Though the functions-based view of school algebra opens up opportunities for students to develop a wider range of solution methods for traditional algebra problems and to understand rationales for the manipulations traditionally taught in school algebra (Schwartz & Yerushalmy, 1992; Yerushalmy & Schwartz, 1993), it has become important to me for another reason: It has aided me in helping students see algebra in the world around them. Earlier, I indicated the students I taught at Holt do not see themselves on trajectories that include education beyond high school (some do not complete high school); algebra cannot be justified to them on the grounds that they will need it in order to go to college. These students were skeptical about school learning, felt that it was remote from their experience, and had not done well in school.

One typical response to the sort of teaching assignment that Sandy and I took on is to imagine that teachers must get involved in an outward-looking inquiry, one focused on their students' lives, not on subject matter; teachers need to learn about their students, find out what is meaningful to the students, and structure their teaching to be "relevant." Though such responses are often promoted as Deweyan, from my perspective, Dewey had something else in mind with the phrase "psychologizing the subject matter." As David Wheeler (1989), the noted Canadian mathematics educator, has written, I believe that Dewey thought "subject matter is a prime source of pedagogical insights" (p. 282). The "relevance" view assumes that a teacher's understanding of subject matter is sufficient to the task of finding connections between school and students' extra-curricular experiences (NCRTL, 1995, April). Attention is focused on understanding the child more deeply and not on developing one's understanding of the curriculum. This view also puts the burden of creating relevance squarely on the teacher's shoulders.

But the standard understanding of school algebra that I had when teaching at the dayschool, a kind of understanding deemed sufficient in traditional modes of algebra instruction, was not up to this task. Even though the functions-based view of school algebra that I had when I began teaching at Holt was a step in the right direction, it was not sufficient. Besides identifying the objects of study in algebra for myself, I needed to be able to see those objects of study in the worlds of my students, if not in their experience then in the experience of people they knew. In Dewey's (1902/1990) terms, I needed to view the subject matter "as an outgrowth of [my students'] present tendencies and activities" (p. 203). Only then could I begin to have a response to the question "What is algebra *all* about?" let alone the question "Why would anyone want to know algebra?"

Choosing relationships between quantities as the central mathematical object of school algebra, and then involving students in the question of relevance, helped when students at Holt asked (either explicitly or implicitly) about the meaning and purpose of school algebra. Since relationships between quantities are mathematical objects the Holt students could learn to see in the world around them (they may be easier to see than some of the more abstract objects of study around which algebra might be organized), the choice of structuring the course around these objects provided Sandy and me with an alternative to looking for relevance. As a product of examination of the curriculum and of our students' experience, what I began to feel I had to offer across the difference between me and my students was a view of the subject matter as a human activity focused on the study of a particular set of objects—relationships between quantities. Rather than assume the complete burden of generating relevance, I could ask students to share this task with me. I could ask them to locate relationships between quantities in the world around them; I could enlist their aid in exploring connections between the mathematics studied in school and their lives. Exploration of the subject matter, in this case school algebra, then became one avenue for having students share with me their experience of the world around them, for them to educate me.

Central Objects of Study and Student Motivation: Three Illustrative Activities. I'll illustrate ways in which exploring school algebra provided Sandy and me with opportunities to learn about our students by presenting three activities we designed. They provide contexts for student exploration of the use of relationships between quantities (functions) in the world around them and lend substance to our desire to use mathematics as a context for learning from our students about their lives. They illustrate strategies for having students take on the burden of relevance and find personally real contexts in which school mathematics is relevant. They also helped us learn about what is experientially real for our students.

In our second year of teaching together, in addition to discussing quantities in students' hobbies, Sandy and I organized a project that involved interviews with local business people about "rules of thumb" used in their work; we sent our students out into their community to do an interview project and job shadowing (Chazan & Bethell, 1998). As one student said, we asked the class to go on a hunt for math in the workplace. We wanted our students to look for situations in which people made computations and to ask themselves a series of questions about what they saw:

- What quantities must have known values (given by measuring, counting, or prior computation) in order to carry out this computation?
- What is the computational procedure or recipe for computing this quantity?
- Why do these people need to do this computation?
- What does finding out the value of this quantity do for them?

Though the technical details of the project were sometimes overwhelming, the students came back with useful information. The school building was being renovated and expanded. So, for example, Rebecca worked with a carpeting contractor who in estimating costs read the dimensions of rectangular rooms off an architect's blueprint, multiplied to find the area of the room in square feet (doing conversions where necessary), then multiplied by a cost per square foot that depended on the type of carpet to compute the cost of the carpet. The purpose of these estimates was to prepare a bid for the architect where the bid had to be as low as possible without making the job unprofitable.

Joe and Mick, also working in construction, found out that in laying pipes, there is a "one-by-one" rule of thumb. When one is digging a trench for the placement of the pipe, the nonparallel sides of the trapezoid have a slope of one foot down for every one foot across. This ratio guarantees that the dirt in the hole will not slide down on itself. Thus, if at the bottom of the hole the trapezoid must have a certain width in order to fit the pipe, then on ground level the hole must be this width plus twice the depth of the hole. Knowing in advance how wide the hole must be avoids lengthy and costly trial and error.

In another activity that Sandy developed that year, we focused on the ways in which Cartesian graphs are meant to communicate descriptions of relationships among quantities in a situation. We had students work in pairs. Each student wrote a story for the other. They then swapped stories and, on an overhead transparency, each student sketched a graph of a relationship between quantities central to the story. Later, students used their graphs to "retell" the story to the rest of the class. The rest of the class then critiqued the graph as a representation of the story.

These stories and graphs told us a lot about our students' interests and about their understandings of graphs (see Chazan & Bethell, 1994). While many of these stories, like the one below, were fanciful, they provide information about the quantities that are salient to our students and experiences they may have had.

ONE STUDENT'S STORY

When I went to florida, I went to visit family. Every day we went to the beach. We were in florida for one week. The first day at the beach I had counted 5 sailboats that were about 3 miles away. The third day I saw about 7 sailboats five miles away. The sixth day there were about 9 sailboats that were six miles away. The last day of my vacation at the beach I saw 10 sailboats that were seven miles away if you were wondering how I could see the sailboats I had binoculars. Graph this. (punctation unchanged)

These stories also raised questions about how best to depict quantities. The student who graphed this story (see Figure 3.17) chose to use discrete points rather than to connect the points. She also chose to ignore how far away the boats were.

Finally, when we focused on linear functions, we had our students design and carry out surveys. In this context, they learned to extrapolate to a population from a sample. This extrapolation involves the assumption of linearity: The predictions for a population are simply a scaled-up version of the responses of the surveyed sample. They chose survey items that interested them; their choices revealed much about their interests and concerns.

Figure 3.17. Another student's graph for this story.

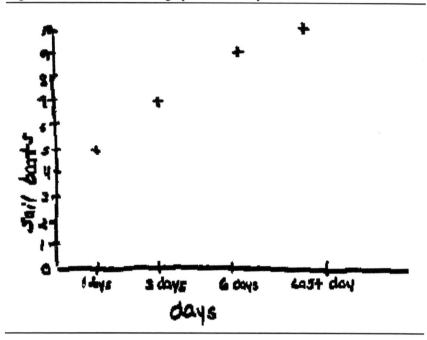

CATEGORIES FOR TABULATING DATA FROM 1992–1993 SURVEY

1F. Number of females who have been pregnant

1M. Number of males who have gotten a female pregnant

1a. Number of females who were pregnant and used drugs during pregnancy

2. Number of students who practice safe sex at all times

3. Number of students concerned about sexually transmitted disease

4. Number of students who have used drugs

5. Number of students who have been under the influence of drugs or alcohol during school hours

6. Numbers of students who have been under the influence of alcohol or other drugs while driving

7. Number of students who support Holt High School being a smoke-free environment (no smoking)

8. Number of students who have thought of or who have attempted suicide

9. Number of students who have brought an illegal or concealed weapon (gun, knife, etc.) to school

After the students collected data from five classes (chosen as representative of the school) and extrapolated their results to the whole student body, our class also took the survey. We compared the predicted and actual results for our class and discussed the composition of different classes and how our class (as a lower-track class) compared with the rest of the school. Finally, we presented a report of the students' extrapolations to the counseling staff for their information.

All three of these activities stem from a common desire to have the students teach us about what is experientially real for them while doing mathematics. Different students will have different experiences. What is experientially real for one student is not necessarily real for another, nor necessarily of immediate interest. Yet all of my previous comments about tensions between students' peer groups notwithstanding, perhaps that which is experientially real for one student can become important to another student. At least there may be value in having students see other students making connections to school subject matter.

But these activities could not have been designed without having a sharp focus on the objects of study in this course. If we could not explain to students what these were, then we would not be able to send students out to look for them. If we could not explain what relationships between quantities were, students would not be able to see them in each other's stories. Without this focus, because of students' interests in the focus of the survey, we might have lost track of the distinction between actual and predicted values.

Having Students Come to Value Symbols

So far, I have suggested that a functions-based approach helped make it possible to explain to students the characteristics of solutions to traditional Algebra One tasks, thus enabling students to explore such problems before learning an algorithm, and that it helped us engage our students in the task of generating relevance for school algebra. By doing so, however, I am not suggesting that we resolved the question of student engagement with Algebra One in our class. I do not mean to imply that we believe that we "solved" the problem of psychologizing the algebra curriculum for our students, and certainly not for all time. As in most teaching situations, ours was filled with missteps and failures. Though there were days of intense engagement, as is common in lower-track mathematics classes, there were many days of low student engagement.

In that sense, it is clear that our work is far from done, that this approach to teaching algebra can still benefit from further elaboration. In particular, there are two issues I believe deserve much further attention. The first continues the discussion of psychologizing the subject matter. While we made progress in helping students see relationships between quantities in the world around them, that does not complete the task. In my negotiations with the principal of the high school, I had accepted the task of creating an alternative Algebra One course. Thus, my students would not only need to be able to see relationships between quantities in the world around them, they would also need to become facile at writing symbolic expressions and manipulating them. But when Sandy and I taught together, I did not feel that our students developed a sufficient facility with symbols. Of course, the matter of just what constitutes sufficient facility with symbols is a matter of debate. In this context, I was concerned with achieving goals of traditional instruction and not altering expectations for student achievement. I am not sure, myself, to what degree I would change these expectations if given the freedom to do so. There is a dilemma that pits my desire to help my students see mathematics as meaningful activity against my desire to make many possible future trajectories open and available to them.

As Sandy and other colleagues at Holt High School have helped me come to appreciate over the last few years, the issue of helping students develop a facility with symbols may again have a component that involves psychologizing the subject matter. Though our students may have come to recognize relationships between quantities as important mathematical objects, that does not mean they saw why facility with one representation of these objects, facility with algebraic symbols, was considered so important. To explore this issue further, though there are many aspects of algebraic work with symbols, I will focus on two: writing linear expressions (the task I used to describe my dayschool teaching in Chapter 1) and the simplification problems discussed earlier in this chapter (I will not discuss the solving of equations explicitly but will include some discussion in the notes).

Writing Linear Expressions. To illustrate both the progress we have made and the issues that remain, I will focus on a central element of the traditional curriculum, which we also address, writing linear expressions (known in the traditional curriculum as "finding the equation of a line").[22] This larger task includes the subtask of determining the slope of linear functions, or constant rates of change, one step of Dolciani and Wooton's (1970/1973) four-step method of finding the "equation" of a line (in slope-y intercept form) between two points (as discussed in Chapter 1). Arguably, this is an example of an extremely complex mathematical concept with many entailments (Moschkovich et al., 1993).

After traditional algebra instruction, students usually have difficulty writing equations of lines. For example, in my own dayschool teaching, writing an equation for the line between two given points was a task students were able to accomplish immediately following instruction, but were no longer able to complete later in the year. Even other, simpler, tasks involving graphs and equations in the "slope intercept form" (where $y = mx + b$; where m represents the slope of the line and b its y-intercept) are difficult for students who have studied algebra traditionally. For example, on the 1990 National Assessment of Educational Progress (NAEP) only 32% of high school seniors were able to draw a line through the origin and parallel to the line for a given equation y-$2x + 5$ (see the dashed line solution in Figure 3.18).

Only 16% could then write the equation $y = 2x$ for this line (reported and discussed in Moschkovich et al., 1993), even though the slope of this line must be 2 (because parallel lines have the same slope) and its y- intercept is 0 because it goes through the origin. Yet these are tasks that I would have hoped a majority of our Holt students could have completed successfully.

At Holt, on our final exams, we regularly posed a related but more difficult task in the context of scales for measuring temperature. Students were asked to develop an equation of a line from scratch, including computation of its slope. I had taken this task from the final exam of a teacher who taught Algebra One out of the UCSMP textbook (McConnell et al., 1990) and rewrote it to make the context clearer (though perhaps its relevance is limited to students who for the most part have not left Michigan).

A FINAL EXAM TASK

In other countries, like Canada, temperature is measured in degrees Celsius. We are familiar with the meaning of temperatures in Fahrenheit. So

Figure 3.18. Solution to the NAEP task.

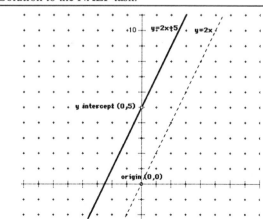

when traveling, it is useful to have a rule for changing temperature from Celsius to Fahrenheit.

The temperature at which water freezes is 0 degrees Celsius and 32 degrees Fahrenheit. The temperature at which water boils is 100 degrees Celsius and 212 degrees Fahrenheit. The relationship between temperature Celsius and temperature Fahrenheit is a linear rule.

Using the information given above:
   a.   Figure out the slope for your rule. Show your work.
   b.   Write a rule that will do the conversion.
   c.   Using your rule, is 40 degrees Celsius the temperature of a hot day?

Our students at Holt found this problem quite challenging; their performance was not as strong as I would have liked. So a Michigan State University colleague, Jack Smith, and I followed up by interviewing students. We interviewed students from a class Sandy taught when Sandy and I were no longer teaching together. Thus, for these students, I was not one of the teachers in the math department. Jack and I interviewed the students in the fall of the year after their study of Algebra One. The results were mixed, both disappointing and satisfying. The interviews revealed that, after the summer break, students could still do much useful and thoughtful work on the problem, beyond what was illustrated on their exam papers. However, they still did not produce correct solutions. Their performance did not put the NAEP results to shame.

To help understand my mixed assessment of this work, recall Danielle, the student my first year at Holt who filled the board with a set of incorrect manipulations. Like many of my students that first year, she came into class with a set of poorly learned algorithms and no criteria for determining whether solutions were correct. The interviews with Sandy's students revealed substantial progress; her students were able to judge their own performance and to determine whether their answers were mathematically sound. They could take a problem, work hard on it for an extended time, and present their work, though they knew it was flawed. They could judge their solutions, but that does not mean that the answers they produced were the "correct" answers required on standardized tests. Some of the basic content of the algebra course remained difficult for them. I was pleased by their ability to know when their answers did not make sense and their capacity to continue working on the problem for a long stretch of time. But I was distressed that they were not, in the end, able to produce a correct solution. Thus, the interviews reinforced the notion that linear functions and slope is a complex domain of learning that will continue to benefit from further study.

I will illustrate what students did in the interviews by reviewing the work of a student I will call Jack. When I observed Sandy's class the previous year, Jack was sometimes a vocal and insightful participant in class discussions, but could also often be disruptive. His academic performance was poor in all of his classes. In some ways, Jack's performance in the interview was strong; unlike many students on the NAEP test, he understood the role of the coefficients or slots in the slope–y-intercept form. While the lion's share of our 50-minute interview was spent on determining the slope between the freezing and boiling points of water in Celsius and Fahrenheit, at the end of the hour, when I asked him to take what he called the "slope" and write a rule, he recognized that the y-intercept was (0,32) and was able to write a rule ($9x + 32$), which was correct except for the slope. Then he was able to judge his performance and diagnose his difficulty. He tested this rule, found it to be incorrect, and diagnosed his difficulty as having determined the slope incorrectly.

While Jack worked on this problem for a full class period and generated an elaborate and correct table of inputs and outputs representing the relationship between temperature in Celsius and Fahrenheit, his understanding of slope still seemed limited and suggests some of the difficulties in teaching students about slope. He seemed not to understand that slope is conceptualized as a rate—by determining the amount of "rise" for every *single unit* of "run"—and he never was able to compute the correct slope. While he used commonsense ways of discussing rates and indicated that the temperature Fahrenheit goes up 180 degrees when the temperature Celsius goes up 100 degrees, or that the temperature Fahrenheit goes up 9 degrees for every 5-degree rise in temperature Celsius, he did not represent this rate of change as a change of 1.8 or 9/5 degrees Fahrenheit for every change of one degree Celsius. Because this problem involves a rate that is not a whole number, it revealed that he did not understand that the "per one unit of 'run'" representation of rate is privileged when slope is defined.

Starting from the information given in the problem (which I have depicted in Figure 3.19), Jack seemed to begin by trying to remember the algorithm for computing slope (subtraction of output from output to determine the rise and input from input to determine the run and then division of the rise by the run). He started subtracting 0 from 32 and 100 from 212, then he stopped, confused about what to do next.

I suggested that he make a table of inputs and outputs. This suggestion seemed to help him draw on the context of temperature.

> *J:* I know the 0 and the 32 should go next to each other because they are both freezing points, and then 100 and 212 should because they are boiling points.

Examining this first cut at a table, Jack subtracted across the columns and decided that the slope would be 32. He then used 32 as the slope and began to go

Figure 3.19. Graphical and tabular representation of the given information.

X	Y
0	32
10	
20	
30	
40	
50	
60	
70	
80	
90	
100	212

by ones from 0 to 100 Celsius, and by 32s from 32 Fahrenheit. Quickly, he realized that the temperature Fahrenheit was rising too rapidly.

I then shifted his attention from the algorithm for computing slope and asked him if he could figure out the temperature Fahrenheit that would correspond to 50 degrees Celsius in his table. After determining that the corresponding Fahrenheit temperature would be 122, he then commented:

J: So then for 150 it would be 302. . . . It's going up 90 every 50.

I asked him if he could then determine how much the temperature Fahrenheit would go up for every 10 degrees Celsius. He quickly responded that it would go up 9 degrees for every 10, because:

J: 90 divided by 10 is 9.

He checked and this did not work. Subsequently, in the context of fleshing out his table, he determined that for every 10 degrees Celsius the temperature Fahrenheit went up 18 degrees and that for every 5 degrees Celsius it went up 9 degrees.

At this point, it became clear that Jack was having difficulty coordinating the two quantities present in slope as a rate. Though he remembered what was discussed in class, he had not integrated that discussion into his own understanding:

DC: So for every 10 it goes by 18 and for every 100 it goes by 180 and for every 50 it goes by 90, for every 5 it goes by 9. Could you say what the slope is?

> *J*: It would be a multiple of nine it would have to be because it's going up a certain amount of nines each time like, nine, eighteen. Ms. Bethell tells us to take it up by one but really the slope could be anything I guess, I mean,
>
> *DC*: The slope could be anything, what. . . . Could you tell my what the slope would be?
>
> *J*: Nine, eighteen, one hundred eighty, ninety, depending on what the inputs are going by.

Jack seemed not to understand that slope is a constant for a linear function, a constant that coordinates the change in the outputs with the change in the inputs, and in this way does not depend on "what the inputs are going by" in the table of values. (For an argument about the importance of such realizations, see Miles, 1992.) The numbers Jack suggested as the slope are simply the changes in the outputs (for a particular sized change in the inputs).

The particulars of this task make it a difficult problem, and thus a good diagnostic tool. While the student interviews convinced me that we had made some progress in having students understand the slope–y-intercept form and treat mathematical tasks meaningfully, they also suggest that we still have much to learn about improving our students' performance, particularly on tasks involving the writing of linear expressions, or equations.

That said, I do not believe that the way toward improvement for a wide range of students lies in a return to direct instruction in Dolciani and Wooton's (1970/1973) four-step procedure. The approach of directly teaching this method seemed not to work in my dayschool teaching. While I had always appreciated students' difficulty with the complex step of finding the y-intercept when it is not given and their complete lack of an understanding for why this step works, I now also have a greater appreciation for conceptual difficulties students may have with the notion of slope. Though students may know, or remember, how to compute slope, they may not understand much about it. For example, they may not understand that the number they have computed is a way to speak in a unified way about the rate of change in output per unit change in input. Given the difficulties involved in these two steps of Dolciani and Wooton's method, the task of writing a linear equation through two points, though it may on the surface seem simple, remains an extremely difficult task for a wide range of students master and retain (see Schoenfeld et al., 1990, for an elaborate discussion of one student's work and a similar argument for the complexity of this domain).

Why Write Symbols? Conversations with Sandy and other members of the Holt High School Mathematics Department have helped me understand other dimensions to the issue of writing linear expressions, in particular its connection to the ongoing issue of psychologizing the subject matter. Though this skill may be difficult cognitively for several reasons, it may also be difficult for students because students do not appreciate the purpose in mastering this skill.

Teachers in the department report that while student engagement is strong at various points during the year, it tends to drop when there is prolonged work on writing symbolic expressions. Students do not seem to want to master this skill; instead, even though they are not proficient, they want to move on. It reminds me of the kind of conflict I experienced with my students early during my first year of teaching at Holt.

In discussing this phenomenon, the teachers turned to their own subject matter understandings, to the justifications they had for such work. Their comments about this aspect of the course reminded of my feelings about the course as a whole when I taught at the dayschool. They felt uncomfortable with their justifications for the importance of this skill. They had some justifications that were in the present tense, for example, graphing calculators understand only symbolic input and thus it is useful to be able to write symbolic expressions; the capacity to write symbolic expressions allows one to use a graphing calculator and the variety of tools it offers. But most of their justifications were future-oriented, justifications dependent on continued mathematics course-taking. Though they could help students see relationships among quantities in the world around them, they could not similarly help students see the value of being able to represent such relationships with symbolic expressions, rather than "rules of thumb," graphs, or tables. In fact, when Sandy and I sent our students out into the world of work to find relationships between quantities, such relationships were rarely captured in symbols and we did not have any examples of someone creating a symbolic expression. Symbolic expressions when present were pre-packaged "black boxes." The closest we could come was when someone, like an accountant in an example to be discussed below, created his own rule of thumb.

Why Manipulate Symbols? According to the Holt teachers, there are similar issues around tasks involving the manipulation of symbols. Though students can sometimes become intrigued, as Bob was, by a task involving the rewriting of an expression in different forms, again their experience over time is that students seem to resist developing facility at such tasks. This is another place where I think our teaching could develop. As outlined in the section "Meaning for Symbol Manipulation," a relationships-between-quantities approach helped us think of such tasks as writing an alternative expression for the same function. As I will outline below, this approach also began to help us explore why a person would want to write an expression in a different, but equivalent, form. However, our justifications still seem insufficient.

Earlier I suggested that a relationships-between-quantities approach suggests that "simplifying" exercises are really asking for different symbolic expression for the same function. While this understanding is useful in explaining the goal of such "decontextualized" problems to students, it does not yet help me see the activity of writing different expressions for the same function in the world around me. However, with this view in mind, it is possible to recognize such activity.

I'll illustrate this point with a story that Nancy Alexander, a mathematician and graduate student in education, brought to my attention after she heard about the kinds of interviews Sandy and I asked our students to do in workplaces. She was talking with her husband, who is an accountant, about calculations he carried out. (The story comes from the days when the tax rate in Michigan was 4%.) Frequently, accountants need to recover the tax paid by clients from receipts for the total bill where the tax is not listed. The traditional method is:

Take the total bill, divide it by 1.04 to find out what the original sales price was, then subtract the original sales price from the total bill to find the tax.

This method requires the entry of the total bill twice, as well as the use of two operations. In doing this procedure, year in and year out, her husband had noticed a pattern. It seemed that there was an alternative, shorter method:

Take the total bill and divide by 26 to find the tax directly.

On the surface, these two procedures seemed very different, so he did not trust the shortcut and would only use it during his first pass through a tax return. On the second pass, he would use the traditional method.

Algebraic manipulations of the kind we were teaching in class can be used to demonstrate that these two procedures will always generate the same results for a given total bill, that they are alternative expressions for the same function. We were able to use this example with our students to clarify why for computer programmers finding "fast" algorithms is important. We were then able to use this understanding of equivalent expressions to design activities for students. We devised situations in which students created alternative procedures to get the same result. Manipulation of their expressions then let us "prove" that two procedures really were equivalent. But this still did not seem satisfying. The students created alternative procedures in many different trial-and-error ways; they were not using the manipulations to create alternative expressions. Manipulation was being used as justification, but we could also verify that the procedures gave the same results by making tables and graphs.

Earlier I indicated another way that a relationship-between-quantities approach provides meaning for manipulations: It suggests that writing alternative expressions for the same function is a way of highlighting different aspects of the function. But, again, such a rationale is not completely satisfying. After all, these different aspects of the function are available in its graphical and tabular representations as well. Why is it important to learn to manipulate expressions in order to make these aspects of the function salient in the symbolic expression? (This issue is also discussed in Chazan, 1995.) I'll illustrate my lack of satisfaction by exploring this rationale in the context of a problem we gave students about loans.

When manipulating expressions, there is more than the question of which expression is most efficient; when one keeps in mind the meaning of the coefficients in a mathematical model or description, manipulating expressions can also give insight into the situation being modeled.[23] Sandy and I realized one day that the different forms of expressions where the variable is time can be thought of as descriptions from particular moments in time. Here is a task we explored with our students:

Different Forms and Situational Meaning

You take out a car loan at 0% financing [zero percent financing was in the media at this time as car companies sought to increase sales] and then repay it by paying the same amount each month. Here are three mathematical descriptions of the balance that you owe and how it changes over time:

Balance of account (time) $= 215t - 4300$
Balance of account (time) $= 215(t - 10) - 2150$
Balance of account (time) $= 215(t - 20)$
where t represents time in months.

- Make tables and graphs for these rules.
- How much are you paying off each month (payment rate)? Explain and circle the part of the rules that tells you this information.
- How long will it take you to pay it off at this rate? Explain and circle the part of the rules, the table, and the graph that shows this information.
- How much did you borrow at first? Explain and circle the part of the rules, the table, and the graph that shows this information.
- What else can you say about this situation?

The first two expressions have two terms. An easy balance to compute is the one where the first term is zero; the result is then simply the second term. For this reason, the first expression can be thought of as written from the perspective of time zero when the balance of the debt is $4,300; while the middle expression is written from the perspective of 10 months out, when $2,150 is owed. The last expression has only one term and thus is from the time (20 months out) when the balance is paid off ($0). This observation suggested to us that manipulation of expressions can help one "travel" in time, to write descriptions of a situation from different moments in time. But, again, the question remains, why would one want to do so?

Thus, while a relationships-between-quantities approach provides a way of telling students what Algebra One might be about, we have not completed the task of psychologizing the subject matter. Because there are other canonical representations of functions, the issue of justifying to students (in the present tense) the importance of work with the symbolic representation must continue to be addressed.[24]

The Nature of Classroom Mathematics: Proof in School Algebra

A second fundamental way in which I would like to develop the approach that Sandy and I used is quite different. To anticipate some of the issues that will be discussed in the next chapter, it involves the nature of the mathematical activity in which students participate. As in the discussion above of students' work with symbols, it is not that traditional approaches are more successful than we were. Rather, difficulties also present in traditional approaches remained for us as well. I am concerned about the sorts of reasoning that students are asked to do in algebra classrooms. In particular, I am perturbed by the absence of the peculiar way of knowing/reasoning that is known as mathematical proof.

Using the phrases *psychologizing the subject matter* and *mathematical objects of study* in this chapter, I have explored how Sandy and I presented school algebra to our students. As Schwab (1978) emphasizes, however, in our representation of the subject matter, we were doing more than simply representing the objects of study in algebra (the substantive in his terms); we were also representing to students how mathematics is done (syntactical aspects of the discipline, in his parlance) by the nature of the mathematical activity we tried to create in the classroom. Just as in our choice of objects of study for our course, there were pedagogical choices to be made in "psychologizing" this aspect of the subject matter; the tricky task for the teacher is to balance authentic representation of the discipline, the nature of the interactions one wants to have with students, and one's students' needs as learners. When designing mathematical activity for the classroom, one central consideration is how one represents the practice of mathematical reasoning and proof, both in their roles of justifying and explaining results (Hanna, 1989).

Mathematical proof has been represented in school curricula in a variety of ways. (For discussion and critique of recent trends, see reviews by Canadian mathematics educator Gila Hanna, 1983, 1995.) This variety represents differences in views of learning, of appropriate roles for teachers and students, of the nature of mathematical proof, of the role of proof in mathematical activity, and of the relative weights these different views should receive (for an examination of different views on the nature of mathematical proof and its role in mathematics, see the discussion in the next chapter). For example, in discussing his choice to present results and postpone demonstrations in his geometry text, Robert Recorde, author of early and influential mathematics textbooks in English, emphasizes a theory of learning: "So shall men best understand things: first to learn that such things are to be wrought, and secondarily what they are, and what they do import, and then thirdly what is the cause thereof" (quoted in Fauvel, 1989, p. 3). By way of contrast, the New Math movement at the secondary school level stressed formal logic and rigorous proof as crucial to the authentic representation of mathematics (Hanna, 1983).

The NCTM Standards documents base their recommendations related to proof both on views of learning and on views of mathematics as a discipline. Sometimes, perhaps as a result of different weightings of these views, there seemingly are tensions between recommendations in different parts of the standards. Thus, for example, *Professional Standards for Teaching Mathematics* (NCTM, 1991) recommends, across curricular areas, that mathematics teachers choose tasks that "require students to speculate, . . . to face decisions about whether or not their approaches are valid" (p. 26) and to create classrooms in which students are expected to explain and justify their ideas (pp. 35–36). In the context of high school geometry, *Curriculum and Evaluation Standards* (NCTM, 1989) calls for decreased attention to two-column proofs and increased attention to alternative expressions of mathematical argument (p. 126).[25]

In seeking to balance tensions between authentically representing the discipline, helping students' think for themselves, and meeting students' needs, for me, it seems important that a year-long course like Algebra One, which aims to represent the discipline, have some sort of place for mathematical proof and involve students in mathematical argumentation. Indeed, this is one particular aspect of the concern I had about my dayschool students and their lack of opportunities to think for themselves in Algebra One as opposed to other subjects. But I think it is important to be aware that attempts to include mathematical proof in the classroom as a reflection of mathematical practice can unwittingly be undermined by classroom contexts. As often happens in high school geometry courses, writing proofs can become a ritual unreflective of the practice it is on some level meant to represent (Herbst, 1998). In order to understand the particular difficulties involved in representing proof in the context of school algebra, it is useful, once again, to contrast high school algebra and geometry, though admittedly algebra and geometry are different types of mathematical activity.

When teaching high school geometry with *The Geometric Supposer* (Schwartz et al., 1985), it was relatively easy to ask students to develop their own theorems. There were many theorems to be discovered and students could prove many of their results. One simply provided students with a construction and asked them to create conjectures (e.g., explore what happens when you draw in all three medians in a triangle, as discussed early in Chapter 1). Students used their empirical exploration of figures to locate a relationship between parts of the diagram and to explore the conditions under which it held. These discoveries were formulated as conjectures. Students then utilized their developing understanding of the postulates and key theorems of Euclidean geometry to write arguments to justify their conjectures and to explain why they held. In this way, students had an opportunity to learn about mathematical proof and rigor.

In school algebra, usually, the situation is quite different. In a traditional text, like the one I used when teaching at the dayschool, there are few theorems. Texts that take a more formal approach, based in Abstract Algebra, may identify axioms for the field of real numbers, but students are not usually asked to write proofs.[26] Thus there is a big difference between the kinds of tasks students do in school algebra and geometry. In algebra, students carry out algorithms they have been taught, while (in theory if not practice) in geometry, students are not engaged in a ritualistic activity involving the listing of statements and reasons. Instead, when writing a proof, they are involved in activity that cannot be described algorithmically and that draws on their understandings of geometrical relationships. As articulated by the renowned French mathematician Rene Thom (1986) in his reflection on curricular developments in school mathematics:

> While there are geometry problems, there are no algebra problems. A so-called algebra problem can only be a simple exercise requiring the blind application of arithmetical rules and of a pre-established procedure. With rare exceptions, one cannot ask a student to prove an algebra theorem; either the requested answer is almost obvious and can be arrived at by direct substitution of definitions, or the problem falls into the category of theoretical algebra and its solution exceeds the capacities of even the most gifted student. Exaggerating only slightly, one can say that any question in algebra is either trivial or impossible to solve. By contrast, the classic problems of geometry present a wide range of challenges. (p. 70)

Thus, in traditional school algebra, it is hard to illustrate mathematical standards of rigor and the central role of mathematical proof in both justifying results and understanding them.

In our approach to school algebra, as a result of the identification of the "objects of study," we were able to pose problems to students before they had been taught algorithms. Thus students were often tackling problems that did not involve the "blind application of arithmetical rules." But few of the problems we posed to our students asked them to develop a theorem.[27] Unlike the Euclidean geometry course, we did not have a structure of axioms and key theorems that students could then use to prove results. Thus, in our algebra class, students still did not have an opportunity to learn about the role of mathematical proof in the doing of mathematics. And for those students who did not continue on to study Euclidean geometry, it is likely that there would be no such opportunity in school.

REFLECTION AND LOOKING AHEAD

Having a stance on the fundamental objects of study in algebra, or perhaps having this particular stance, has been an importance resource in changing my teaching of algebra. Deborah Ball's (1992) reflections on her own teaching, in an essay titled "Teaching Mathematics for Understanding: What Do Teachers Need to Know About the Subject Matter?," support this observation. She suggests that teachers need knowledge of mathematics (the body of disciplinary knowledge), knowledge about mathematics (the disciplinary activity), and knowledge about mathematics in society. In elaborating the first of these categories, she argues that teachers' knowledge of mathematics must be correct, but beyond correctness, teachers must have an understanding of mathematical meanings that underlie mathematical procedures and a sense of the connectedness of mathematics. Similarly, in describing the conflicts experienced by teachers with *The Geometric Supposers* (Schwartz et al., 1985), Magdalene Lampert (1995, p. 228) uses the metaphor of a map to describe how teachers needed to understand the geometry curriculum in order to make connections between their students' explorations and conjectures and the topics of the standard curriculum.

It is this map or sense of the connectedness that I, like most algebra teachers, lacked. For many years, I could not give anyone an overview of what algebra was about. Any description would quickly become bogged down in the specifics of the manipulations taught in each chapter. I also had difficulty reading the table of contents of algebra books. The words did not carry much meaning. The course progressed tediously through the standard set of manipulations. I dreaded the usually unasked question of what this was all about.

Having a characterization of the central object of the course has changed that situation dramatically. I now can describe how I conceptualize a year's work in Algebra One. I can look through materials and place a particular activity in my view of the unfolding of the course; I do not have to rely on the textbook to structure the course. I can contemplate alternative paths through the material in response to particular interests or comments of students. I can write materials making use of the particular interests or comments of students to explore the topics of the curriculum. I can also explore with students the reasons people might have for finding the study of these objects useful, important, or illuminating. Identifying a central object of study for the course has been a crucial step

(margin annotation: What teachers need)

in beginning to imagine students and the curriculum as Dewey's (1902/1990) two limits that define a single process.

Yet the work is far from complete. Though Sandy and I were able to help students see relationships between quantities in the world around them, we were not as successful in helping them see a rationale for the mastering of certain symbolic skills. The rationales that we have developed were not sufficient. Similarly, we were not yet happy with the structure we had for aiding students in their reasoning about relationships between quantities.

Our pursuit of a deeper understanding of school algebra had other dimensions as well. It was also related to our desire to have different sorts of interactions in our classroom. Sandy wanted to see our students' competencies developing in the way her students' competencies grew in her Spanish classes. I wanted to see our students as involved in their studies and as willing to question and be intellectually independent as my dayschool students had been in my nonmathematics classes.

How is a teacher's understanding of subject matter related to the nature of classroom interaction? Working in the Deweyan tradition, science educator David Hawkins (1974) reinterprets Martin Buber's (1970) theological categories—I, Thou, and It—to illuminate this connection. In his reinterpretation, I is the teacher, Thou the student, and It the subject matter. He suggests that each of these three terms is crucial in teaching for a "stable bond of communication, of shared concern" between teacher and students. When all three are present, "the child comes alive for the teacher as well as the teacher for the child. They have a common theme for discussion, they are involved together in the world" (pp. 57–58).

Our attempts to identify the fundamental objects of study in algebra and to help students identify these objects of study in the world around them was an attempt to provide students with independent access to the It of our Algebra One class. We did not want the It, algebra, to be primarily the province of the teacher, and not of the student. However, students' active engagement in classroom interaction is not solely a matter of a teacher's conceptual understanding of the curriculum and naming of central objects of study. There is the matter of teachers' and students' conceptions of their roles in classroom discussion. I take up this theme in the following chapter.

Chapter 4

Developing Conversations in the Mathematics Classroom

The National Council of Teachers of Mathematics (NCTM) (1991) *Professional Standards for Teaching Mathematics* calls for major changes in the environment of mathematics classrooms. In doing so, the document draws attention to teachers' and students' classroom roles and implicitly paints a portrait of standard practice in mathematics classrooms. This implied description of standard practice suggests that mathematics classroom interaction, particularly at the secondary level, most often consists of teacher exposition, teachers' evaluative questioning of student, and student requests for clarification. It suggests classrooms in which the teacher is the sole authority for right answers and students memorize procedures and mechanically find answers; it implies that most classrooms are collections of individuals in which mathematics is portrayed as a body of isolated concepts and procedures.[1] It suggests that students are, at least outwardly, passive and that conversation[2]—in the sense of "informal spoken exchanges of thoughts and feelings" (Morris, 1976)—is rare in mathematics classrooms, that the lack of conversation in my dayschool mathematics classes was not an idiosyncratic issue of my own teaching practice. (For evidence supporting this portrayal of U.S. classrooms, see, for example, Stigler & Hiebert, 1997; Welch, 1978.) Furthermore, the rhetoric of the NCTM document indicates that changing teaching is not a simple task, that it requires attention and effort.

The document argues that desirable changes in typical classroom roles of students and teachers entail five major shifts:

- toward classrooms as mathematical communities—away from classrooms as simply a collection of individuals;
- toward logic and mathematical evidence as verification—away from the teacher as the sole authority for right answers;
- toward mathematical reasoning—away from merely memorizing procedures;
- toward conjecturing, inventing, and problem solving—away from an emphasis on mechanistic answer-finding;

112

- toward connecting mathematics, its ideas, and its applications—away from treating mathematics as a body of isolated concepts and procedures. (NCTM, 1991, p. 3)

Assuming some change is necessary, why these five shifts? Two factors stand out for me. One impetus is mathematical. There is a mismatch between NCTM's (1991) description of standard mathematics classroom practice and reasons for valuing mathematics as a part of schooling. Part of what is valued about mathematics as a discipline is its emphasis on logical reasoning, the notion that mathematical ideas are not to be accepted on faith, but can (indeed must) be supported with argument that others accept. But, as my dayschool teaching illustrates, in standard mathematics classroom practice, much is taken on faith. (In Chapter 3 I have also argued that this is a dimension along which I would like to improve the teaching that Sandy and I did.) As a result, students do not learn to be mathematical and do not develop confidence in their own reasoning powers.

Another key factor behind NCTM's (1991) call for change in classroom roles is rooted in insights from cognitive psychology. As psychological theories of learning increasingly have emphasized the active nature of the role of learners, educators have begun to pay more serious attention to the conceptions students bring with them to the classroom; this psychological insight suggests that teachers must gain knowledge of their students' conceptions in order to influence them. Knowledge of these conceptions can be gained by changing the nature of classroom interaction, by opening up conversational space for students to make their ideas public, by creating what historian of education Larry Cuban calls "student centered instruction" (1993, p. 7).

As the decision to publish the *Professional Standards for Teaching Mathematics* (NCTM, 1991) indicates, this sort of change requires development in mathematics teaching methods. Simply put, though there are counterexamples here and there, as a community, mathematics teachers have little experience in making these five shifts and supporting informal exchanges of mathematical thoughts in the classroom. As a result of the attempts that Sandy and I have made to create mathematical conversations in the secondary classroom, I explore in this chapter such questions as: Why is mathematics seemingly resistant to conversation and to student-centered instruction? What obstacles to student-centered instruction are especially prevalent in lower-track secondary school mathematics classrooms? What resources are available for the development of such approaches to teaching in such settings? What challenges arise when attempting to develop such teaching?

Building on one of Cuban's (1993, p. 9) arguments for the endurance of teacher-centered instruction in the face of reform efforts, I argue that our cultural beliefs about mathematical knowledge play a key role in the seeming resistance of mathematics to student-centered mathematics instruction. At the same time, I see resources for change. Recent developments in elementary school mathematics teaching and in the history and philosophy of mathematics critique standard views and present important practical and theoretical resources for designing alternative forms of mathematics instruction in secondary school classrooms. But this work is in its infancy; the task of developing this sort of mathematics teaching is a complex one that will require much time and effort.

CULTURAL BELIEFS ABOUT THE NATURE OF MATHEMATICAL KNOWLEDGE

There are major stumbling blocks on the road toward a lower-track Algebra One class in which students are vocal and actively engaged and in which their mathematical reasoning, and *not* the unquestioned authority of the teacher, determines what is correct and incorrect. I will focus initially on one of six explanations that Larry Cuban (1993) gives for the patterns of constancy and change in instruction revealed by his study of teaching from the 1880s to 1990. Cuban finds that, though educational reformers have asked teachers to create classrooms in which students can be active learners, a small number of student-centered practices have been incorporated into elementary school teaching. In contrast to elementary school classrooms, one of his central findings at the secondary level is that "high school instruction has largely remained teacher-centered" (p. 272). In attempting to explain this finding, and others, Cuban suggests that

> cultural beliefs about the nature of knowledge, how teaching should occur, and how children should learn are so widespread and deeply rooted that they steer the thinking of policymakers, practitioners, parents, and citizens toward certain forms of instruction. [I would add students to Cuban's list of important actors.] (p. 14)[3]

He suggests that modern public education evolved from European and American religious educational traditions in which knowledge was stable, unchanging, and unproblematic, traditions in which the role of the teacher was to inform the uninformed (see especially pp. 14, 248).

Building on Cuban's (1993) view of the role of cultural beliefs, I suggest that his explanation for the stability of teacher-centered instruction has a special flavor when one focuses on mathematics instruction. In Western views of knowledge, mathematics is often described as the most certain branch of human knowledge, one in which it is easy to distinguish "right" from "wrong." I argue that, as a result, there is a complex web of beliefs about mathematical knowledge and mathematics instruction that has developed over time and that is integral to the difficulty of teaching secondary school mathematics in a student-centered manner. Central to this set of beliefs about mathematics instruction are the notions that:

- all statements of school mathematics can be judged unequivocally right or wrong;
- a central role of the teacher is to exercise this judgment;
- these judgments can be used effectively to label students' "ability" or aptitude in mathematics.

In my view, these beliefs make it difficult for a teacher to create authentic conversations with students about mathematics. Briefly, if the teacher knows what is right and what is wrong, what is there to discuss? To understand this set of cultural beliefs more deeply and to appreciate the difficulties it poses for instruction, I turn to a quick survey of Western views of mathematical knowledge and their relationship to teacher-centered instruction. Subsequently, I will explore resources that might support an alternative practice.

CERTAINTY IN MATHEMATICS AND ITS RELATIONSHIP TO EDUCATIONAL PRACTICES

In Western societies, there is a complex web of mutually reinforcing societal attitudes toward mathematics that affects instruction. Though careful rationalists stress that no human knowledge can be certain (e.g., Scheffler, 1965), mathematical knowledge has traditionally been seen as certain and unchanging, transparent and unproblematic. Other fields of human endeavor—even science—might strive for the certainty of $2 + 2 = 4$, but cannot achieve it. In this vein, historian of mathematics Morris Kline (1980) suggests that mathematics is our exemplar of "certitude and exactness of reasoning" (p. 4). According to this view, mathematics is not culture-bound; it is universal, accessible (or perhaps inaccessible!) to one and all regardless of their race, gender, nationality, and creed.[4]

Philosophers in Western culture, from the Greeks on, have wondered what is responsible for this special, seemingly incontrovertible quality of mathematical knowledge. Explanations have varied. For Plato, mathematics owes its special epistemological status to its relationship with ideal forms. These forms exist in a world of "reality" only indirectly accessible to our senses, grounded as they are in the world of experience. For example, in *The Republic* Plato outlines his reasons for including arithmetic and geometry in the quadrivium. In his view, arithmetic and geometry lead the mind upward and away from the mundane world of experience (see Fauvel & Gray, 1987, pp. 68–70). The mathematical figures that we draw (e.g., a particular triangle) are but pale shadows of the ideal forms (the Triangle); while a particular diagram passes, the geometrical objects it describes are eternal. Thus, Plato posits that the noncontingent nature of our geometrical knowledge is due to the character of the objects it describes. (According to Davis and Hersh, 1981, p. 70, these are the weekday beliefs of most working mathematicians.)

The 18th-century German philosopher Immanuel Kant, in contrast, bases the certainty of our mathematical knowledge on a presumably shared human capacity for true intuitions. He would agree with Plato that mathematics, unlike science, has access to truths as a result of its nonempirical nature, but argues for a different basis for that nonempirical nature of mathematics. Rather than describing objects "in the world of reality," for Kant mathematical concepts are built around "an intuition which it [mathematics] presents *a priori*, that is, which it has constructed" (quoted in Fauvel & Gray, 1987, p. 516). We intuit the fundamental true principles—for example, the axioms of Euclidean geometry— and then make truth-preserving deductive arguments based on these axioms (what Lakatos, 1986, calls a "Euclidean" view of mathematics). In such a way, our mathematical knowledge is rock-solid, based on the bedrock of true intuitions.[5]

After the development of non-Euclidean geometries challenged the solidity of human mathematical intuitions—by suggesting that there are other logical and legitimate alternatives to the notion that given a point and a line there is always one and only one line through the given point parallel to the given line—early in this century, different programs were pursued to reconstruct a rock-solid foundation for mathematical knowledge. Some followed Kant and sought to elucidate bedrock intuitions on which mathematics was founded. Others looked to logic, and others to the consistency of formal systems, to explain the nature of mathematical knowledge. Though there were important differences among these programs, all sought to explain the peculiarly different nature of mathematical knowledge, often contrasting it with empirical, and thus necessarily contingent, scientific knowledge (programs for the foundations of mathematics are outlined in Benacerraf & Putnam, 1964/1983).[6]

In schools, historical views about the certainty of mathematics and its importance mesh with views of school subject matter as fundamental, unambiguous, and unproblematically factual[7] to shape teacher-centered mathematics instruction. In contrast to matters of opinion or interpretation, the validity of answers to arithmetic, algebraic, or geometric questions is seen as amenable to judgment in simple and noncontroversial ways. There is no need for interpretation and adjudication. Two plus two is four, and will always be four; one can subtract the greater from the lesser. Zero is a number like any other number; the sum of the interior angles of a triangle is 180 degrees; the derivative can be used to compute the instantaneous velocity of an object in motion; and so on.

Mathematical statements, particularly elementary mathematical statements of the kind examined in school, are either true or false.

In keeping with this view of mathematical knowledge, in schools there is a heavy emphasis on truth and correctness. The notion that the truth of these statements is contingent on one's definitions is ignored. For example, for Frend and Maseres—the Cambridge-educated 19th century mathematicians discussed in Chapter 3, who restricted their definition of number to what we would call the positive rational numbers—one cannot subtract the greater from the lesser *and still obtain a number.* Similarly, there are non-Euclidean geometries in which the sum of the measures of a triangle is different from 180 degrees (for a related point in relation to intelligence testing, see Brown & Langer, 1990).

In typical secondary-level teacher-centered instruction, such issues are not deemed important. A large chunk of instructional time regularly is devoted to teacher lectures. (For descriptions of such practice see Good, Grouws, & Eb-meier, 1983; Goodlad, 1984; Welch, 1978.) The notion is that, in these lectures, teachers are presenting true information efficiently; the mathematics of the teacher or textbook is not contested, or contestable, knowledge.[8] Of course, students can ask the teacher questions of clarification or request further explanation, but students' confusions, or perhaps disagreements with what is being taught, are considered problematic. The teacher actively tries to clear up confusions as quickly as possible. Usually incorrect ideas are labeled "errors" and then dismissed, lest the teacher seem to sanction them; traditional descriptions provide no rationale for focusing attention on incorrect ideas and suggest that the teacher must indicate clearly which notions are correct and which are not. And there is always pressure to "cover" the material. There is so much for students to know. Even if one would like students to be more active in class, because of time constraints, one cannot reasonably expect students in school to blunder inefficiently as they attempt to recreate mathematics it has taken generations of talented mathematicians to create.

For these reasons, the shifts advocated by the National Council of Teachers of Mathematics toward student reasoning, logic, and evidence as support for statements, and away from teacher authority, represent dramatic changes and can be threatening—for teachers, students, parents, and policymakers. But there are other reasons as well. Though students often leave traditional mathematics classes with mistaken conceptions, the idea of having students leave a class session before the teacher has announced what is true, or not, contravenes traditional views of the teacher's role; knowingly letting students leave a particular class session with "wrong" conceptions seems, according to traditional practice, the height of pedagogical irresponsibility. It even smacks of relativism, namely, that there are no solid grounds for preferring certain conceptions over others, that everything, including mathematics, is relative.

Finally, in teacher-centered classroom instruction, "problems" or "exercises" have a well-defined role; students do problems *after* new material has been introduced. Since there are unambiguously correct answers to problems, the purpose of doing a problem is for teacher and students to evaluate whether students have learned the presented material, *not* to uncover new material or create a discussion of students' own mathematical ideas. Based on the teacher's presentation of the material, students are expected to be able to do the assignment correctly. Wrong answers indicate that the material has not been learned and that further explanation or practice is required.

These beliefs about mathematical knowledge and teaching are part of a web of cultural conceptions of mathematics that extends beyond the walls of the classroom. There are other educational practices, like aptitude testing and tracking by "ability," that also depend on the possibility of judging mathematical statements unambiguously as either right or wrong. It is a common experience to find that some people are "wrong" in mathematics more often than others. Indeed, some people find the whole subject impenetrable and have difficulty with proportional reasoning throughout their lives (even after valiant attempts and the efforts of teachers year after year). Others seem to have special mathematical talents or intuition—there are prodigies who at age eight are conversant with the calculus;[9] we do not all seem to have the same access to the supposed truth of mathematical statements. But, in contrast to other societies that may emphasize effort rather than ability, in the United States, we give much weight to ability (Stevenson, Lummis, Lee, & Stigler, 1990). Thus, to explain differences in achievement in mathematics, common wisdom holds that mathematical aptitude or ability is an attribute of people amenable to assessment and evaluation.

The combination of the view of mathematical knowledge as certain and the notion of mathematical aptitude or ability results in harsh assessments of people, like the students Sandy and I taught at Holt, who do not do well on tests of school mathematics. People who do not give the right answers, for whatever reasons, are not successful in mathematics and are considered of "low ability." They do not "see" or intuit what is so clearly "seen" by those with mathematical ability. They do not achieve on tests and as a result are shunted aside when the college-intending track is created in secondary school.[10]

These notions about mathematical ability or aptitude are woven into our decisions about how to allocate opportunities for continued, or specialized, education and the economic possibilities that such education may bring. Beginning in the late 1930s, and especially since World War II, in the United States, aptitude and intelligence testing has played an important part in regulating people's opportunities for continued formal education.[11] I am intrigued by the role— *unique among school subject matters*—that mathematics plays in such testing. All of the standardized college admission tests have sections to assess mathematical aptitude. There is no other assessed aptitude linked as directly to a school subject. Those who wish to pursue noncompulsory postsecondary education in colleges or universities must attain a level of mathematical achievement that varies with the selectivity and cachet of the institution. There is no other school subject matter put to similar use.[12]

This use of assessment of mathematical aptitude in allocating opportunity reveals the complex ways in which the parts of our web of commonsense views about mathematics reinforce each other.[13] The certainty of mathematical knowledge makes it possible to create questions for which there is a single answer that can be scored quickly, easily, and cheaply by machine. (In reviewing literature on testing, Carroll, 1978, suggests that these are important characteristics of standardized test questions.) Furthermore, since mathematical knowledge, unlike historical or scientific knowledge, for example, is not considered culture-bound, tests made up of such questions are viewed as unbiased, merit-based assessments of aptitude.[14] These tests do not test matters of opinion. The tasks on such tests are not open to interpretation and do not have multiple answers. Further, the graded difficulty of mathematics and differences in individual talents and interests suggest that there will be a range of scores on such mathematics tests. People who have mathematical aptitude will score well, and those who do not will score poorly. For these reasons, some characterize the use of mathematics in educational settings as a filter, or gatekeeper; it is used to allow those with aptitude to continue on, while those without aptitude are held back (for a discussion of this metaphor, see Mathematical Sciences Education Board, 1989, pp. 1–16). And, because of its role in determining college entrance, perhaps there is no mathematical filter as important as the one we call algebra (Moses, Kamii, Swap, & Howard, 1989; Usiskin, 1995).

LOWER-TRACK MATHEMATICS CLASSES AND THIS CULTURAL WEB OF BELIEFS AND PRACTICES

When I began to teach at Holt, this web of beliefs and educational practices was one of the obstacles to the creation of student-centered instruction in lower-track secondary school mathematics classrooms. The notion of ability was clearly problematic. On the one hand, there was evidence to label my students "low ability"; they did poorly on standardized tests. But acquiescence to this labeling had negative consequences. When my students accepted this label, they had a ready-made explanation for expecting that tasks posed for them were too difficult to attempt. If I accepted this labeling, my energies and efforts at understanding my students were undercut. Instead, I found myself battling harsh judgments of their ability and emphasizing the mathematical strengths they brought to

class, particularly the ways in which they insisted on sensible uses of mathematics in situated contexts (for an examination of such strengths, see Chazan, 1996a).

In addition, in lower-track secondary school mathematics classrooms, the notion of ability has an impact on the dynamics of classroom interaction. At first, the students that Sandy and I taught sometimes seemed reluctant to share their thinking with us. They had been placed in our class as a result of their achievement in prior courses; their achievement had been evaluated and found wanting. They were accustomed to the teacher as evaluator. We were teachers, members of a group that had previously judged them to be of "low ability." Perhaps they were concerned that if they shared their thinking, we might once again judge that they knew little.

Second, we often found that our students were not in the habit of listening to one another. This, again, seemed related to the notion of ability. It can be especially difficult to help students in a lower-track class see a purpose in listening to each other. If all the students in the room have been placed in this class because they have done poorly in mathematics, students may wonder why they should listen to each other's comments.

For teachers who want to create classroom conversation, these two dynamics result in a serious concern about student participation. In Chapter 2, I discussed Mary Metz's (1993) notion of the teacher's dependence on students. Yet her argument about the teacher's dependence on students' learning is situated in the context of traditional instruction. Student-centered teaching makes the teacher all the more dependent on students. Not only were we dependent on our students to learn, but we also depended on them to help produce classroom interaction, or our lessons could come to a grinding halt.

CHANGING THE ROLE OF THE "PROBLEM"

How does one begin to change the mathematics classroom to create different roles for teachers and students? The shifts called for by the NCTM *Professional Standards for Teaching Mathematics* (1991) are not widespread in secondary school mathematics classrooms, but there has been some progress in developing and instantiating alternative stances toward mathematical knowledge in the practice of elementary school mathematics instruction.[15] For example, Magdalene Lampert, an educator known for changing the nature of the interaction in her own elementary mathematics classroom, builds explicitly on views of mathematical practice. In a piece titled "When the Problem Is Not the Question and the Solution Is Not the Answer: Mathematical Knowing and Teaching" (1990) she describes her own classroom stance. As a teacher, Lampert steps away from the role of sole arbiter of mathematical truth and insists that students help decide what is true. Rather than have students memorize procedures for finding solutions, she asks students to conjecture and invent as they solve problems.[16] Instead of textbooks, homework, and fill-in-the-blank worksheets, her instruction includes a bound student notebook in which students write with pens so they will not erase their reasoning (one small indication to students of the importance placed on their reasoning); a format for organizing work in this notebook; the introduction and use of the terms *conjecture, hypothesis, revise, agree, disagree,* and *prove*; norms for the respect of others' ideas; and whole-class discussions as a central element.

However, in order to carry out these changes, there must be something to discuss; the contents of the lesson cannot be "cut and dried." To paraphrase Lampert (1990), "doing mathematics" can no longer mean following the rules laid down by the teacher; "knowing mathematics" can no longer mean remembering and applying the correct rule when the teacher asks a question; and "mathematical truth" can no longer be determined when the answer is ratified by the teacher (p. 32).

While Lampert makes many changes in her instruction, I will focus on the way she changes the role of the problem in mathematics instruction. On the surface, she seems to assign traditional problems/exercises to students; seemingly, like most of the problems assigned in school, her problems "are well formulated, present no ambiguity, admit a few objective solutions, and can be solved by the application of a suitable combination of learned algorithms" (Borasi, 1992, p. 167). But closer examination reveals this not to be true. As the title of Lampert's article suggests, in her classroom, "the problem is not the question and the solution is not the answer"; hidden beneath the seemingly cut-and-dried problem is an instructional design and a set of classroom expectations that elicit a multiplicity of student strategies.

In her teaching, Lampert changes the role of the problem by making a clever inversion. Rather than have mathematics problems follow direct instruction of algorithms that solve these problems and use problems solely as an assessment tool to determine whether students have learned the "covered" material, she assigns a problem before an algorithm for its solution is taught and uses student exploration of such problems as a central way for students to learn the mathematics she seeks to teach.[17] In typical instruction, once an efficient algorithm is taught, there is a press to use this algorithm rather than idiosyncratic solution methods. When a seemingly unambiguous problem is used before an algorithm has been taught, it is no longer cut-and-dried; it often can be approached in different and innovative ways.

In Lampert's instruction, student exploration of a problem comes prior to classroom discussion during which students share the results of their exploration. Through the discussion of their results, the class as a whole (the teacher included) develops a shared set of mathematical understandings. Since the problems she uses may have a limited number of answers, while students may develop a range of solution procedures, they must come to grips with each other's ideas as they come to consensus about the correct answers. It is the resulting conversation around the problem, students' solution methods, and their developing mathematical ideas that are important. Direct instruction, if carried out at all, might follow up on a discussion of student results, indicating how these results relate to accepted mathematical thought, or underlining the consensus that has developed in the group.

Thus, in her instruction, Lampert portrays school mathematics like the discipline itself, as a living and growing field in which developments occur when people create solutions to problems. She encourages her students to see mathematics as a field in which one makes hypotheses and revises them. Since she asks students to tackle problems before having taught them algorithmic solutions to problems of these kind, right and wrong are less central categories in her teaching than in traditional teaching; students are not expected to be able to come to correct answers in their first attempts at a problem of a particular kind. Incorrect answers are as deserving of classroom attention as correct ones (without implying that they are correct); what matters is the nature of students' mathematical reasoning and its evolution.

A SAMPLE HIGH SCHOOL ALGEBRA LESSON

In "When the Problem Is Not the Question and the Solution Is Not the Answer: Mathematical Knowing and Teaching," Lampert (1990) exemplifies her instructional design by describing a session devoted to discussion of the following problem: "What is the last digit in 5^4? 6^4? 7^4?" In order to illustrate the ways in which Sandy and I were inspired by her example and to indicate the sorts of discussions that occurred when we followed a similar format in our high school class, I will describe a class session in which we asked students to read from graphs (see Figure 4.1).

We asked students to tackle these questions early in their study of how the Cartesian coordinate system can be used to represent relationships between two quantities. Our students had used sketches of graphs to illustrate how the relationships between quantities changed. They had used more precise graphs to record information from tables and algebraic rules. But this was the first time they were being asked to use specific qualitative graphical information to make quantitative comparisons. They had no algorithm for producing a response; using their understanding of the nature of the Cartesian coordinate system, they would have to decide which aspects of the graph should be used to help answer each of the questions.

Although on the surface there are single, correct answers to each of the

Figure 4.1. An Algebra One problem.

Here are the graphs for the rates for four **different** pumps, which are emptying four **different** pools.

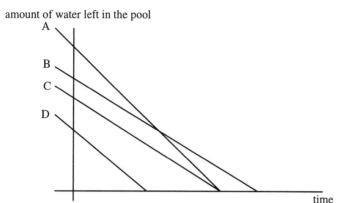

amount of water left in the pool

Explain all of your answers!
1. Which pool had the most water to start with?
2. Which pump completed its task first?
3. Which pump pumps the most water in a given time?

three questions, as in Lampert's (1990) instruction, our questions "put the solver in the position of devising all or part of the solution procedure" (p. 40). Our interest, like Lampert's, was not in the answers to the particular questions we asked, but, rather, in the nature of the rationales that students gave for their answers and the development of these rationales. Students' explanations for their choices would help us learn about their understanding of the use of the Cartesian coordinate system for representing relationships between two quantities.

Typically, after allowing students time for exploration, one of Lampert's classes might spend 30 to 40 minutes discussing such a problem and the ways in which people are thinking about the solution to the problem (see Figure 4.2).

While some might argue that such an emphasis on whole-group discussion forces students of different abilities to move at the same "pace," the beauty of this commitment of time to group discussion is that it can support the shift away from the teacher as sole arbiter of mathematical truth and toward the class as a mathematical community. In-depth discussion of problems can bring out the different ways in which students understand a problem, some of them mathemat-

Figure 4.2. The schedule of a typical lesson.

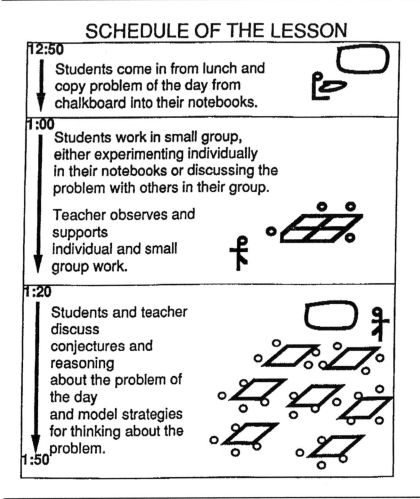

SCHEDULE OF THE LESSON

12:50
Students come in from lunch and copy problem of the day from chalkboard into their notebooks.

1:00
Students work in small group, either experimenting individually in their notebooks or discussing the problem with others in their group.

Teacher observes and supports individual and small group work.

1:20
Students and teacher discuss conjectures and reasoning about the problem of the day and model strategies for thinking about the problem.

1:50

Source: Lampert (1991a)

ically correct and others mathematically incorrect. When a range of views is available to the class, students can then use logic and mathematical evidence to decide which answers and approaches they trust and value.

But orchestrating these whole-class discussions of a problem is not easy; good discussions do not occur spontaneously. In particular, such whole-group discussions require that students articulate their mathematical points of view clearly enough that the rest of the class can understand. The atmosphere in the class must help students not feel bad for offering "wrong" answers, but instead feel that such answers are steps along the way to the development of a deeper understanding—that offering wrong answers is part of the role of the student. Then, for the teacher, the challenge of leading the discussion is to keep students' ideas developing and growing toward deeper understanding.[18] When there are disagreements, the classroom community, the teacher included, has to support students in revising their initial conjectures.

The session in our class devoted to the discussion of the four-pump problem illustrates the nature of conversations when Sandy and I did not take on the role of arbiter of mathematical truth and instead left students to engage with each other's ideas. The students all chose pump A for the first question, seemingly for similar reasons. However, when we moved to the second question (which pump finished first?), it became clear that there were three reasons for choosing D, some correct and others incorrect. Jackie indicated that D was "first" on the y-axis; Christin chose D because it was the shortest line from y-intercept to x-intercept; and Bob thought D was the closest to (0,0), along the time axis.

As a result of seeing these different rationales for the same answer, students took it on themselves to decide which of these rationales would in general be correct. As part of that discussion, Bob argued that Christin's reasoning was not sound and attempted to develop an example that would distinguish his reasoning from hers (in my judgment, he was ultimately not successful). He hoped that doing so would provide mathematical evidence that would convince her that her rationale was not, in general, correct.

> *Bob*: You can put something before this [D], it's a longer line, but still it's done first. So it doesn't really matter. Like watch. . . . Okay, like that [draws in line E; see Figure 4.3]. This [E] is longer than this one [D], but it [E] got done first.
> *Christin*: That's not in it [the problem] though.
> *DC*: So Bob has made up another graph, this one here, we can call it "E." (C: My point . . . [inaudible]) We can call it "E," and he says, Christin, that it's a counterexample to what you say. Joe?
> *Joe*: It may not be an example in this time [this problem?], but still it's

Figure 4.3. Bob's pump E.

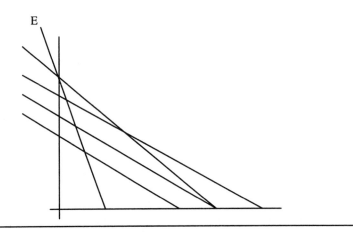

an example that you can't use that rule all the time that "it's the shortest one."

We moved to the third question, which I thought was about the "efficiency" of the pumps, but which students interpreted as deciding which pump was best in some sense. There were different answers, not only different reasons for the same answer. To some degree, these different answers reflected different views of the question.

> *Mark*: I think number three's A because it has the most water, even though it had the most water, no matter what place it came in, it would always pump the most water.
>
> *Angela*: I think it's D. . . . Because it's the one who got done first. I mean, it pumps, even though it has less water than everybody else's, . . . I think it was a better pump and it pumped faster.
>
> *Joe*: A is the best, that has the most amount of water, and it still finished first, so no matter what you do it's just better, it's going to pump the most water at any given time.

However, as students discussed these three answers, they did not address directly the different interpretations of the question that their answers reveal. Instead, adherents of the third response tried to indicate how their response was different from the other two. In what seemed to be the most convincing turn,

Bob again came to the board and presented an argument that asked the other students to compare the different pumps by doing a thought experiment and changing aspects of the given problem.

> *Bob*: The way I look at it, you've got to look at the angles. Now say [Angela: Here's our mathematician!] say, take angle D [Bob places a ruler over line D] and put it up here [moves the left-hand edge of the ruler to the *y*-intercept of A, while keeping it parallel to D. See Figure 4.4]. This [A] still has a steeper angle, it will be done first. Take angle C, do the same thing, A has a steeper angle again, still, and do the same thing for this one [B], and it still has a steeper angle, so this is always going to get done first because it has a steeper angle than the rest.

This class session fascinates me. On the one hand, it illustrates connections between changes in the role of a problem (Lampert, 1990), the shifts in classroom roles proposed by NCTM (1991), and the nature of classroom conversation. Students do not have an algorithm for solving these questions. As a result, attention is focused less on the answers to the questions and more on the rationales for student responses. For example, even though on the second question everyone agrees that the answer is D, students still discuss the various rationales presented. In doing so, they make use of logic and evidence to attempt to convince each other to revise their points of view. In this discussion, students speak

Figure 4.4. Bob's use of the ruler.

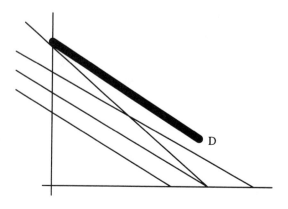

to each other and take longer conversational turns than those common in most classrooms, and some students, like Bob, come to the board to represent their thinking in that public space. There is conversation in the mathematics classroom!

On the other hand, some of the tensions and complexities of our classroom are just below the surface. What does Angela's comment about Bob—"Here comes our mathematician"—mean? Is Angela expressing anger because Bob is arguing against her point of view? Is there an issue of gender that underlies the ways in which Bob argues against Angela and Christin's point of view? On the other hand, Angela, Bob, and Christin are all smokers. They tend to care about each other's point of view in class. Would Bob have bothered to argue against Christin's rationale if instead it had been articulated by a preppie? Is this why Angela calls him "our" mathematician? And what about the rationales students give? Are these articulated well enough to convince others?

BEYOND THE ROLE OF THE PROBLEM: TACKLING "RIGHT" AND "WRONG"

There is more to Lampert's (1990) teaching (and to the example I have just given) than reworking the pedagogical role of problems. Lampert's teaching is guided by mathematician George Polya (1945) and philosopher Imre Lakatos' (1976) descriptions of mathematics as a discipline, descriptions that differ from the conceptions of mathematics I have outlined earlier in this chapter. Simply changing the role of the problem is not enough. It is not enough for teachers to refrain from judging students' ideas. In line with Cuban's (1993) argument, I believe that one's beliefs about the nature of knowledge are central. In the case of mathematics, the categories of "right" and "wrong" have to be reexamined.

To illustrate, I'll return to the Algebra One classroom. In my first year of teaching at Holt, as I tried to create a student-centered classroom, a disquiet developed for me, focused on my role in evaluating students' comments and strategies. On the one hand, when I thought something was right or wrong, it seemed disingenuous to refrain from commenting, to withhold my views, particularly when students, concerned about knowing right from wrong, asked me directly. (These issues are explored in Chazan & Ball, 1999.) While I wanted to respect students' mathematical ideas, I did not want to retreat into an every-idea-is-of-equal-value brand of relativism; I did not want my students "taught" incorrect ideas.

On the other hand, I had three concerns about how to indicate, even subtly, that a comment or strategy was wrong. First, I was concerned that, if I told students flat out that they were wrong, they might give up and decide they were not able to make progress. Unlike students who have been successful in school and who have a strong belief in the value of school knowledge, my students were not goaded by a negative evaluation to return to their work and puzzle out where they had "gone wrong." Second, though I thought there was value in examining students' incorrect ideas, I was concerned that if I labeled an idea wrong, my students would no longer want to spend time on it. With my students' prior experiences of schooling, how would I justify spending time on something that was wrong? Finally, I was concerned I might undercut the dynamics leading to classroom conversation. If I simply told students what was right and wrong, why would they bother to listen to each other? After all, as the teacher, my judgment should be trustworthy, while students were in this class because they had not done well in mathematics. If I was going to tell them what was right and what was wrong, then wouldn't it be simpler and more efficient for me to do this without forcing them to work so hard? But, if I did that, I would be back in the role I had when teaching at the dayschool!

Propelled by these sorts of issues in the Holt teaching, I felt that I had to rethink my understandings of right and wrong and how I would present these categories to students. In this rethinking, I have drawn on recent debates about the nature of mathematical knowledge.[19]

CRITICISMS OF MATHEMATICAL CERTAINTY
AND THEIR RAMIFICATIONS

Views of the nature of mathematical knowledge are becoming subject to the same sorts of examination as views of other kinds of knowledge (for example, the examinations of science associated with Thomas Kuhn, 1962, and of knowledge more generally associated with Richard Rorty, 1991). As a result, there are controversial challenges to the set of attitudes about mathematics that I outlined earlier. Most mathematicians would still characterize mathematics as "a field where things are either right or wrong . . . [where] the decisions are usually clean and straightforward" (Devlin, 1997, p. 2). But, for me, these challenges suggest that the edges around this set of conceptions are fraying. In my view, these challenges are resources for the development of new instruction in secondary school mathematics classrooms; with the reexamination of the nature of mathematical knowledge come opportunities to rework educational practices central to the teaching of mathematics.

At the heart of these critiques, the very notion of mathematical certainty, of the special character of mathematical knowledge, is being questioned and reevaluated. Critics of mathematical certainty, *pace* Devlin (1997), argue that labeling mathematical statements unambiguously right or wrong is not always a straightforward affair; the existence of a mathematical proof does not necessarily decide the matter once and for all. They argue that overdrawing the difference between mathematical and scientific knowledge fundamentally misrepresents mathematics.

Such critics are not suggesting that $2 + 2$ does not equal 4, but instead that this sort of statement is not the best reflection of all of mathematics—that representations of mathematics also need to reflect other aspects of mathematics. For example, with regard to $2 + 2 = 4$, mathematical thinking also involves understanding how arithmetic operations have been conceptualized. As a result, representations of mathematical knowledge also must encompass the sorts of knowledge needed to understand why the fact that two shirts and two pants yield four possible outfits is an example of $2 * 2 = 4$, and not $2 + 2 = 4$.

Critiques of mathematical certainty by mathematicians, historians of mathematics, and philosophers of mathematics began in the 19th century. The development of non-Euclidean geometries—geometries based on intuitions quite different from the philosopher Kant's—initiated what Morris Kline (1980) characterizes as "The Loss of Certainty."[20] Mathematicians developed alternatives to Euclid that were internally consistent, but whose assumptions directly contradicted Euclid's, as did many of the theorems that stemmed from them. These developments contradicted Kant's views of the *a priori* "truth" of the intuitions embedded in Euclid's parallel postulate. How could those intuitions be "true" when opposing views are "true" as well?

Later, during the turn of the century, there was a crisis in the foundations of mathematics (Benacerraf & Putnam, 1964/1983). Different programs were developed to provide an epistemologically sound foundation for mathematics, but these programs designed to explain the peculiar certainty of mathematics—as opposed, for example, to the fallibility of science—all failed. Some tried to reduce mathematics to logic, which would then be proven true. As Frege completed his masterpiece, the young Bertrand Russell presented a paradox that undermined the very basis of this program, of Frege's life's work. (This tale is recounted movingly in Kline, 1980, pp. 205ff.) Russell and Whitehead reduced mathematics to arithmetic and constructed their *Principia* to provide a basis for arithmetic, only later to have Goedel present mathematical arguments suggesting that their quest was unachievable (Kline, 1980, pp. 258–277).

Not only has the seeming certainty of mathematics remained unexplained, but the very enterprise of providing foundations for mathematical knowledge has been questioned. Rather than emphasizing differences between science and mathematics, some philosophers of mathematics, mathematicians, and historians of mathematics have been exploring the notion that mathematics is "fallibilistic," and in that sense similar to science. These thinkers emphasize ways in which the practice of mathematicians diverges from the descriptions of philosophers. Mathematical proofs are not as unshakable as they might seem: Real proofs are never produced in exhaustive detail; much is left to the reader; consequently, proofs often have errors; difficulties with a proof may be more serious;

incorrect results are published and counterexamples are developed to results that have been proven (Davis, 1986; Lakatos, 1976); and, finally, social factors, like a mathematician's reputation or the popularity of a mathematical field, play an important role in the acceptance of advances (Hanna, 1983).

This examination of mathematical practice challenges the notion that mathematics, because of the mechanism of mathematical proof, is certain and uncontested (though some still argue that it has a qualitatively different feel from other kinds of knowledge).[21] It changes the important philosophical questions. According to Brian Rotman (1993), what needs to be explained is not why mathematics is more certain than other kinds of knowledge, but why it is that we perceive this to be so.[22]

These developments in epistemology are reflected in recent debates about what makes for good history of mathematics. In portraying new trends in the writing of the history of mathematics, David Rowe (1996) analyzes a standing tension among two camps, which he calls cultural historians and mathematical historians.

In Rowe's (1996) view, mathematical historians know what mathematics is—it is the knowledge currently recognized as mathematics—and document who discovered it. They produce histories that "present the development of mathematical ideas as a steadily unfolding search for Platonic truths that transcend the particular cultural contexts in which these ideas arose" (p. 1). Mathematical historians want to know who first discovered a particular theorem. They are less interested in understanding exactly what led the person to focus on this area of study, or in characterizing the general level of mathematical activity in a culture. Using the words of Sabbetai Unguru, Rowe suggests that mathematical historians focus on the evolutions that lead to modern mathematics and write the "mathematics of history."[23]

By way of contrast, cultural historians are interested in the idiosyncratic development of mathematics in particular cultures and investigate the "history of mathematics." They are less sure of what exactly in a culture is mathematical and what, for example, is religious or mystical (e.g., Cohen, 1999). They are interested in a wide variety of mathematical activity, not only what is innovative or correct by our standards. Thus, cultural historians criticize the histories produced by mathematical historians and object that such histories are produced "only by discounting the rich variety of meanings that accompanied this [mathematical] work" (Rowe, 1996, p. 10).

Tensions of these kinds have played out around the depiction of change in mathematics. Our cultural conceptions of mathematics have little room for revolutionary change in mathematics, only incremental accretion of new results. However, challenged by Thomas Kuhn's (1962) identification of revolutions in scientific thought, historians of mathematics have debated whether there are revolutions in mathematical thought. In the 1970s, Michael Crowe (1975) suggested that "revolutions never occur in mathematics" and stipulated that in a revolution, "some previously existing entity must be overthrown and irrevocably discarded" (p. 166). While agreeing that in mathematics previous notions are not "irrevocably discarded," other historians have subsequently argued that there are dramatic shifts in mathematical thought and that Crowe's definition of a revolution is too limiting when it rules out such episodes. Instead, Joseph Dauben (1992) has argued that revolutions are "discontinuities of such magnitude as to constitute definite breaks with the past" (p. 51). (For an exposition of the Crowe-Dauben debate, see the introduction to Gillies, 1992.) Thus, for Dauben,

> mathematics is not a simple progression of results leading in a continuous, unbroken chain from Antiquity to the present. It has its own revolutionary moments, and these are as necessary to its progress as revolutions have been to all of science. (p. 81)

Though there still is much controversy about the existence and nature of revolutions in mathematics, even Crowe (1992) agrees that recent developments in the history of mathematics demonstrate that "the new [Kuhnian] historiography of science can be usefully applied to the history of mathematics" (p. 316).

To give an idea of the evidence that leads to this conclusion, I will outline the argument given in one study, an essay titled "Is Mathematical Truth Time-dependent?" In this essay, Judith Grabiner (1986) argues against our immediate impulse to answer in the negative by examining 19th-century changes in criteria for mathematical proof and rigor, particularly in the field of analysis. She argues that from the 18th to the 19th century there were substantial changes in standards for truth in analysis.[24] Eighteenth-century mathematicians were more focused on obtaining results, many of which are now known by their names, than on determining the foundations of the subject. Their proofs do not meet modern standards. Though we know the results by the names of the 18th-century mathematicians who first published them, Grabiner argues that these initial results are quite different from the ones we know today: "Chances are good that these results were originally obtained in ways utterly different from the ways we prove them today" (p. 203). Today's proofs—utilizing limits, convergence, and continuity—are 19th-century arguments that reject the methods used in 18th-century proofs. Examination of these mathematical developments leads Grabiner to conclude that "perhaps mathematical truth is eternal, but our knowledge of it is not. . . . Mathematics is *not* the unique science without revolutions" (pp. 211–212).

In addition to philosophers and historians of mathematics, mathematics educators have also been experiencing discomfort with the notion that mathematical knowledge is timelessly certain and easily categorized as right or wrong.[25]

Psychologists and educators working under the rubric of the psychology of mathematics education have focused on students' mistakes and, attributing sense-making capabilities to students (in the spirit of Piaget), have investigated the rationales and conceptions that underlie mistaken answers. In 1976, the International Group for the Psychology of Mathematics Education was founded as an umbrella organization for those working in this field. Nesher and Kilpatrick (1990) present much of the work done by members of this group to a wider audience. Initially under the rubric of "misconceptions," researchers turned up many sensible and coherent conceptions supporting mistakes. For example, when people say that zero is not a number, they are trying to capture an essential difference between zero and numbers with which they are familiar. In applied contexts, zero represents the absence of quantity. In that respect, it seems strange to think of it as a number. (For elaborate examinations of this point, see Rotman, 1987, and Boyer, 1944.) Or, when students in calculus courses resist the notion of instantaneous velocity, they are confronting a contradiction between their commonsense definition of velocity, which involved a distance traveled over an interval of time, with the seemingly oxymoronic term instantaneous velocity. (Speiser and Walter, 1994, investigated this point creatively by having college calculus students analyze the photographer Muybridge's stroboscopic photographs of a cat walking.) As a result, many students resist the mathematical definition of this term.

Once educators have uncovered the bases for students' views, it becomes more difficult for them to label these views "misconceptions"; many misconceptions seem both defensible and sensible. As a result, within the psychology of mathematics education, the term *misconceptions* has come under attack and is being replaced by the term "alternative conceptions" (Hammer, 1996; Smith, diSessa, & Roschelle, 1993). This change in terms signals a lack of comfort with the notion that accepted mathematical ideas are necessarily "correct," while conflicting ideas of students are "incorrect."

CLASSROOM RAMIFICATIONS

As a mathematics teacher, I find that these critiques have a certain initial face validity. First, theoretical pronouncements about the certainty of mathematical knowledge are not concerned with the actual statements people speak. In mathematics classes, we often speak in shorthand; it is much harder than one might think to make statements in mathematics without implicitly making assumptions. Often statements that are taken as correct at one level of study, if not qualified, are seen as incorrect later. (The necessity of this dynamic is one aspect of the concept of "epistemological obstacles" as discussed in Brousseau, 1997.) As I indicated earlier, one cannot subtract the greater from the lesser *if one is working within the set of positive rational numbers*, and the sum of the interior angles of a triangle is 180 degrees *in Euclidean geometry*. Without the phrases in italics, the statements are neither simply right nor wrong. One must decide how they are to be qualified and interpreted.

Second, categorizing elementary mathematical statements in the classroom as simply and timelessly right and wrong often seems unproductive and sometimes misleading. Contrary to the presentation of mathematics as certain, as "cut-and-dried," there are places where ambiguity, rather than clarity, is important in mathematics.[26] Earlier, I presented the solution to a typical algebra word problem in which the role of x was ambiguous; x was at once variable and particular unknown. Paradoxically, much of the power of x is this very chameleon quality. This quality is what allows different branches of mathematics to make use of the very same symbolism. Similarly, mathematics is often mysterious. Mathematics often involves reasoning with the result of concluding an infinite process. Such reasoning challenges our imagination and often defies our expectations.

In addition, these philosophical, historical, and psychological critiques of commonplace views of mathematics are of value to me because they challenge the basis of many traditional educational practices and thus provide resources for changing instruction. While I recognize ways in which mathematical knowledge seems different from other kinds of knowledge, if mathematical knowledge is indeed more like scientific knowledge than previously thought, if mathematical knowledge is not necessarily infallible and timeless, then we might rethink the ways in which the categories of right and wrong are used in the mathematics classroom. Perhaps the traditional authority of teacher, text, and test could be asserted more modestly, and, as a result of this rethinking, perhaps mathematics classrooms could become more hospitable places for conversation. If students' wrong responses have important logic to them and if teachers can no longer claim to tell students what is right and wrong in the timeless and completely certain sense of traditional practice, there are opportunities to diminish the traditional disparity between the teacher's intellectual authority and that of students'. In this way, one might accomplish the NCTM's (1991) desired shift toward logic and mathematical evidence as verification and away from the teacher as sole authority.

Yet the desire to portray mathematics as more fluid (and not certain) and to avoid categorizing mathematical statements as right or wrong does *not* mean one need be a relativist; I do *not* want to suggest to my students that the views that have traditionally been labeled wrong are just as valid as those that have been labeled right. I feel a responsibility to teach my students the accepted mathematics of our day, as we explore why people believe it to be true.

With this in mind, based on these recent critiques, how might one actually reconceptualize right and wrong in the math classroom? Instead of right and wrong, one might suggest to students that there are the accepted views of the mathematical community (however we define this amorphous group[27]), traditionally labeled right, and other views.[28] If mathematical knowledge, like other knowledge, is socially constructed and is a product of culture, then it is not timelessly right or wrong, but may be contested or disputed. (To convey the notion that mathematics is a culturally situated practice, D'ambrosio, 1994, coined the term "ethnomathematics.") Rather than dissenting views' being dismissed as wrong or as the rantings and ravings of cranks, they may be seen as examples of disagreement; sometimes people do not agree with the accepted views of the mathematics community. However, this is a community that collectively has thought long and hard about mathematical issues. Its views are not to be dismissed lightly.

I find such a conceptualization of the teacher's role vis-a-vis right and wrong useful, particularly when one is attempting to help the sorts of students Sandy and I taught engage with mathematics; it opens up the possibility of labeling disagreements between the general public and the mathematics community about mathematical topics. As a result, mathematics becomes a contested field of knowledge.

That said, having taught and been taught in classrooms in which right and wrong were treated traditionally, enacting a different approach in the classroom can be challenging. To flesh out this reconceptualization of right and wrong, as well as difficulties enacting it, I will illustrate two dynamics: In a paradoxical order, they involve responding to students and listening to students. I will use zero as a thread to connect the different examples.

WHEN STUDENTS INSIST: RESPONDING TO, BUT NOT DISMISSING, "WRONG" IDEAS

Portraying mathematics as fluid and at the same time not retreating to complete relativism becomes a tricky task when students are strongly committed to notions that are traditionally labeled wrong.[29] If, following the epistemological critiques outlined above, I view mathematical proofs as social acts that do not necessarily guarantee the truth of a statement, how do I justify to students differentiating between statements (e.g., *pi* is irrational) that have been proven (perhaps by no one they know and in a form that they cannot follow) and those they believe strongly but are traditionally considered wrong (e.g., that zero is not a number)? Or, what do I do when students are not willing to take on the assumptions or definitions upon which accepted mathematics is based?

This last question periodically concerned me in my teaching at Holt. For example, as I mentioned before, many people have difficulty thinking of zero as a number. In October 1991, Sandy and I had just begun to teach together when we stumbled on an instance of this issue. After reviewing basic arithmetic skills and discussing negative numbers, we began to examine "number recipes" such as:

> Take the input, multiply it by −3, and then add 2.
> Take the input, multiply it by −2, and then add 3.
> Take the input, multiply it times itself. Take the opposite of the result and then add 4.
> Take the input times itself and then add 4.
> Take the input, find its distance, along the number line, from zero.
> Take the input and multiply it by −1.
> Start with the number 1 and divide it by the input.

We had students practice carrying out these sorts of recipes by hand and with a calculator. We taught students how to write such recipes with symbols. And, in order to explore the types of numbers students were using as inputs, we asked students to find the inputs that would generate an output of zero. We expected that for a recipe like the first one, many students would limit their inputs to whole numbers, or to truncated decimal representations of numbers on their calculators, and would argue that there is no number that can be used in this recipe to generate exactly zero.

Our discussion of this aspect of the problem created the need to talk about different systems for classifying numbers. We asked students to talk about the different ways they knew to describe numbers, and particularly to describe the kinds of numbers they were using as inputs. Many categories were raised: odd and even numbers, fractions and decimals,[30] whole numbers and fractions, positive and negative numbers. To investigate these categories, we gave students a list of numbers to categorize, and zero was one of them.

Two of the students, Scott and Jerry, were particularly intrigued by zero. While others argued about whether zero was a positive or a negative number, they broke in and explained that it could not be either because it was not a number, because it represents the absence of quantity. For them zero was a symbol that represented the phrase "no value." Rather than tell them that they were wrong, and that zero *is* a number, Sandy and I let Scott and Jerry be. At first jokingly (perhaps they were out to test us), but more seriously as the week progressed, since zero was, for them, a symbol but not a number, they began writing the words "no value" as its output in their tables of values (see Figure 4.5). If one tried to use it as an input to a function, since it was not a number, one could not generate a result (though their calculators were quite happy to do so!).

Recognizing that Scott and Jerry were pursuing a different mathematical tack, other students began to tease them about needing to write their own mathematics book, which would not have zero as a number.

Figure 4.5. Scott's tables of values for x^2 and $-x$.

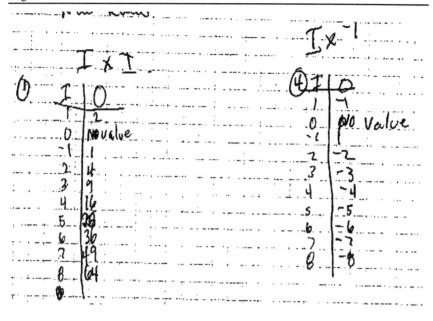

In making the decision to let Scott and Jerry be for the time being, Sandy and I sought to acknowledge their disagreement with the accepted mathematical view and not to dismiss it. At the same time, Scott and Jerry knew that we did not share their view; neither did their classmates, nor the people who had created their calculators. Over time, we returned to this issue when an opportunity arose. For example, we returned to it when discussing mathematicians' views of the result of using zero as an input to the rule "Start with the number 1 and divide it by the input."[31]

The decision not to dismiss their view—not to use our authority as teachers to force them to acquiesce publicly and say that zero is a number, but instead to keep their disagreement in our consciousness—was based in the conceptualization of mathematics teaching as a cultural transaction (Bishop, 1988) that can travel in both directions. In this conceptualization, students can learn about the views of the mathematical community, but teachers, if they desire, have an opportunity to learn about students' views as well.

So, with Scott and Jerry—though we had a responsibility to tell them that on standardized tests zero is a number—the question for us no longer was whether zero *is* or *is not* a number. Instead, we thought it was important for

Scott and Jerry to understand what people mean when they say that zero is or is not a number. We thought that it was important for our students to learn that within accepted mathematical discourse when people say that zero is a number, they mean that like other numbers it can be added, subtracted, multiplied, and divided. (Notice that this makes it quite complicated to decide what a number truly is. At what point do mathematical objects—e.g., matrices—that can be operated on with these operations cease to be numbers?) Indeed, the use of zero as a number allows mathematicians to define these operations in aesthetically pleasing ways (as long as one avoids dividing by 0). As teachers, we felt our role was to inform our students about accepted views and to try to help them appreciate the aesthetic that leads mathematicians to view zero as a number. At the same time, we wanted to acknowledge their insights—that zero has a different relationship to counting and to quantity than the numbers 1, 2, 3, 4, . . . and that it is impossible to divide an object into zero pieces. We did not want to get caught in the familiar trap of extolling the virtues of our way without appreciating alternative insights.

While such a stance builds on the critiques of mathematical certainty I just surveyed in this chapter, it adds another dimension. The historians and philosophers of mathematics I have surveyed all concentrate narrowly on disagreements and conflicts among mathematicians of repute; they simply ignore people whose views are traditionally labeled wrong. It is mathematicians whose disagreements count.[32] People who do not agree that zero is a number and still hold this position after years of schooling are simply wrong. Therefore, their disagreement is of no account, even when a large majority of the general populace are wrong, or disagree. (For example, mathematicians hold many beliefs that are incomprehensible to the general public, e.g., that infinite sets come in more than one "size.") As a result, in the disputes cited by historians, none of the positions can simply be dismissed as the opinions of the uninformed, but at the same time only small parts of mathematics seem to be contested. The majority of mathematics seems unquestioned, and, consequently, revisionists are vulnerable to the charge that serious disagreements are uncharacteristic of mathematics as a whole (Conway, 1995; Hanna, 1995).

But when one includes people who are outside the mathematical community, disagreements become more prevalent, and many such disagreements are not easily dismissed. They are not created solely by people's naive "mistakes" in logic or reasoning. Many people simply are not willing to countenance basic assumptions made in the mathematics community. For example, there are accepted mathematical definitions that make no sense to many—for example, instantaneous velocity. People sometimes work from definitions different from those implicit in basic mathematical "facts"—for example, when my students argue that zero is *not* a number. And some people simply do not believe proofs they cannot understand—for example, some 19-century Americans refused to believe European mathematical results, thought that the circle could be squared (that it was possible with compass and straight-edge to construct a square with the same area as a given circle), and tried to legislate particular rational values for *pi* (Fuller, 1893; Hallerberg, 1977).

While I am not advocating that such positions be taken as true, the teaching that I have done at Holt has challenged me to take a broad perspective that makes a place for the reasoning of the "uninformed," of those who—like my students and their parents—are not professional mathematicians and for whom mathematicians are *not* living and breathing human beings, or members of their extended social network.[33] My students, and their parents, often hold positions that are at odds with those of mathematicians. When viewing mathematics as a social product, rather than simply ignoring such disagreements by saying that my students and their parents are wrong and that therefore their views do not count, as a teacher I can instead at least acknowledge their views by indicating that they disagree with the views of the mathematics community, to which I, as a mathematics teacher, have an allegiance.[34]

How does this reconceptualization of right and wrong and the acknowledgment of disagreements between mathematicians and nonmathematicians affect the mathematics classroom? I see such acknowledgment providing another rationale for attention to students' ideas and supporting an emphasis on mathematical reasoning. According to this reconceptualization, in the mathematics classroom, rather than learning what is right and wrong in some timelessly true sense, students are being enculturated into the views and established practices of the mathematics community, a community that collectively has thought long and hard about mathematical issues but that may on occasion be at odds with students and their parents. Thus, as a teacher, when responding to views that are not accepted as correct, rather than simply telling students that they are wrong or that mathematicians think differently, whenever possible I must listen carefully and sympathetically to students' reasoning and help students appreciate *why* the mathematics community has come to a particular perspective even though it is one the students find unlikely or unconvincing. Besides presenting mathematical evidence and logical reasoning and encouraging students to do the same, I need to help students appreciate the rationales behind choices of definitions and axioms.

LISTENING PAST MY OWN ENCULTURATION

In the example of Scott and Jerry and zero, though Sandy and I had to figure out how to respect their disagreement, it was relatively easy for us to hear what they had to say. The definition of number has been contested historically; Frend and Maseres argued that there could be no quantities less than "nothing." Scott and Jerry's view of zero seems similar to that of 19-century English mathematicians Frend and Maseres. But at other times in our class, it was much more challenging to listen to statements that were wrong and to appreciate the logic behind such statements. (As suggested by Cobb and Steffe, 1983, this is also a difficulty for cognitive psychologists doing clinical interviews.)

Again, the notions of mathematics as a cultural product and teaching as a cultural transaction are helpful conceptually. As a teacher, I have become an enculturated member of the mathematical community; I am used to certain ways of thinking about mathematical tasks and topics. (Thomas Kuhn (1977) argues that the purpose of problem sets in science classes—e.g., physics—is to accomplish exactly this sort of enculturation. Pointing and naming, or ostention, thus play an important role in his theory of teaching and learning. See especially the chapter "Second Thoughts on Paradigms.") When students' statements conflict with conventional mathematical wisdom, it is very difficult for me not to dismiss these statements simply as wrong. Listening to such views required that I somehow overcome my own enculturation to accepted views and develop an understanding of the alternative conceptions on which the statements are based. Yet maybe that is precisely what some lower-track students have to offer: alternative conceptions and ways of seeing. Following up on the topic of zero, here are two short examples where I struggled to understand what my students had to say and came to appreciate ways in which they were being quite rigorous in their thinking, even when I, with my training in mathematics, did not agree.

A large part of the curriculum in our Algebra One class was devoted to learning to read standard mathematical representations of relationships between quantities: graphs, tables, and symbols. With respect to graphs, one area we worked on intensively was the role of the labels on the axes that indicate the quantities that are being discussed or represented. Traditionally, such labels are elliptical, one-word descriptors, like "time" or "distance," yet one-word descriptors are not sufficient. A more complete description would include the origin from which time or distance is being measured or counted. It is also important to know whether the values of the quantity are being accumulated.

These points about quantities were driven home to me in thinking about the following "silly" story that the class constructed collaboratively.

A Collaboratively Written "Silly" Story

Chris bungee jumped from 200 ft. He jumped and at 100 ft. above ground the cord snapped (after 4 seconds). He fell 15 more feet in 2 seconds and then grabbed a bird. The bird carried him 100 ft. up in 7 seconds.

Initially students made tables and graphs of distance and time. Focusing on distance, there were two interpretations: vector and scalar notions, which are not well distinguished in English. One view of distance was how far Chris was above the ground. According to this view, Chris starts out at 200 feet above ground, falls to 100 feet above ground, keeps falling to 85 feet above ground, and then is carried up to 185 feet above ground. Another view of distance was how far (total distance) he had fallen or traveled. According to this view, Chris was at a starting point, he then traveled 100 feet to the point that his cord broke, he fell 15 more feet before the bird picked him up, and then the bird carried him 100 more feet. These different views led to different values and different graphs. They are very different quantities hiding under the word *distance*.

As a result, I made it my practice to try to specify more carefully the quantities that appeared as labels on the axes of graphs. I hoped that by being more specific I would help my students. In the following example, I learned that more elaborate descriptions sometimes added their own complications.

A common practice in our class was to read through problems before students got to work singly, in pairs, or in small groups. One of the reasons we started this practice was to help students in the class who had great difficulty reading. It also helped us clarify misunderstandings before students got to work.

It was the day that we worked on the problem about the four pumps (see Figure 4.1). In retrospect, there are all sorts of assumptions being made if one answers that pump A had the most water to start with and pump D emptied its pool first. First, though there are no numerical scales on the graph, I am implicitly assuming that the intersection of the two axes, the origin, is at the point (0, 0) and that this point represents the starting time and an empty pool. Second, notice that I have a more elaborate phrase on the *y*-axis than on the *x*-axis; I still am using "time" as shorthand. In my shorthand, I assumed that along the *x*-axis time begins (at 0) when the pumps start (and that they start at the same time). However, in order to avoid asking my students to decipher my handwriting, I created this problem on the computer. I pasted the graph from a graphing program without taking care to erase the extensions of the lines beyond the first quadrant. While the extensions beyond the *y*-axis help me attach a letter unambiguously to each line graph, combined with my lack of specificity about the *x*-axis, they could be taken to indicate that we are entering the story in the middle, that at the time indicated by the intersection of the *y*-axis with the *x*-axis, the pumps had already been working. Finally, I am assuming that the zero on the *y*-axis represents the emptying of the pool. However, my students seemed to share my assumptions about the graph. They "saw" graphs in the first quadrant of the Cartesian plane only. Something else caused them trouble.

Calie, who I thought understood the material very well, immediately began raising questions:

> I'm confused about the graph. I don't understand the graph. . . . I don't understand where the part of the, where the most water to start with. . . . Where is the start of the water being emptied, or where. . . . Because it says the amount of water left in the pool.

I could not understand what the problem was. Couldn't Calie see that the place to look for the answer to the first question was along the *y*-axis, at the start, where time (along the *x*-axis) was zero? Perhaps I had overestimated my students' understandings of Cartesian graphs?

I fumbled around. I asked Calie if she understood what the *x*-axis represented. She understood quite well. I tried to get other students involved in understanding the question. They all seemed to share her question, but I could not understand what it was. Finally, she asked if A would be the correct answer. She explained why she thought it would be. Rather than evaluating her answer or sharing my own view, I emphasized that the graph is meant to show us how much water is left according to how much time has passed. The students began to work on the questions.

While they were working, Ginger, a student often given to testing the boundaries of school discipline, came up to me and said she could explain Calie's question. The difficulty she said was the word *left* on the vertical axis. If this axis represents "the amount of water *left* in the pool," how does one find out the amount of water in the pool just before the pump started working? When the pump has not started working, it does not make sense to talk about the amount of water *left* in the pool, but rather the amount of water in the pool. According to her view of the description on the *y*-axis, the amount of water in the pool when the pump started would not be displayed on this graph. She suggested simply dropping the word *left*.

For me, Ginger's comment illuminated the exchange with Calie. I realized that here was another example related to zero, to what Boyer (1944) calls the "concept" of zero—zero the number as a representation of absence of magnitude. Affected by my training in mathematics, I had set up a correspondence between the number line and "time"; zero appears on the number line and is associated with the start time. For me, zero is a number like any other number and absence of magnitude is itself a particular magnitude; therefore, the starting time was a time like any other time. Since, for other moments in time, the notion of how much water was left in the pool is a sensible one, for me, it was also a reasonable label for the starting time as well. But for many of my students, zero is qualitatively different from other numbers and requires special consideration. Thus, they were troubled by my reasoning across the difference between the start and subsequent times, across the difference between zero and other numbers.

For me, Ginger's comment also illustrates the benefit of opening up classroom conversations and not treating mathematics as the province of the timelessly right and wrong. If one believes that mathematical statements are easily characterized as right or wrong, in order to make sure that one is correct, one becomes quite focused on the wording of statements. From this sort of perspective, one might interpret Ginger's comment as an uncharacteristically gentle correction. She was showing me my error and how to fix it. Having learned from her, I should now fix the wording of this problem for future use. The belief underlying this sort of interpretation—that one can find a wording that is completely above reproach—is common in mathematics education. Because, in practice, it is so difficult to create such wordings, I believe this belief is responsible for the often convoluted ways in which mathematical ideas are presented in textbooks. Texts often try to guard against being incorrect by including details and qualifications that at first blush are mysterious to students. But there is an alternative. If mathematical statements often require clarification and qualification, perhaps Ginger was helping me understand Calie, rather than correcting me. And perhaps rather than providing students with complicated statements, intended to avert any potential misunderstanding, as a teacher, I can rely on interaction with my students and their interpretations of problem texts to make my meaning clear.

However, if I rely on such interaction, I have to be able to hear what students say. In this case, it took me a long time to be able to listen past my own enculturation and hear my students, though what they were saying was quite sensible. This dynamic, my difficulty listening past my own enculturation—in this case my own view of zero as a number like any other number—was not an isolated occurrence; it came up in other contexts as well. "Taking the average" (by that I mean the arithmetic mean, and not the median or mode) is a procedure with which our students were familiar when they came to our high school algebra classroom; they knew how to add up the numbers and divide by the number of numbers. When people take the average of a set of numbers—imagine that these numbers represent different bonuses given to employees in a company—they are deciding to reimagine the situation as one where the same amount of money was distributed, but where every person got the same bonus. When people take the average they are determining the amount of bonus that everyone would get in the "equal bonus" scenario. It is this reimagining, or hypothetical, or "abstract," quality of the arithmetic mean that, I believe, causes much difficulty for students. We are talking about a situation not as it really is, but as it might be reimagined. (For research on students' views of the arithmetic mean, see Mokros & Russell, 1995; Pollatsek, Lima, & Well, 1981; Strauss & Bichler, 1988.)

Like some of the students described in the educational research literature (especially Mokros & Russell, 1995), our students came into Algebra One knowing "the average" as a procedure for averaging a set of numbers (a data set). They could say little about what the final number, the arithmetic mean, said about the data set. Some also thought it was impossible to determine the average if all the "numbers" were not given. Yet people often do this. For example, if we know that a company distributed $5,000 in bonuses to 10 employees, we can still determine the average bonus by dividing 5,000 by 10.

To explore this issue, I have offered the following situation on a number of occasions.

A PROBLEM ABOUT AVERAGES

The owner of a small business has $5,000 to give out in bonuses to her 10 employees. One option is to give everyone an equal bonus. Alternatively, she could give some people higher bonuses and some people lower ones. In this case, we might ask what the average bonus would be.

With students, I explore what would happen if she gave everyone the same bonus, whether it is possible to decide what the average bonus is without having further information, as well as computing the average for a couple of different scenarios.

One year, Sandy and I gave the distribution of bonuses in Figure 4.6 to students to explore (see Chazan & Ball, 1999, for more detail). The discussion went back and forth. Some students, like Victoria, thought the 0 bonus did not add anything and should not be counted, resulting in an average of $555.56 when $5,000 is split among nine people. Some students, like Christin, wanted to count the 10th person (the one who got a bonus of zero dollars) and have the average bonus be $500.

If you're going to average this, wouldn't you have to average in the last person, because it's still a person? They're just not getting any money. See what I'm saying?

The disagreement, once again, centered on zero. Some, like Victoria, thought the zero should not be counted because it is not a number: "It's nothing"; others, like Lynn, because it cannot represent a bonus: "You can't really use the zero.

Figure 4.6. A distribution of 10 bonuses.

| 100 | 200 | 300 | 400 | 600 | 700 | 800 | 900 | 1000 | 0 |

It's not standing for anything." Jose thought that the zero can represent the "money they [the people] didn't get." Calie, Buzz, and Joe argued that the average bonus should be $500 no matter how the money is distributed.

As the discussion evolved, I had to listen hard to understand students' arguments. I understood why some students would argue that the average bonus would be $500 no matter how the money is distributed. Their reasoning accords with the mathematically accepted argument.

Why were students arguing that the average bonus should be $555.56? Why should you divide by 9 and not by 10? Only after considerable discussion did this become clearer. Students were saying it is silly to say that one person got a bonus of zero dollars, instead of saying that the person did *not* get a bonus and therefore should not be considered when computing the average bonus. They were insisting that our mathematical treatment of the situation be sensible. Again, some of my students wanted to treat zero as qualitatively different from other numbers and to distinguish between magnitude and absence of magnitude, reserving number for magnitude and not its absence. Before the discussion, I had not quite thought about it that way. I would never have thought about dividing by 9 instead of by 10. For me, once again, absence of magnitude was itself a particular magnitude.

REFLECTION AND LOOKING AHEAD

As these classroom episodes illustrate, there are important challenges for teachers as they try to exercise their mathematical authority in the classroom less often, to deemphasize the categories of right and wrong, to encourage students to express their ideas, and to ask the class to become a mathematical community that will exercise its own standards of logic and evidence. It can be hard to hear and understand what students are saying, and then one must figure out how to respond—in particular to students whose ideas are problematic or nonstandard without simply dismissing or disrespecting them. In our teaching, Sandy and I just began to develop practical responses to these issues. As these shifts in classroom interaction become more widespread in mathematics classrooms, perhaps a rich practitioner's lore and technical vocabulary will develop in which these challenges will be addressed (see Chazan & Ball, 1999, for one such attempt).

At the same time, these classroom episodes also illustrate the potential benefits released by changes in our view of mathematical knowledge. Changing to a less certain and more fluid view of mathematics played an important role in allowing for discussion; potentially, there was something to discuss. As the teacher, if all elementary mathematical statements cannot necessarily be labeled as timelessly right or wrong, perhaps during engagement with students and their mathematical ideas I might be stimulated to reexamine some of my own beliefs and perspectives. Such a possibility changes the nature of the interaction in the classroom and allows for the sorts of exchange of thoughts and ideas that Sandy and I wanted to have in our classroom.

In our class, the resulting discussions were different from usual student participation in a lower-track secondary school mathematics classroom. The discussion generated by the question about average bonuses, for example, was a particularly good one (for a more elaborate description of this discussion and of my role during the discussion, see Chazan & Ball, 1999): Many students participated; students listened to each other and responded to each other's comments. The students were deeply engaged in a discussion in which they attempted to make sense of an application of mathematics. Such discussions, while not of this caliber every day, were a regular occurrence in our class. While there is much room for improvement and development in my teaching practice, during these discussions I no longer was an unquestioned, and unquestionable, authority in the mathematics classroom and mathematics was not cut-and-dried; perhaps as a result, there was conversation.

Looking further back, this chapter and the two that preceded it have brought you into the class Sandy and I taught and have focused on a particular example of the interaction of teacher, students, and subject matter—of the interactions among Sandy and me, our high school students, and Algebra One. The first of these chapters began by focusing on the students we taught and our attempts to learn more about them. The student-researcher project helped make us aware of student peer groups and their relationship to engagement with school. Examination of student experience of the curriculum and of levels of students' classroom engagement led us to questions about the role of homework and the nature of real-world problems.

The next chapter described our evolving relationship to Algebra One as we carried out a curricular innovation. Interaction with our students around a functions-based approach to algebra led us to a yet deeper examination of our curricular understandings. The aim of this examination was to locate resources in our understandings that would help our students forge strong connections to algebra. While I was pleased with our capacity to help students see relationships between quantities—our choice for the central object of study in the course—in their own experiences, issues remained. In particular, I focused on students' appreciation of manipulation of symbols and of the nature of argumentation in mathematics. Finally, in this chapter, relationships among teacher, students, and subject matter all came together in an examination of the dynamics of classroom conversations.

Throughout these three chapters, I have taken a particular stance toward teaching. While I have described what I believe I have learned from teaching with Sandy, I have also tried to give pride of place to our uncertainties and questions, alongside our conclusions. For example, though we learned about the smokers, many questions remain. Perhaps if we had learned more about the preppies we might have yet different insights into Algebra One at Holt High School. Similarly, the functions-based approach to school algebra we took may have particular benefits, but in its current instantiation it also has important limitations. Perhaps most important, while we were able to engage students in classroom conversation on some days, there still are important questions concerning the many challenging days when students did not engage with the class. And, when students participated, we also wondered how to respond responsibly to some of their ideas and contributions.

To bring the book to a conclusion, the following chapter shifts the focus from the interaction of teacher, students, and subject matter in the classes that Sandy and I taught to an examination of the nature of discussions about teaching. Using our experience, as a high school teacher and a university researcher who took shared responsibility for teaching students, and the experiences of the Holt High School Mathematics Department more generally, it examines dynamics that lead to a vocabulary of certainty when discussing teaching, and others that might help sustain the portrayal of teaching as an uncertain craft.

Chapter 5

Portraying Teaching as
an Uncertain Craft

In discourse about educational issues, there are conflicts about the nature of educational research and its potential in establishing the relative strengths and weaknesses of educational practices. For people who have a profound respect for the benefits of basic scientific research, some discussions of research in education seem quite confusing. Why would an author in the premier U.S. mathematics education research journal argue that "What is 'best' cannot be proven by research" (Hiebert, 1999, p. 5)? Why aren't there cut-and-dried, once-and-forever answers to questions like "Is it better for students to use calculators or not to use calculators in elementary school?" (p. 5)?

In *Teaching: Making Sense of an Uncertain Craft*, educator and school reformer Joe McDonald (1992) provides one response. For him, there are basic truths about the nature of teaching that must be considered. He describes teaching as located inside an elastic triangle whose vertices are teacher, students, and subject matter—Hawkins's (1974) I, Thou, and It. Because relations in the triangle are always in interaction, in flux, McDonald's triangle does not have the structural integrity of a triangular steel truss. What is the nature of the relationship between teacher and students? What is the teacher's view of the subject matter? What subject matter should the teacher try to teach these students? How does the teacher use his or her own knowledge of the subject matter and of the students to bring these students into a relationship with this subject matter? For McDonald, none of the answers to these questions are bedrock on which one can build a solid structure. Instead, the answers to each of these questions shift, for example, as the teacher learns and changes. And, since answers to these questions are dependent on each other, changes in perspective reverberate through the triangle.

McDonald's (1992) description of teaching captures the complexity of my experience teaching Algebra One at Holt High School. As detailed earlier, *lower-track, suburban*, and *algebra* cannot be taken for granted as reliable descriptors in discussing teaching. My students at Holt treated me differently as a teacher than my students had previously; I was learning to conceptualize the subject matter differently; these differences led to other changes that in turn influenced my relationship with students and my understanding of the subject matter. In my telling of this experience, I have separated artificially what I learned about my students from what I learned about algebra from what I learned about orchestrating conversation in a mathematics class. But these separations are for the sake of the retelling; my experience was not divided in this way. I was learning on all of these fronts at all times; each lesson I learned echoed through the triangle and had an impact on my thinking in other areas. There was no simple order to this learning; I did not move through a progression of learning about students, about algebra, and then about classroom conversation.

And I do not expect that my experience generates a set of findings that can readily be applied by others. That said, this sort of stance toward teaching does not imply that one cannot draw conclusions from experience; insisting on the uncertainty of teaching does not consign discussion to the realm of mysticism. McDonald (1992), for example, argues forcefully that, as with other crafts, there can still be critical dialogue that does not treat teaching as technique.

For example, mind sets and stances can be critiqued for their impact on teachers' ability to reach professed goals. In the previous three chapters, I have found fault with commonplace views of mathematics for their chilling effect on discussion in the mathematics classroom; I have traced some of teachers' difficulties helping students appreciate algebra to philosophical positions that describe mathematics as a "meaningless" activity; and I have argued that teachers' own subject matter understandings are central in tackling issues of motivation and relevance. By doing so, I hope to have contributed to a growing literature in which problems of teaching practice are viewed from the perspective of the teacher and seen as intellectually challenging and important, without implying that such problems have "solutions." (In addition to the work of Ball, Duckworth, Lampert, and McDonald that I have mentioned earlier, others whose work might be viewed as part of this tradition include Gallas, 1994, 1995; Heaton, 1994; Lensmire, 1994; Paley, 1979; Schifter, 1996; Simon, 1995; Wilson, in press.)

Yet, though there are educators who take a stance like McDonald's (1992) or Hiebert's (1999), many discussions of education in the United States are quite different. Some, particularly those involving policymakers and often teachers, are characterized by a technical vocabulary about teaching. In such discussions, research results concerning student learning are taken to "prove" the effectiveness of a particular approach. In this chapter, I will explore some reasons for this phenomenon. This discussion will bring to the fore issues of school restructuring that I have left in the background until now. Based on my experience teaching with Sandy, and subsequent experience with other members of the Holt High School Mathematics Department, I will argue that current arrangements shield many educators from the uncertainty of teaching practice. I will argue for the importance of structural arrangements, like shared teaching assignments, that bring people face-to-face with both the necessity of action and the uncertainty of practice.

DYNAMICS THAT SUSTAIN A DISCOURSE OF CERTAINTY

In some educational research on teaching, there is a narrow focus on the student and the subject matter. The rest of the triangle can even slip from view; research has often focused on results (measured by scores on tests) and made recommendations for practice with only cursory examination of the interaction among students, teachers, and subject matter. Perhaps this happens because there are two conflicting, commonsense usages of the familiar verb *to teach*—for both the activity of interacting with students and the accomplishment of one goal of this activity, student learning (for an elaborate discussion of this distinction, see Scheffler, 1960).

Yet even when the process of interacting with students about subject matter remains in focus, uncertainty is not necessarily embraced. Often there is a technical vocabulary for talking about teaching that fixes the relationships in McDonald's (1992) elastic triangle. For example, via the constructs of "ability" and "motivation," students' achievement—which encompasses a variety of relations between student and subject matter, teacher and subject matter, and student and teacher—becomes solely a function of the student. Motivation and ability are "things" that students have, that can be assessed, and that explain their achievement. Together these sorts of words help create the familiar culture of school mathematics teaching in which the subject matter is the material that is in the book, answers can always be judged unproblematically right or wrong, and the curriculum is continually justified as preparation for future courses.

If one finds McDonald's (1992) portrayal of teaching compelling, one might wonder why such educational discourse portrays teaching as certain. Recognizing the uncertainty for which practice, as opposed to theory, has traditionally been denigrated, in "The Quest for Certainty: A Study of the Relation of Knowledge and Action," John Dewey (1929) places this educational tendency in a larger context. He argues that "insecurity generates the quest for certainty" (p. 254). As a confident American pragmatist, he advocates instead a "Copernican revolution which looks to security amid change instead of to certainty in attachment to the fixed" (p. 307). From Dewey's point of view, such a revolution would blur the boundaries between theory and practice, would articulate ways in which knowledge can be conceptualized as a species of action, and would lead to a greater appreciation of the uncertainty of all knowledge, as well as of opportunities for rational dialogue about problems of practice.

This blurring spurs Dewey (1929) to champion the application of something like the "scientific method"—a "disciplined mind," "being on the alert for problems," or a "scientific attitude"—to problems of everyday practice, to the wide field of human activity. Since Dewey's desire to dissolve differences between theory and practice has not carried the day, ironically, applications of scientific method to problems of educational practice have had the reverse effect. Method, and the power it conveys to the results of researchers, as opposed to the anecdotes of teachers, contributes to complaints about the lack of connections between theory and practice and to institutional insulation of many educational actors—like curriculum developers, assessment professionals, teacher educators, educational researchers, and policymakers—from the everyday messiness of teaching practice.

But why do teachers themselves develop a vocabulary of certainty to describe their own work? McDonald (1992) suggests that this is not so surprising. As a teacher, one must act; one is forced to "temporarily repress uncertainty in a believing persona" (p. 2). Thus,

> whenever they teach, teachers must to some extent swallow the uncertainty they feel, believe wholeheartedly in their goals and efforts, even though riddled by doubt. Otherwise, the class fails to move and may fall apart for lack of trust in the leader: Who is he to tell me what to do, when he doesn't even believe in himself? (p. 6)

Beyond the particular class session, there is continuing pressure to maintain this persona, to turn craft into technique, to ignore complexity, and to assume that one can meet all of one's commitments without having them conflict (Lampert, 1985, argues that such conflictless teaching is not possible). Though some teachers resist this pressure, teachers who acknowledge frustrations with the utility of their own subject matter knowledge for teaching provide fodder for a critic's charge of "poor subject matter preparation," rather than produce grist for an illuminating examination of the nature of the subject matter knowledge useful in teaching (Gormas, 1998). Teachers who acknowledge the pervasive struggles of lower-track classes open themselves to charges of "lack of control," rather than set the stage for an examination of the nature of schooling for students who are skeptical of school knowledge. Teachers who open up problems of practice to an audience of educators are liable to be told how to "solve" the problem, rather than to be engaged in dialogue about the complexity of managing it.[1]

There is an analogy here to the mathematics classroom. Just as an overreliance on the categories of "right" and "wrong" inhibits discussion in mathematics classrooms, a technical vocabulary of teaching with its certainty inhibits discussion of teaching practice. It provides no rationale, even among teachers, for discussion of problems of practice in all of their particularity and complexity. Why should we discuss a particular case in detail if "research shows" what should be done in such cases?

SUPPORTING ACKNOWLEDGMENT OF
THE UNCERTAINTY OF TEACHING

How might a discussion of teaching that respects uncertainty in teaching be sustained? Reflecting on my experiences sharing a teaching assignment and the experience of the Holt High School Mathematics Department, I will argue that one crucial dynamic is providing opportunities that bring people face-to-face with teaching situations that require both action and collegial scrutiny of those actions. But such opportunities can also raise tensions inside a group, like a department, that must come to joint decisions.

Reflection on Sharing a Teaching Assignment

For me, remaining close to the messiness of practice and having my work open to the scrutiny of colleagues has made it difficult to adopt a language of certainty. As a university researcher and teacher educator, sharing a yearlong, difficult teaching assignment—a pressing issue of practice—with a teacher in a relatively ordinary public school[2] grounded me in the uncertainty of teaching. Paradoxically, it did this by forcing me to make commitments and choices about how to act. In addition, when Sandy and I agreed to share a teaching assignment, two sorts of isolation were breached: the isolation of the teacher working alone in a classroom and the isolation of the university professor from day-to-day work in schools.

As Sandy and I explored the issues examined in the last three chapters, we were teachers; we had responsibilities to and for our students; we had to act. We could not think and think and think about what school algebra should be. We had to make bets, both big and small, in our planning and on the fly, and then act on them. Having ultimately to follow a particular course of action meant that we could not go our own separate ways. Thus, when we disagreed, we ended up having to follow a particular course. Someone (or both of us) would get to see the ramifications of something he or she would not otherwise have done.

Because we shared the teaching assignment, our actions were viewed not just by our students, but by another teacher as well; Sandy could view the ramfications of my actions, and vice versa. By its very nature practice is humbling. Sometimes we were pleased with our choices; however, since we had taken on a difficult assignment, many times we were not (though we were not always sure what would have been a better choice). If either one of us had pretended to be certain about our actions, the complexity of our day-to-day practice would have quickly pointed out the fraud. We could not pretend to be certain that we had done the "right" thing.

Finally, it seems important that we worked together for two full years. We had time to get to know each other well and to develop trust in each other as we struggled with this difficult assignment. Sometimes, simply having someone to work with gave us the confidence to try something that we otherwise might not have attempted. And, while each day was a new day and presented new opportunities, we also had the opportunity to repeat a year-long curriculum, while making different choices.

For me, there was another way in which the press of practice drove home the uncertainty of teaching. Being back in the classroom forced me to integrate strands of educational research and thought that tend to remain separate in academe. At one and the same time, as a result of teaching, I was interested in students' experience of learning and student peer groups—issues commonly studied without a subject matter focus by researchers in educational psychology; algebra curriculum—the turf of curriculum developers, mathematics educators, and mathematicians; history and philosophy of mathematics—fields that often are not seen as directly relevant to issues of schooling; and discussion in the classroom—a burgeoning field both inside and outside mathematics education. The work of teaching challenged me to become broadly conversant with research in these fields, though I knew I could not possibly become an expert in all of them (for a similar sentiment, see Lampert, 1991c).

Reflecting on the Experience of the
Holt High School Mathematics Department

In retrospect, Sandy and I had a unique opportunity. Not only did we share a teaching assignment (across what normally are insurmountable institutional boundaries), but we were also both members of a high school and a university with a long-term agreement to have a Professional Development School (PDS) relationship. The Holmes Group, a consortium of leading U.S. schools of education, originally proposed such relationships. According to the rhetoric of that group, the Professional Development School is a new institution designed in part to breach the boundaries of theory and practice that separate universities from schools. The PDS is "for the development of novice professionals, for continuing development of experienced professionals and *for the research and development of the teaching profession*" (Holmes Group, 1990, p. 1; emphasis in original). We shared our teaching assignment in the context of such an institution, dedicated to "thoughtful long-term inquiry into teaching and learning" (p. 2). In the next sections, I reflect on my experiences with the continuing efforts of the Holt High School Mathematics Department to engage in the sorts of inquiry outlined by the Holmes Group. Analyzing these experiences suggests that while shared teaching assignments, like the one that Sandy and I had, are potentially of tremendous value, at the level of a department there are other dynamics to be overcome, pressures that can inhibit acknowledgment of the uncertainty of teaching.

Shared Teaching Assignments Focused on an Approach to a Problem of Practice. The PDS initiative at Holt High School predated my work with Sandy. Since I know it best, I will focus on the mathematics department's work. The Michigan State University PDS effort at Holt High School, and even within the mathematics department, is extremely complex; there are many important initiatives that have supported each other over time. For example, while Sandy and I were working together, there were other PDS projects within the mathematics department on alternative assessment and on issues of students' self-esteem.

At times, there have been tensions among the projects; some of the projects have different orientations toward teaching, which reflect differences inside the department. For example, though a functions-based approach to Algebra One seems to have gained wide acceptance in the department, the degree to which a functions-based approach to algebraic thinking is a useful approach more broadly has been controversial. In the years since I taught, debate has centered on whether a functions-based approach should be extended to Algebra Two and Precalculus. However, there is widespread agreement on some matters. According-ing to the teachers in the department, the opportunity for shared teaching assign-ments stands out as a unique and highly valued aspect of the PDS initative. Here, for example, is one teacher's comment:

> Team Teaching has provided for me opportunities that have alleviated much of my frustration as a teacher. Traditional methods of professional development—one day workshops, research articles, etc.—were a large part of the frustrations I had felt as a teacher trying to improve my practice. For me, they helped foster a notion that to become an excellent teacher, I needed only see someone do it right and then copy their technique. . . . I know that for me and my colleagues at Holt High School teaching together on a daily basis (with the same courses and students) has helped us grow as professionals in the field of mathematics and teaching in innumerable ways. I now see good teachers as people who constantly reevaluate their under-standing of the subject, constantly struggle with activities and lessons, and who seek their colleagues as resources. (quoted in Chazan, Ben-haim, & Gormas, 1998, p. 694)

Thus, I will focus my attention on this particular initiative.

Having watched Sandy and me work together, other teachers in the Holt math department found the model of sharing a teaching assignment worth imitating; this arrangement would provide members of the department with opportunities to observe each other's practice firsthand, rather than simply to discuss the happenings of their separate classrooms. As a result, during the second year that Sandy and I shared a teaching assignment, two small Algebra One classes were consolidated during second semester to allow two teachers to work together. Over the next four years, Professional Development School funds and other funds supported six shared teaching assignments focused on the exploration of a functions-based revision of the algebra curriculum. Two other shared teaching assignments were created around the teaching of high school geometry: one to explore computer-aided design and the other to explore computer-aided student conjecturing. Finally, these shared assignments were augmented by the hiring of two recent MSU graduates who had done their internships at the high school and had thus shared yearlong teaching assignments with at least one teacher. Over a six-year period, every teacher shared at least one teaching assignment with another teacher (see Figure 5.1 for a schematic representation of the shared assignments, including internships).

While there are many factors that had an impact on these shared assignments (beliefs and personalities of individuals, administrative support rather than compulsion of teachers, the role of the department chair, general school resources, and more), in my view, there are four characteristics of these assignments that made them valuable to the teachers: identified problems of practice, something to try, shared attempts at practice, and time for development of trust and reflection.

When I came to teach at Holt, there was an identified problem of practice: Algebra One in all of its complexity was an issue. Frustration and desire for change were already present—indeed, this desire to change was part of what brought me to Holt. Much of the impetus came from people's personal experiences with the teaching of lower-track algebra classes. I continually hold in mind a vivid description of Algebra One teaching given by one colleague. He described it as akin to being charged with the responsibility for "pulling students' teeth out, through the backs of their heads." In addition to the teachers' frustrations, initial PDS activities focused on developing teachers' awareness of issues of student learning. For example, in one PDS project, some members of the department interviewed each other's students. These interviews indicated both students' power of thought and their lack of conventional mathematical understandings. Of course, there were also communal and administrative pressures to increase the scores of all students and to increase the numbers of students receiving state-certified diplomas. There also was a general sense of a need for mathematics education reform in the air. For all of these reasons, when shared teaching assignments were possible, the members of the department were eager to participate. The problem always has been not having enough

Figure 5.1. Shared assignments among teachers in the mathematics department.

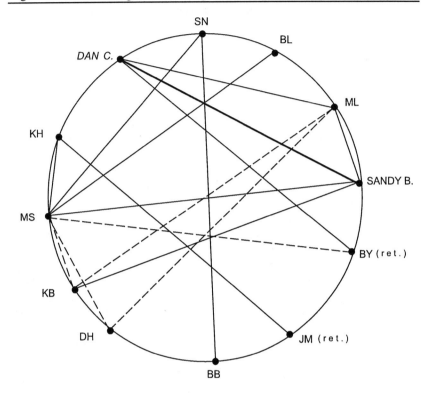

resources to support all of the shared assignments that people thought would be valuable.

But awareness of limitations of a school's program or frustration with one's own teaching may not necessarily provide an impetus for change; one can feel powerless and blame others. Even if there is an impetus for change, there may not be resources to support tackling serious teaching issues.

At Holt, I brought something to try—not a solution, but a set of mathematical and pedagogical ideas that might present a resource in tackling the problem. In order to try out these ideas, Sandy and I had to make a commitment to attempt a functions-based approach. These ideas were initially quite controversial inside the department, but, over time, about half of the department has found them useful and has moved to a functions-based approach to algebraic symbols in Algebra One, Algebra Two, Precalculus, or Calculus.

Focusing teachers' attention on a set of mathematical ideas seems well suited to a high school mathematics department. High school mathematics teachers pride themselves on being subject matter specialists. Separate from the particular merits and drawbacks of a relationship-between-quantities approach to algebra, for those who examined it carefully, myself included, the presence of an alternative view of the familiar subject matter had many beneficial effects. By its very presence, this view focused attention on one's own mathematical understanding. Even though we were subject matter specialists, the presence of this view made us learners and explorers of familiar content (Chazan, 1999). We were relearning school algebra. Unlike standard reports from pre-service teachers who find it difficult to connect advanced study of mathematics in the university with their future teaching, as a result of examining this approach, we were able to see connections between what we learned and the mathematics we were teaching. Seeing ourselves as learners of this content changed our stance toward the content and worked to undermine the typical ways in which high school mathematics is seen as cut-and-dried, completely understood.

But, even taken together, a desire for change, a commitment to some course of action, and mathematical ideas as resources for change are not necessarily sufficient to support teachers' change. The opportunity to share an instructional assignment, to practice together, was pivotal. Reflecting on the two shared assignments during the 1994–1995 school year, the four participating teachers suggested three dynamics that explain how the shared responsibilities in the same classroom created opportunities for substantial professional growth (Chazan et al., 1998). First, they focused on the opportunity to become an observer of students one is teaching. Rather than having to always act, they could rely on each other and take turns sitting back, watching students, and reflecting on the nature of their own students' learning. Second, the shared experience was complex, much more complex than the vocabulary one has for talking about teaching. Sharing an experience, being able to point, rather than to describe, allowed teachers to learn from each other in ways that were simply not possible when relying on words to share classroom experience. Third, since the responsibilities were held jointly, there was a need to come to decisions and to act. Thus, teachers were forced to work together in ways that are not necessary, even when teaching parallel sections of the same course.

Finally, while sometimes there was not enough time during the day for reflection on the shared teaching and planning (one reason such work can be stressful), the shared teaching assignment was a yearlong affair. While the joint responsibility led to some friction, the friction had to be worked through, in order to continue working together. The length of the commitment also played a role in helping people develop trust in each other and having opportunities to appreciate the results of actions they might not have taken on their own.

The Holt High School Mathematics Department and McDonald's Triangle. The Holt High School Mathematics Department has struggled continually to create, recreate, and sustain an environment of thoughtful inquiry into teaching and learning. The department has worked hard to become a place where the uncertainty of teaching is acknowledged, not repressed; where teachers can raise important issues of practice and can work together on these issues. While there have always been tensions and conflicts inside the department, the degree to which there has been success in creating such an environment is, in my view, due in large measure to the opportunity for shared teaching assignments and the mutual respect and understanding such assignments fostered. To illustrate the type of environment that has been created in this department, I'll use the three sides of McDonald's (1992) triangle (teacher and subject matter; student and subject matter; teacher and student) to describe a range of issues that have become focal in the work of the department.

First, members of the department have been deepening their own relationship to the subject matter they teach. As some members of the department have explored a functions-based approach to algebra, curricular exploration has helped make the familiar content strange. As it did for Sandy and me, this effort has stimulated members of the department to reexamine their own mathematical understandings. For example, here is a comment from one teacher:

> I think that's one of the best things about team teaching, you're getting together with other math teachers and just being able to talk about math and talk about new ideas. (Chazan et al., 1998, p. 695)

As a result, members of the department are more explicitly and less bashfully learners of mathematics.

One indication of this ongoing mathematical exploration by teachers is that the department is now taking greater responsibility for the mathematics curriculum. For example, the department has become more and more active in attempts to align the curriculum throughout the district. For another example, in Algebra One classes, teachers in the department have taken on a greater responsibility for the curriculum than simply choosing a textbook, supplementing a textbook with favorite activities, or changing the order in which textbook chapters are covered. Classes are structured by teachers around discussion problems that they have developed or that were developed by other members of the department. Rather than following a textbook and leaving that level of curricular decision making to a remote author, the teachers use their collection of activities to construct a text with their classes, partially in response to the ideas and questions of their students. Units begin with the introduction of a dynamic table of contents that students fill out as activities are done in class. The resulting text is the record of class activity. Rather than supplementing a textbook, teacher-developed materials are now supplemented by a range of prepared materials. Some teachers have done similar things in Geometry, Algebra Two, and Precalculus, but in these courses there is less departmental consensus. To support this process and share material, for the last few years, the department has been experimenting with an internal computer network to share problems written to stimulate classroom discussions. In order for teachers to search for problems relevant to their teaching, over time, this repository has developed a course and unit structure that supports the sharing of materials.

It is not that members of the department agree on everything. The focus on curriculum has led to much debate and many initiatives: What aspects of algebra might be left unaddressed by a functions-based approach? What is the relationship between geometry in the high school mathematics curriculum and the algebraic work that dominates the rest of the curriculum? In what ways can (sometimes artificial) disciplinary boundaries be blurred to allow mathematics to be integrated with the teaching of other subject matters? Is this a desirable goal? To what extent and in what ways might technology be used to support student activity toward curricular goals? How does a department share its evolving understandings of the mathematical content of the high school curriculum with new colleagues? In what ways might technology support teachers' own curricular understanding? What sort of teaching at the elementary, middle, and junior high school levels would prepare students for the sort of work now expected at the high school? How does a high school mathematics department create a vital and ongoing connection with teachers throughout a district? How does one engage a district and its community in discussion of issues central to the mathematics curriculum? Can issues of individual student assessment and larger program evaluation (including the state's proficiency test) be used as forums to involve the community in the work of the school?

Second, in terms of students and subject matter, the department has gradually worked toward a situation in which all students are involved in courses that the department considers academically sound, but that seek to connect academic content to students' experience. At the high school, in a break with past practice, students do not continue to study arithmetic, but instead begin with Algebra One. There have also been substantial efforts to increase the numbers of students studying mathematics and the number of courses that individual students take.

Sensitivity to the diversity of student aspirations in the high school population has also led to a series of debates: How do teachers learn about students' social groups and their aspirations? What is the role of homework in mathematics teaching as one seeks to have high standards for all students? What is the role of tracking? For example, should honors be a grading option rather than a separate class? How might the high school mathematics department create connections with the local area vocational education center and the curriculum it teaches to many students? How might the high school respond to the perceived needs of local businesses? What is the relationship between collegiate mathematics reform efforts and the high school's efforts? Should there be alternatives to calculus for college-intending students? For students who come to the high school with little chance of attending college, how does one help create opportunities for those who wish to learn enough mathematics to make college possible?

Finally, in terms of interaction between teachers and students around subject matter, there has been an increasing desire to build coursework around discussion of students' ideas. I have mentioned the internal network and the sharing of problems intended to provoke classroom discussion. This has led to a shift in teaching practice that students have begun to notice. For example, when interviewed about a team-taught class, one student said:

> You know, old math class you sit down, they give you the book, there's usually one teacher in the room and all you do is just write out problems all day long. This one, you do a little bit of explaining and thinking. It gets your head moving, your brain working. (quoted in Chazan et al., 1998, p. 692)

This focus on discussion of students' ideas has also raised a series of questions for the department: What are teachers' responsibilities in terms of helping students learn others' ideas—for example, to learn to read textbook materials—and how might such responsibilities be met? Is there a conflict between having students explore and come to understand their own reasoning and having them have access to the ideas of others? For example, can a Calculus class emphasize success on the College Board's Advanced Placement exam by mastering material in the textbook *and* focus on having students' develop their own understandings of the ideas central to the calculus? Or do these two goals conflict? If they do conflict, how does one choose? Just how does one orchestrate a discussion?

Complexities of Departmental Discourse About Teaching. This quick summary of some of the issues of teaching being examined and debated at the high school does not do justice to the work of the department, but I hope that I have illustrated that the department has taken on issues central to mathematics teaching.

Nonetheless, for teachers in the department, this work has not been easy. While shared teaching assignments may sustain a recognition of the uncertainty of teaching, there are pressures on a department to repress uncertainty and act in unison. Just as teachers in their own classrooms must adopt a believing persona, so must departments—though perhaps in the context of curricular decision making a discourse of uncertainty seems even less tenable. On the one hand, departmental commitments may represent common understandings of what can and should be done for students, and can create contexts for collaboration. But such departmental commitments can also become the focus of tensions as choices are made and some paths not taken, when departmental commitments conflict with personal commitments.

With a state proficiency exam and college entrance exams looming, and with notions of mathematics as a hierarchical subject, curricular decisions in mathematics, as opposed to subjects commonly viewed as optional or subjective, can become the locus for fierce battles. Departments are often torn into camps by decisions about implementing new curricula, and coordination across schools inside a district can become hazardous when schools make different commitments. At times, such issues have surfaced at Holt. In order to understand the way in which departmental organization can add to the predicaments of a high school teacher, I'll analyze some of the dynamics that have led to this sort of tension at Holt.

For the teachers who have been exploring a functions-based approach to Algebra One, Algebra Two, and Precalculus, curricular work no longer consists of deciding which textbook series to adopt and follow. Instead, there is a commitment to developing personal understandings of the mathematical ideas at the core of the curriculum and using these understandings to build curriculum that is responsive to students' ideas. In their interpretation, this commitment entails a curriculum that changes yearly, and differs from third hour to fourth hour, in recognition of the different students in each section. It also evolves as the mathematical understandings of the departmental faculty evolve.[3]

Among some members of the department such descriptions of teaching send off alarm bells. How does one teach Precalculus when you do not know what exactly was "covered" in Algebra Two? What does a teacher do if students come into Algebra Two with quite different approaches to, and understandings of, solving equations? How does a department make sure that it is indeed doing well by its students if different teachers take different approaches to courses based on their own understandings?

But for other members of the department, recognition of this complexity and uncertainty has been celebrated. Discussions of the materials stored on the school's internal network have included concerns not to reify particular orders of the units or of the problems, lest such reification evolve into a curriculum no longer constructed in response to the students in a particular class (Gormas, 1998).

Paradoxically, the notion that teachers should be constantly reevaluating their subject matter understanding is championed by those teachers who have committed to a functions-based perspective on school algebra. While this commitment closes off discussion of some issues, it seems to open up discussion of others. It has been the shared commitment to this perspective that has allowed some members of the department to be open to different orderings of topics and tasks inside a given course.

On the other hand, the commitment to this view of school algebra has been one of the key factors generating tension inside the department. It is hard to accommodate difference inside a department. Most school systems do not tolerate publicly the notion of differences between different sections of a course. It is hard to imagine, in the face of scheduling constraints, administrative support for courses in which sections took radically different approaches. Indeed, for this reason, at Holt, the Algebra One that Sandy and I taught had to be presented as the "same" Algebra One as everyone else's. Thus, though there is no desire inside the Holt Mathematics Department to force individual teachers to teach algebra in particular ways, there are structural dynamics inside a high school department that make any innovation scary; for individual teachers, an innovation inside the department may mean coming under pressure to change the way they teach.[4]

LOOKING BACK

Stepping back from what for me has been a vital and engaging experience, I now recognize that the clinical faculty position that I came to MSU to fill was special in more ways than I recognized at the time. The position provided me with support to do research on teaching by teaching mathematics in a K–12 setting. It allowed me to be a professor, devoted to inquiry into teaching, and at the same time to also be a teacher, someone responsible for teaching particular children. As a result, I learned more about teaching and algebra than I think I could have in many other ways.

The position did all this, but it also provided opportunities for exploring the potential of such inquiry for promoting conversations about some of the difficult challenges of teaching. There were opportunities both to reflect on practice and to act together with colleagues in a high school department. Finally, though I have not discussed this aspect of the arrangement, pre-service teacher education candidates could be folded into the conversation as well. They could learn to teach in settings where practicing teachers were involved in serious, sustained, and collegial attempts to make progress on central challenges of secondary mathematics teaching.

The setting is clearly special. It represents a series of long-term commitments and investments on the part of both the high school and the university.[5] With the limited resources of many public schools in mind, an initial reaction might be to ask how lessons learned in such a setting are related to larger-scale possibilities. However, my own bent is different. Instead, perhaps this is where our classroom work links to—indeed is dependent on—school restructuring. Perhaps insights from our work might even have implications for the design of such restructuring.

The longer I have been involved deeply in the life of one school's mathematics department, the more I have come to respect the scope and complexity of the problems of mathematics education today. For example: How do we create a system where substantially more students are doing acceptable work and are not failing, while being held to rigorous standards? How can we create assessments of student learning that will help us specify our standards, that will specify what is meant by the sometimes vague desire of employers for high school graduates with "mathematical common sense," and reveal when we are or are not achieving this goal? How do we create a conversation about mathematics teaching and learning, involving a wide range of community members, that maintains a focus on the serious and particular challenges of teaching, without degenerating into an impassioned but ultimately unproductive rhetoric of "reform" or "back to the basics"? How does one create realistic structures for parents and educators to discuss future plans with individual students and ensure that students have access to needed coursework and the resources to be successful? How does one create circumstances that would make possible all the conversations necessary to align curriculum, assessment, and teaching across a district? How do teachers attempt to tackle such challenges in two or three preparations with approximately 150 students?

For me these sorts of questions suggest that, in order to tackle the difficult challenges of teaching, the individual resources of a teacher isolated in a room of a school are simply not sufficient. There needs to be an accessible conversation about the challenges of teaching, which will provide teachers with the resources and support that other teachers can provide. But I believe the experience at Holt suggests that such conversations should not be limited to teachers. Such conversations can benefit from the involvement and expertise of other educational actors: parents, community leaders, curriculum developers, mathematicians, assessment professionals, researchers into student learning, students of adolescence in our society, and those devoted to inquiry into teaching. Opportunities to interact with others outside the school community who are also passionately engaged with issues of teaching and curriculum can be a helpful antidote to the isolation experienced by many teachers.

Thus, rather than asking how conversations about important challenges of teaching might be supported in contexts in which teachers are isolated from each other and from other educational actors, I think it is more important to ask how to break down this sort of isolation.[6] The Holmes Group (1990) vision, which guided the establishment of the PDSs, forms an interesting model. In this model, the school and the university both identify pressing problems of their own practice and realize how collaborative activity can strengthen each institution in its mission. The school provides university faculty with grounding in the realities of practice, which serve to enhance teacher education and research. The university offers a long-term commitment to aiding schools with the professional development of teachers and resources for the improvement of K–12 teaching. Thus, rather than dismissing the work at Holt as a too-special case, I hope that is a harbinger of future institutional affiliations. Perhaps other educational institutions in the future will do a similar calculation and decide that there are important benefits for sustaining long-term collaborations with schools. And perhaps schools will invent methods for allocating resources, methods that allow teachers time to share assignments in which they tackle important problems of practice and reflect on their attempts to do so.

Coda

Predicaments of High School Mathematics Teaching

The introduction to this book began with an invitation, an invitation to return to the Algebra One classroom and to come to understand the predicaments of its teachers. I hope that I have accomplished this task and that you have a greater appreciation for the task of the high school mathematics teacher.

This task has many dimensions shared with other sorts of teaching. High school mathematics teachers have few opportunities to come to know their students well. They teach subject matter in a compulsory setting. Most often, they teach alone with little time for interaction with colleagues. In many situations, they teach students who are disengaged from schooling.

The teaching of mathematics also has its own peculiarities. Mathematical knowledge is high-status knowledge in our society. But there are some negative ramifications of this status. Our cultural notions of ability together with our views of the status of mathematics outfit many students with reasons to feel that the subject matter is alien to them. Furthermore, this set of cultural views also puts distance between mathematics teachers (who presumably value mathematics highly) and some of their students. In addition, high school mathematics teachers must come to grips with the discipline's ambivalence toward meaning, as well as commonplace views of mathematical knowledge as "cut-and-dried." These views do not provide teachers with resources to tackle difficult issues of student engagement.

Finally, high school mathematics teachers struggle with all of this in a politically charged cultural environment where there are conflicts over how mathematics should be taught. These debates often ignore the complexities of teaching, while sometimes putting a premium on reform of teaching and improved achievement for all students. The task is truly daunting!

In this book, I have argued that dealing with these predicaments of high school mathematics teaching involves challenging ways in which we commonly speak. The challenges that I have proposed include objection to "ability" and "motivation" as fixed characteristics of individuals, mathematics as a "meaningless" game played with symbols, school mathematics as consisting of statements that can be judged unequivocally "right" or "wrong," and teaching as a craft in which actions can be judged unambiguously "good" or "bad." If we can develop other ways of speaking about mathematics teaching, we may create an environment more conducive to mathematics classrooms in which students are engaged in serious examination of their own mathematical ideas and the fit of their ideas with the ideas of other members of our culture. For teachers, learning to create such classrooms and to teach in them will present a host of new challenges, energizing ones, perhaps.

Notes

Introduction

1. These ideas are so counterintuitive to students that Ephraim Fischbein (1982), a founder of the International Group for the Psychology of Mathematics Education, argues that "the concept of formal proof is completely outside the main stream of behavior" (p. 17) and that it requires a complete reorganization of one's intuitions.

2. The phrase in quotation marks is due to Thomas Henry Huxley and was not meant as a compliment. For J. J. Sylvester's response, see Newman (1956/1988, vol. 3, pp. 1727–1737). For a seminal essay on the unreasonable effectiveness of mathematics, see Wigner (1984).

Chapter 1

1. In this vein, Jack Smith (1996) argues that teachers implementing reform-based visions of mathematics teaching may feel a reduced sense of efficacy and that it is imperative to create new "moorings" for teachers' sense of efficacy.

2. This text bears interesting marks of the influence of the mathematics education reforms of the 1960s, as it also tries to address concerns about students' "basic" skills. For a more focused comparison of my teaching with this text with my teaching of a functions-based approach, see Chazan (1999).

3. Many of my Holt students find this terminology terribly confusing. They wish it were "y-intersect" or "y-intersection" instead.

4. An alternative explanation is to say that determining the y-intercept is finding the y-coordinate of the point on the y-axis that together with the point $(5, 2)$ creates a slope of 1. Since the x-coordinate of the y-intercept is known to be 0, there is only one missing number that students can then compute $(2 - b)/(5 - 0) = 1$.

5. For those who might want to go farther afield, I also did not engage students in critiquing the implicit notion that there is only one line connecting the two given points. In applying this procedure for finding an equation to a nonplanar context, like that of latitude and longitude, it is important to recognize that there are many "straight" paths between two points on a globe. I did not address such issues at all.

6. The small number of diagrams in textbooks may also be the result of 19th-century developments in geometry. As non-Euclidean geometries were developed, diagrams became suspect. See the discussion in Greenberg (1980).

7. According to mathematicians, the "slope" of x^2 at a particular point is $2x$ not x. I wondered if there was any way to explain this calculus result to a class of Algebra

Two students. I have been playing on and off with this question since and have explored a series of avenues for explaining the "2" in $2x$. See Chazan (1990b).

8. Perry Lanier, a Michigan State colleague, first introduced me to the mathematics department at Holt High School. Perry had been working on teacher education and research projects with members of the department since the mid-1980s. I was initially attracted to the school because members of the mathematics department expressed a strong commitment to revamping the algebra curriculum.

9. This is a quote from my teaching journal of Sept. 4, 1990.

10. Zalman Usiskin (1995), one of the codirectors of the University of Chicago School Mathematics Project, has attempted to address these issues in a way that practitioners find recognizable (see also Davis, 1995).

Chapter 2

1. Descriptions of this sort of design for instruction are found in many places in the literature, but these two articles were particularly influential for me and for Sandy.

2. Sometimes, these sorts of problems are called "applications" (for example, see Sharron [1979]). Here the dichotomy is between abstract and applied. The terminology also suggests a pedagogical order; first one teaches the abstractions, the mathematics, and then, for motivational reasons and to practice correct application, one assigns problems in which the mathematics is applied. These problems tacitly suggest that the mathematics is useful since it can be applied. Another version of this distinction, one that does not suggest a pedagogical order, is between contextualized and decontextualized problems. A decontextualized problem is posed without reference to a situation outside of the mathematical relations under consideration—e.g., Simplify $3(x - 4)$.

3. One complication, however, is that ways in which people solve problems in everyday life and in school are often quite different. See, for example, Jean Lave's (1988) work on arithmetic in shopping, especially Part II.

4. Also, the compromises forced by the structure of high schools were particularly apparent and problematic to me. In my teaching at the university, opportunities for individual interaction with students were much greater. When students were disengaged in my university courses, I could create opportunities to discuss the issue with students and attempt to understand their concerns.

5. This quote is from a conversation on 7/14/93.

6. Ibid.

7. Even within the non-college-bound track, there are important issues of status as I alluded to in Chapter 1 with Darlene's comment about Sam. Similarly, on the second day of class in my first year at Holt, when John was talking, Sara told a neighbor that he was a Practical Math student and should be ignored. Students seemed to have greater respect for younger students who had come from more academic classes, like Pre-Algebra at the junior high school, than for older students coming from Practical Math at the high school.

8. For example, we had a student in our class who expected to go to the most prestigious law school in the state. She did not realize that her academic standing made such a future extremely unlikely.

9. In fact, because of the nature of certification in Michigan, at Holt High School all of the mathematics teachers were mathematics majors in college. While nationwide this may not always be the case, the general point about success in mathematics coursework still holds.

10. In addition to our concerns about students completing the work, we also became more and more skeptical of the traditional rationales for homework and were in the process of rethinking our approach to homework.

11. From our conversation on 6/16/93.

12. Ibid.

13. From our conversation on 7/14/93.

14. Ibid.

15. This difficulty plagues developers of widely used curricular materials. The diversity of student experience creates difficulties for curriculum developers who wish to create "real" problems for widespread use across the United States.

Chapter 3

1. For example, though deductive proof is emphasized (sometimes in trivializing ways), the curriculum is not designed on the basis of Hilbert's famous comment (for example, as reported in Kline, 1980, p. 191) that the undefined terms in geometry—point, line, plane—could just as well be beer mugs, chairs, or any other objects, provided they obey the stated axioms.

2. A separate difficulty is the imprecision of the definition of an equation. In the traditional course, strings of literal symbols (x's and y's) that include an equal sign are called equations. Yet, while this definition allows one to pick out examples of equations, it describes strings that are treated very differently. In the traditional course, one can operate on both sides of $y = 3x - 4$, but not on both sides of $f(x) = 3x - 4$; the f is a very different creature than the x or the y; the = sign in $f(x) = 3x - 4$ does not stand for numerical equality, but instead for naming—there is a function f of the variable x whose definition is "take whatever x is, multiply it by three, and subtract four." See Chazan (1993) for an examination of the definition of "equation." For this reason, some have called the traditional algebra curriculum intellectually incoherent. See, for example, Schwartz & Yerushalmy (1992); Yerushalmy & Schwartz (1993). In this spirit, Freudenthal (1973) critiques different uses of the = sign and suggests the introduction of alternative symbols.

3. I view Husserl's (1970) attempt to locate the origin of geometry in human activity as an attempt to (re)infuse schooled knowledge with an animating sense of human purpose and meaning. In that sense, it seems consistent with Dewey's program. See especially appendix 6, pp. 353–378.

4. It is the caricature of such views that led Bertrand Russell to characterize mathematics "as the subject in which no one knows what he is talking about" (Russell, 1956/ 1988, p. 1551; see also Boyer, 1968/1985 p. 649).

5. According to Boyer (1968/1985), this title refers (in modern notation) to "the transposition of subtracted terms to the other side of an equation . . . [and] 'reduction' or 'balancing'—that is, the cancellation of like terms on opposite sides of the equation."

$$x^2 + 2x - 3 = 2x + 1$$

$$x^2 - 3 = 1 \quad \text{(reduction)}$$

$$x^2 = 1 + 3 \quad \text{(transposition)}$$

$$\ldots = \ldots$$

The techniques of "Al-jabr wa'l Muqabalah" are the familiar ones now taught in high school algebra. They are useful for synthesis, for moving from the unknown x to the known, the solution (either 2 or −2). Al-Khowarizmi's equations were written in words, not symbols. The equations seen in a high school course are manipulated in the same way that al-Khowarizmi manipulated his problems, but they are recorded in a system of symbols that began to evolve in France some 400 years after the time of al-Khowarizmi (pp. 252–253).

6. I use the descriptor "essential" to indicate an affinity between this question and the goals pursued by the Coalition of Essential Schools.

7. This question builds on a philosophical criterion for possessing a concept—the "ability to pick out or distinguish that to which an expression applies." See Runes (1983, p. 69). For a critique of this choice, see Confrey & Costa, 1996.

8. These examples come from a course on disciplinary knowledge that I taught with G. Williamson McDiarmid.

9. To anticipate a later discussion, Schwab (1978) seems to think that in mathematics there may only be one such structure. It is this commonplace view of mathematics that I will challenge below as we explore fields associated with school algebra. But already we have seen a tension between the views of Aleksandrov (1956/1963) and Hilbert, the German mathematician, about the fundamental nature of geometry and, more generally, between formalist views of mathematics and recent developments in the philosophy of mathematics. Similarly, there are important tensions between applied and pure approaches to mathematics.

10. This dynamic created difficulties for the NCTM task force (NCTM, 1994) charged with writing a vision of school algebra. As a result, the task force deliberately avoided the question of defining what school algebra is.

11. Furthermore, the techniques taught in school algebra for solving equations apply only to a subset of the equations now used in mathematics and science. For example, there is no closed form solution to an equation like $\tan x = x$.

12. Since 1989, the Office of Educational Research and Improvement–sponsored National Center for Research in Mathematical Sciences Education located at the University of Wisconsin has sponsored an electronic mail working group that has grappled with this question. One direction proposed by this group (Kaput, 1995) is the integration of algebra as a strand in elementary school mathematics.

13. This sort of work has pushed me to try to develop greater historical appreciation of the evolution of mathematical subdisciplines. I have found conversations with Al Cuoco particularly helpful in appreciating the nature of Abstract Algebra.

14. These solution procedures were described by illustrating them on a particular problem described in words. Thus, the work in what now might be called the Theory of

Equations that precedes Viete's introduction of symbols is often referred to as rhetorical algebra. For example, see Kramer (1981) or Sfard (1995). For a full description of the historical development of algebra, see van der Waerden (1985).

15. Analysis is a large field of mathematics with a complicated history. For an overview of the evolution of the meaning of the term *analysis* and how it became the name for a field of mathematics, see Boyer (1954). For descriptions of the various subfields of mathematical study that now fall under this title, see entry: "analysis" in McHenry (1992).

16. In that sense, analysts might argue that algebraists do not have a monopoly on interpreting early historical work in algebra, that modern algebra and analysis both have the right to claim the work of Viete, who called algebra the analytic art (Chazan, 1996b).

17. Number systems that Cuoco uses include those commonly studied in school, like the integers, the rational numbers, the real numbers, and the complex numbers, as well as those not traditionally studied in school, like the numbers that can be represented as $a + \sqrt{2}b$ for a and b rational numbers, or those that can be written as a (modulus b) where a is an integer. He asks students to use programming to explore how the properties of these calculation procedures differ depending on the properties of the number system on which they are carried out. What are the number of solutions of $x(30 - 2x)^2 = 0$ in a number system, like the integers (mod 6), where the fact that two numbers when multiplied equal zero does not indicate that one of the two numbers must be 0—e.g., $2 * 3 = 0$ (mod 6)?

18. A standard example given in arithmetic of real numbers is that multiplication is commutative for any two numbers: $a * b$ is the same as $b * a$, while division is not: a/b is not the same as b/a for any a and b.

19. Now there are other ways to do these sorts of activities. There are sensors that can be attached to graphing calculators. The calculators generate a graph of the data collected by the sensor. Students can be asked to "draw" graphs by manipulating the sensors. For descriptions of such work, see Nemirovsky (1994). A different tactic to sketching graphs is taken in *The Algebra Sketchbook* (Yerushalmy & Shternberg, 1994). See Schwartz & Yerushalmy (1995) for a description of this work.

20. In Davis's (1984) analysis of this common faulty rule, these students are doing much that is correct. They are responding with an appropriate kind of answer; they are presenting another expression. He suggests they are simply overgeneralizing the distributive law and creating their own nonstandard law. On the other hand, while there is evidence of much knowledge, these students seem to be missing one of the most important ingredients. They seem not to know criteria for determining whether their answer is correct (or they are not sufficiently self-monitoring); they do not seem to be thinking about what is supposed to remain the same as they rewrite the expression in a different form; they are not checking their work.

21. If we give "x" a value, like 5, $(x + 5)^2$ and $x^2 + 25$ are not names for the same number; $(x + 5)^2$ produces 100, while $x^2 + 25$ produces 50. Notice, however, that both expressions give the same result for an input of 0. Checking is helpful, but it is not a guarantee!

22. Calling such a string of symbols an equation is based on an insufficiently pre-

cise definition of an equation, one that neglects the different kinds of equal signs. By being more precise for the moment in distinguishing two kinds of uses of the equal sign (à la Freudenthal, 1973), I hope to help students keep track of functions as the central object of study in the course.

23. Keeping the meaning of symbols in mind flies directly in the face of some of the rationales originally given for using symbols. According to some, use of symbols allows us to forget what it is we are talking about and thus come to see answers to problems too complex to solve while retaining meaning in mind. Such a view is implicit in descriptions of mathematical modeling that suggest a movement from "a real-world situation" to "a formal system" in which manipulations are done to produce "a mathematical result," which is then reinterpreted in terms of the "real-world situation." For diagrams that schematize such a view, and for criticism of such views, see Schoenfeld (1991, p. 313) and Davis and Hersh (1986, p. 59). Like those authors, I am arguing instead for a process that involves more back and forth between mathematical descriptions and that which they are meant to describe, and against postponing reinterpretation of mathematical results to the end of the process. See Pimm (1995) for a similar argument on insight through symbol manipulation in purely symbolic contexts.

24. Michal Yerushalmy (1997; Yerushalmy & Gilead, 1997) in Israel has had some better success in having college-intending students adopt the use of symbols in a functions-based approach, although she does note individual differences in propensity to work with algebraic symbols. She also describes a similar dynamic with a functions-based approach (and its multiple representations) and the solving of equations. Solving equations can no longer simply be justified in terms of finding solutions, because solutions can be found directly using other representations and tools. Solving equations needs a different sort of justification.

25. As controversy has developed around the reform movement, such calls for reduced attention to rigorous proof have been viewed with concern by some mathematicians and have created tensions between mathematicians and mathematics educators (Ross, 1998; Wu, 1997).

26. Some algebra texts from the era of the New Math presented simplification problems as proofs. One proves that one expression is equivalent to another by justifying every step in the simplification (see Herbst [1998] for further discussion).

27. Students can develop some theorems that are similar to those of the theory of equations. They can reflect on their methods for solving an equation with particular coefficients and generalize their strategy and create solution methods for an equation in a particular form. More recently, teachers at Holt have been using parameters to help students articulate conjectures about, for example, all quadratic functions which can be written as $A(x + h_1)(x + h_2)$.

Chapter 4

1. There is a paradox here. Mathematics classes are usually described as among the most intellectually rigorous and demanding; students often find mathematical thinking difficult and fail mathematics courses. Yet the *Professional Standards* (NCTM, 1991) depicts typical mathematics classes as teacher-centered contexts in which students are

not actively engaged in intellectual work. Paradoxically, both descriptions are accurate in their own ways.

2. I am using the term *conversation* here rather than the more common and technical term *discourse* for two reasons. First, I am focusing on oral, face-to-face communication and not the full range of exchanges that discourse involves. Second, the term *conversation*, for me, focuses attention on the sense of exchange that I seek in classroom interaction.

3. Cuban later suggests that this explanation does not explain why some practitioners in elementary schools, as opposed to high schools, have taken up some student-centered practices and not others. I would suggest that his assessment is overly harsh. Buttressed by developmental psychological theory, elementary school teachers are somewhat insulated from the force of cultural beliefs about the nature of knowledge in a way that high school teachers are not. And some student-centered practices may be more appealing than others because of their connections to other beliefs teachers hold.

4. Indeed for this reason, Davis and Hersh's (1981) "Ideal Mathematician" believes that the surest way to communicate with extraterrestrial beings is to broadcast the expansion of *pi*. On the other hand, some argue that for this reason mathematics has been an avenue for individuals from low-status groups seeking advancement within Western society. As evidence, one could point to the ways in which Ramanujan's mathematical ideas have had a great impact, though arguably his economic and social situation made such a contribution on his part unlikely. Making use of this view of mathematics in this way is part of the strategy of the Algebra Project's focus on mathematics as a way to ameliorate the situation of African Americans; see Moses (1994).

5. The crisis caused by non-Euclidean geometries was that the negation of a fundamentally true *a priori* principle also leads to a consistent mathematical system. For this reason, the development of non-Euclidean geometries, and the view of axioms as arbitrary choices, had such a large impact on epistemology.

6. I am focusing here on the special characteristics ascribed to mathematics. Mathematical knowledge is also prestigious knowledge in Western society because of its involvement in scientific endeavors. Advances in scientific fields and their use of mathematics have led to many tools for interacting with our environment. These tools—from the watch to the microprocessor—have had tremendous impact on our society, not the least of which has been financial. Thus, politicians exhort their populace to become mathematically literate for the sake of national economic competitiveness. Indicative of this kind of exhortation is the title of the report of the Commission on the Skills of the American Workforce (1990), "America's Choice: High Skills or Low Wages!" Similar economic arguments are advanced in such reform documents as Mathematical Sciences Education Board (1989). For a critique of such exhortations, see Secada (1990).

7. Cuban traces these views of school knowledge to the important role of churches in founding schools. An alternative theory might focus on the pressure against controversy generated by compulsory public schooling.

8. This is one of the insights that French researchers have codified in their description of "the didactical contract" (Brousseau, 1997). Yet, paradoxically, what is taught in school is often true only in a limited way. One *can* take away a larger number

from a smaller number. Not all triangles have angles whose measures sum to 180 degrees.

9. I once taught such a prodigy, who at age three, using a circular disk cut into fractional parts, had explained adding, subtracting, multiplying, and dividing fractions to his surprised father.

10. Associated with differences in ability, mathematical topics also seem to be graded in difficulty. It is common lore that some mathematical topics are hard to grasp. There are some notions that are simply difficult and that may not be understood until one teaches them. See, for example, Davis and Hersh (1981), pp. 274–284. The commonsense view is that the order of the school curriculum is graded according to difficulty. As a result, there are predictable places in the curriculum where people will have difficulty. Some people drop out when they reach the x's of algebra; for others, it is the proofs of high school geometry; less well known, but just as deadly, are the hurdles of Linear Algebra and Abstract Algebra. Thus, the notion is that the further one progresses along the curriculum, the more hurdles have been jumped, the more able one is.

11. Interestingly, testing of this kind is not as widely used in other societies. In a chapter titled "The Peculiarities of the English," Sutherland (1984) suggests that standardized multiple choice tests have not been as widely developed in England as a result of different cultural perspectives on merit.

12. This role of mathematics in testing seems ripe for study. Some potential questions include: How does mathematics come to play such a central role in aptitude testing and thus in access to a college education? How does this role illuminate our society's views about mathematics? What kinds of cultural assumptions about mathematics can be revealed by an analysis of the role that mathematics plays in such tests? And finally, how might the use of mathematics in these tests affect our society's views of the subject?

13. It is this web of societal attitudes that leads Bob Moses (1994) to argue forcefully that algebra and the college-track high school mathematics curriculum is the literacy test of the nineties. For example, he argues that "the ongoing struggle for citizenship and equality for minority people is now linked to an issue of math and science literacy" (p. 107). In making this statement, Moses is arguing for the use of a set of cultural attitudes as a lever to attack discrimination. Achievement in mathematics is considered incontrovertible. It is a sign of ability or aptitude. Thus, if African American students are able to achieve in mathematics, they will be demonstrating in an incontrovertible manner that they are able and deserve entry to college. In Moses' analysis, achievement in mathematics is currently being used as a gatekeeper that denies African American students access to continued education, but if the achievement of African American students can be raised it can be used in the future as a lever to increase access to college education.

14. In a loosely coupled system, at least in theory without a national curriculum, college admissions tests should not be biased toward students with particular kinds of preparation. Such tests should provide a meritocratic basis for college admission, an objective standard. Such a standard would allow "able" students from lower classes to rise to the level of their ability. It also legitimizes the achievement of students from the upper classes as being reflective of their "aptitude."

15. For examples of such instruction, see Schifter (1996), Ball (1993a, 1993b), and Burns (1992). On the other hand, such changes are not the norm. For example, for a

critical examination of the types of reforms carried out in California's elementary school classrooms, see the papers from the Educational Policy and Practice Study collected in *Educational Evaluation and Policy Analysis, 12*(3).

16. Though the phrase *problem solving* has different usages, some work done under this banner fits with the discussion in this section. For reviews of this sort of problem solving and research on classrooms taught in this way, see Lester (1994) and Lester and Garofalo (1982).

17. Others use a similar strategy, but more explicitly change the nature of the task students are working on. Brown and Walter (1983) suggest that rather than searching after correct answers to problems posed by the teacher or text, students should pose the problems they then seek to solve. Their book suggests strategies for helping students learn to pose problems. While Brown and Walter stress developing questions, Michal Yerushalmy and Judah Schwartz's vision of doing mathematics is centered around the creation of conjectures. Schwartz (1989) outlines how *The Geometric Supposer* (Schwartz et al., 1985) can be used to pose tasks unlike typical school tasks. Another scheme for changing the nature of classroom mathematical tasks is the Middle Grade Mathematics Program's Launch–Explore–Summary model (Lappan & Ferrini-Mundy, 1993).

18. The commitment to respecting students' ideas often comes in conflict with being true to the discipline. Deborah Ball (1993b) and Magdalene Lampert (1985) discuss this conflict by using the language of "dilemmas," where one does not choose one value over another.

19. Most recently, these debates have surfaced in the popular press following the publication of Alan Sokol's hoax in the journal *Social Text*. For a review of the controversy, see Weinberg (1996). While I, like Weinberg, find it difficult to see how it is a hoax to publish views one does not hold, I disagree with Weinberg's view of the nature of scientific and mathematical knowledge.

20. Kline (1980) argues that "the concept of a universally accepted, infallible body of reason—the majestic mathematics of 1800 and the pride of man—is a grand illusion. Uncertainty and doubt concerning the future of mathematics have replaced the certainties and complacency of the past" (p. 6).

21. This trend is represented by the work of Davis and Hersh (1981, 1986); Kitcher (1983); Lakatos (1976); Rotman (1987, 1993); and Tymoczko (1986). All of these thinkers take a skeptical view of the certainty of mathematical knowledge and prefer to see mathematical knowledge as socially constructed. For a review of this work and its relationship to mathematics teaching, see Chazan (1990a).

22. In *Ad Infinitum: The Ghost in Turing's Machine: Taking God Out of Mathematics and Putting the Body Back In*, Rotman (1993) undertakes a semiotic analysis of mathematical practice and suggests that the nature of mathematical rhetoric helps explain our perceptions of the certainty of mathematical knowledge.

23. This tension came to the fore publicly in discussions of the nature of the second book of Euclid. In following the evolution of algebraic results, historians whose training was in mathematics saw in the second book of Euclid a series of "algebraic" results "dressed up in geometrical garb without any geometrical motivation at all" (quoted in Rowe, 1996, p. 9). Others objected to the labeling of these results as "algebraic," suggest-

ing that such a reading was historically insensitive and that it did not elucidate how the Greeks conceptualized these results.

24. One of the intriguing aspects of Grabiner's (1986) argument is that the economic circumstances of mathematicians changed in the 19th century. She suggests that while in the 18th century mathematicians were supported by royal courts, in the 19th century they begin to teach in university settings. She believes that teaching played a role in the 19th-century emphasis on rigor and foundational notions. To support her argument, see for example the selection from Dedekind's writings in Calinger (1982), pp. 627–633.

25. For fear that mathematical proof is being deemphasized, Gila Hanna (1995) critiques this trend in mathematics education. Perhaps these views are popular among educators because they mesh nicely with other commitments that educators hold: to more active roles for students in classrooms and to currently accepted theories of learning. Though these theories of learning—from the constructivist, to the social constructivist, to the sociocultural—are not in complete agreement about the relative roles of the individual and the group, there is widespread agreement that individuals in the context of social groups develop their own understandings: that teachers cannot "transmit" their knowledge directly to students, that students must construct understandings for themselves, and that groups provide important resources for these developments. For a discussion of the relationship between these theories of learning, see Cobb (1994).

26. This notion is captured by German theorists of mathematics education by the term "complementarity," consciously built on the notion of particle and wave complimentarity in physics.

27. Is the mathematical community limited to mathematicians? Does it include historians of mathematics, teachers of mathematics, mathematics majors in college, engineers? The notion of community is a difficult one to pin down.

28. In response to the crisis in the foundations of mathematics, this position was developed by Raymond Wilder in the 50s, see Wilder (1986). For a more recent exposition, see Bishop (1988).

29. For me as a teacher, treating mathematical knowledge as certain was less demanding; if there was a proof, even if I hadn't mastered the proof myself (e.g., we teach that *pi* is an irrational number, but few teachers could prove this "fact"), then the statement was true. The existence of the proof would have closed down the discussion (and would have allowed me to say with confidence that *pi* is irrational and that it is not possible to square the circle) even though my confidence, like that of many mathematics teachers, was built on faith.

30. Technically, fractions and decimals are ways of representing numbers and not kinds of numbers in the same way that rational and irrational numbers are kinds of numbers. Yet students are not the only ones who refer to fractions and decimals in this way.

31. They were not troubled by dividing by zero, because they did not want to carry out any arithmetic operations on zero, since it is not a number.

32. Though traditional views of mathematical knowledge implicitly suggest that only mathematicians' views count, such views contradict other impulses in a democratic society. This tension is evident in Mathematical Sciences Education Board (1989).

33. A more general way of stating the issue is that my teaching has raised issues for me about the relationship between Deweyan ideas and social class or local culture. When families do not identify with school knowledge, Dewey's analysis of the child and the curriculum seems incomplete. The family creates a third focal point, which may not be along the continuum Dewey envisions connecting the child and the curriculum.

34. The reverberations of these criticisms continue to echo through the web. If people who disagree are no longer simply wrong, if we think of such people as unenculturated to the point of view of the mathematical community, what happens to our notions of ability? How is such variation among people to be understood?

Chapter 5

1. I have found this to be the case when using videotaped cases from my own teaching as a context for creating discussions of the complexity of teaching, and when watching others try to do the same.

2. While Holt High School is a Professional Development School, unlike a university laboratory school, it was not specially constituted by the university. As a result, its faculty and student body represent the preexisting district conditions. Over time, faculty in the school have had experiences that make them different from many teachers. This theme will be taken up below. I will argue that, rather than thinking of the Holt teachers as special in this regard, it would be useful for many teachers to have such experiences.

3. Initially, this idea was intoxicating to the department. I remember an excited call from Mike Lehman, the department chair, a few years ago. For the first time in his memory, the professional development days before school dealt with mathematics, and not the number of students and textbooks for each section.

4. This dynamic can also explain resistance to change by teachers who have made changes earlier in their careers. For an individual teacher who has invested in a particular innovation (say a new textbook), particularly an innovation that he or she feels meets some important goals, it may be difficult to imagine changing yet again.

5. Though team-teaching is a costly vehicle for professional development, it is important to consider serious investment in teachers' professional growth and development. Cross-cultural examination of mathematics teaching in Japan and China suggests that in those countries mathematics teachers teach polished lessons that are orchestrated around students' ideas, at least in the equivalent to U.S. elementary and middle schools. At the same time, the organization of teaching practice and teaching loads in those countries is quite different. Teachers in those countries teach much larger classes, but also have substantial amounts of time for joint planning of lessons and classroom observations of the teaching of others. It seems important to develop a range of strategies for providing teachers with time for reflection about teaching. Shared responsibility for teaching a section is but one model.

On a practical level, there are different ways to fund and implement such assignments. If such assignments are recognized as professional development, district funds for sabbaticals or professional development might be used for creating release time for teachers. In considering the economics of such choices, it is important to consider how the benefits of particular shared teaching arrangements might amortize over time. Of course, such long-term planning is difficult when teacher turnover is high.

6. An argument might be made that the development of new communication technologies will produce pressure to change the nature of schooling and will work to reduce the isolation of schools. However, such predictions are hard to assess. While in such discussions people often point to the Web, one intriguing development in this regard is the placement of telephones inside classrooms.

References

Aleksandrov, A. D. (1963). A general view of mathematics. In A. Aleksandrov, A. Kolmogorov, & M. Lavrent'ev (Eds.), *Mathematics: Its content, methods, and meaning* (Vol. I; pp. 1–64). Cambridge: Massachusetts Institute of Technology. (Original work published 1956)

Anderson, C. W. (1995). Teaching content in a multicultural milieu. In S. Hopmann & K. Riquarts (Eds.), *Didaktik and/or curriculum* (pp. 365–382). Kiel, Germany: Institut für die Pädagogik der Naturwissenschaften.

Ball, D. L. (1991). Research on teaching mathematics: Making subject-matter knowledge part of the equation. In J. Brophy (Ed.), *Advances in research on teaching* (Vol. 2; pp. 1–48). Greenwich, CT: JAI Press.

Ball, D. L. (1992). Teaching mathematics for understanding: What do teachers need to know about the subject matter? In M. Kennedy (Ed.), *Teaching academic subjects to diverse learners* (pp. 63–83). New York: Teachers College Press.

Ball, D. L. (1993a). Halves, pieces, and twoths: Constructing and using representational contexts in teaching fractions. In T. Carpenter & E. Fennema (Eds.), *Learning, teaching, and assessing rational number constructs* (pp. 157–195). Hillsdale, NJ: Lawrence Erlbaum.

Ball, D. L. (1993b). With an eye on the mathematical horizon: Dilemmas of teaching elementary school mathematics. *The Elementary School Journal, 93*(4), 373–397.

Benacerraf, P., & Putnam, H. (Eds.). (1983). *Philosophy of mathematics: Selected readings*. Cambridge: Cambridge University Press. (Original work published 1964)

Berryman, S. E. (1987). *Breaking out of the circle: Rethinking our assumptions about education and the economy* (Occasional Paper 2). New York: National Center on Education and Employment.

Bethell, S., Chazan, D., Hodges, K., & Schnepp, M. (1995). *Introducing students to representations of functions*. East Lansing: Michigan State University.

Bishop, A. (1988). *Mathematical enculturation: A cultural perspective on mathematics education*. Dordrecht: Kluwer Academic Publishers.

Borasi, R. (1992). *Learning mathematics through inquiry*. Portsmouth, NH: Heinemann.

Boyer, C. (1944). Zero: The symbol, the concept, the number. *National Mathematics Magazine, 18*, 323–330.

Boyer, C. (1954). Analysis: Notes on the evolution of a subject and a name. *Mathematics Teacher, 47*(8), 450–462.

Boyer, C. (1985). *A history of mathematics*. Princeton, NJ: Princeton University Press. (Original work published 1968)

Brantlinger, E. A. (1993a). Adolescents' interpretation of social class influences on schooling. *Journal of Classroom Interaction, 28*(1), 1–12.

Brantlinger, E. A. (1993b). *The politics of social class in secondary school: Views of affluent and impoverished youth.* New York: Teachers College Press.

Brousseau, G. (1997). *Theory of didactical situations in mathematics* (N. Balacheff, M. Cooper, R. Sutherland, & V. Warfield, Trans.). Dordrecht: Kluwer.

Brown, J., & Langer, E. (1990). Mindfulness and intelligence: A comparison. *Educational Psychologist, 25*(3 & 4), 305–335.

Brown, S., & Walter, M. (1983). *The art of problem posing.* Philadelphia: Franklin Institute.

Buber, M. (1970). *I and thou.* New York: Scribner.

Burns, M. (1992). *About teaching mathematics: A K–8 resource.* Sausalito: Math Solutions Publications.

Calinger, R. (Ed.). (1982). *Classics of mathematics.* Englewood Cliffs, NJ: Prentice-Hall.

Carroll, J. (1978). On the theory-practice interface in the measurement of intellectual abilities. In P. Suppes (Ed.), *Impact of research on education: Some case studies* (pp. 1–106). Washington, DC: National Academy of Education.

Chazan, D. (1990a). Quasi-empirical views of mathematics and mathematics teaching. *Interchange, 21*, 14–23.

Chazan, D. (1990b). *The "slope" of monomials and other functions: An exploration and method based on a student's idea.* Unpublished manuscript, Michigan State University, East Lansing.

Chazan, D. (1993). F(*x*) = G(*x*)?: An approach to modeling with algebra. *For the Learning of Mathematics, 13*(3), 22–26.

Chazan, D. (1995). Five questions about algebra reform (and a thought experiment). In C. LaCampagne, W. Blair, & J. Kaput (Eds.), *The algebra initiative colloquium* (Vol. 2; pp. 19–26). Washington, DC: U.S. Department of Education.

Chazan, D. (1996a). Algebra for all students? *Journal of Mathematical Behavior, 15*(3), 455–477.

Chazan, D. (1996b). Historical developments in algebra and analysis: Resources for algebra reform. *Proceedings of the Third International Conference on the History and Philosophy of Science in Science Teaching.* Minneapolis, MN: University of Minnesota.

Chazan, D. (1999). On teachers' mathematical knowledge and student exploration: A personal story about teaching a technologically supported approach to school algebra. *International Journal of Computers for Mathematical Learning, 4.*

Chazan, D., & Ball, D. L. (1999). Beyond being told not to tell. *For the Learning of Mathematics, 19*(2), 2–10.

Chazan, D., Ben-haim, D., & Gormas, J., with Schepp, M., Lehman, M., Bethell, S., & Neurither, S. (1998). Shared teaching assignments in the service of mathematics reform: Situated professional development. *Journal of Teaching and Teacher Education, 14*(7), 687–702.

Chazan, D., & Bethell, S. (1994). Sketching graphs of an independent and a dependent quantity: Difficulties in learning to make stylized, conventional "pictures." In J. P. da Ponte & J. F. Matos (Eds.), *Proceedings of the Eighteenth Annual Conference of the International Group for the Psychology of Mathematics Education* (Vol. II; pp. 212–220). Lisbon, Portugal: PME Program Committee.

Chazan, D., & Bethell, S. (1998). Working with algebra. In Mathematical Sciences Education Board (Ed.), *High school mathematics at work: Essays and examples from workplace contexts to strengthen the mathematical education of all students* (pp. 35–41). Washington, DC: National Research Council.

Chazan, D., & Yerushalmy, M. (1998). Charting a course for secondary mathematics. In R. Lehrer & D. Chazan (Eds.), *Designing learning environments to develop understanding of geometry and space* (pp. 67–90). Hillsdale, NJ: Lawrence Erlbaum.

Cobb, P. (1994). Where is the mind? Constructivist and sociocultural perspectives on mathematical development. *Educational Researcher, 32*(7), 13–20.

Cobb, P., & Steffe, L. (1983). The constructivist researcher as teacher and model builder. *Journal for Research in Mathematics Education, 14*, 83–94.

Cohen, D. J. (1999). Symbols of heaven, symbols of man: Pure mathematics and Victorian religion. Unpublished doctoral dissertation, Yale University, New Haven, CT.

Cohen, D., McLaughlin, M., & Talbert, J. (Eds.). (1993). *Teaching for understanding: Challenges for policy and practice.* San Francisco: Jossey-Bass.

Commission on the Skills of the American Workforce. (1990). *America's choice: High skills or low wages!* Washington, DC: National Center on Education and the Economy.

Confrey, J., & Costa, S. (1996). A critique of the selection of "mathematical objects" as a central metaphor for advanced mathematical thinking. *International Journal of Computers for Mathematical Learning, 1*, 139–168.

Confrey, J., & Smith, E. (1995). Splitting, covariation, and their role in the development of exponential functions. *Journal for Research in Mathematics Education, 26*(1), 66–86.

Conway, J. (1995). Request for advice: philosophy (email communication). Swarthmore: Geometry Forum.

Crowe, M. (1975). Ten "laws" concerning patterns of change in the history of mathematics. *Historia Mathematica, 2*, 161–166.

Crowe, M. (1992). Afterword: A revolution in the historiography of mathematics? In D. Gillies (Ed.), *Revolutions in mathematics* (pp. 306–315). Oxford: Clarendon.

Cuban, L. (1993). *How teachers taught: Constancy and change in American classrooms, 1890–1990* (2nd ed.). New York: Teachers College Press.

Cuoco, A. (1990). *Investigations in algebra.* Cambridge, MA: MIT.

Cusick, P. (1983). *The egalitarian ideal and the American high school: Studies of three schools.* New York: Longman.

D'ambrosio, U. (1994). Ethno-mathematics, the nature of mathematics, and mathematics education. In P. Ernest (Ed.), *Mathematics, education, and philosophy: An international perspective* (pp. 230–242). London: Falmer.

Dauben, J. (1992). Appendix: Revolutions revisited. In D. Gillies (Ed.), *Revolutions in mathematics* (pp. 72–82). Oxford: Clarendon.

Davis, B. (1995). Why teach mathematics? Mathematics education and enactivist theory. *For the Learning of Mathematics, 15*(2), 2–9.

Davis, P. (1986). Fidelity in mathematical discourse: Is one and one really two? In T. Tymoczko (Ed.), *New directions in the philosophy of mathematics* (pp. 163–176). Boston: Birkhauser.

Davis, P., & Hersh, R. (1981). *The mathematical experience.* Boston: Houghton Mifflin.

Davis, P., & Hersh, R. (1986). *Descartes dream: The world according to mathematics.* San Diego: Harcourt, Brace, Jovanovich.

Davis, R. (1984). *Learning mathematics: The cognitive science approach to mathematics education.* Norwood, NJ: Ablex.

DeLany, B. (1991). Allocation, choice, and stratification within high schools: How the sorting machine copes. *American Educational Research Journal, 28*(1), 181–207.

Demana, F., & Waits, B. (1990). *College algebra and trigonometry.* Reading, MA: Addison Wesley.

Devlin, K. (1997). Editorial: Burning the flag. *Focus: The newsletter of the Mathematical Association of America, 17,* 2.

Dewey, J. (1929). *The quest for certainty: A study of the relation of knowledge and action.* New York: Minton, Balch and Co.

Dewey, J. (1990). *The school and society; The child and the curriculum.* Chicago: University of Chicago Press. (Original work published 1902)

Dolciani, M., & Wooton, W. (1973). *Modern algebra, book one: Structure and method.* Boston: Houghton-Mifflin. (Original work published 1970)

Dryden, D. (1995). Narrative trajectories and the social ecology of opportunity: Authoritative adult guidance and the development of identity. Unpublished manuscript, Duke University, Durham, NC.

Duckworth, E. (1987). *"The having of wonderful ideas" and other essays on teaching and learning.* New York: Teachers College Press.

Duckworth, E. (1991). Twenty four, forty two, and I love you: Keeping it complex. *Harvard Educational Review, 61*(1), 1–24.

Dugdale, S., & Kibbey, D. (1986). *Interpreting graphs* [Computer program]. Pleasantville, NY: Sunburst.

Eckert, P. (1989). *Jocks and burnouts: Social categories and identity in the high school.* New York: Teachers College Press.

Erickson, F., & Shultz, J. (1991). Students' experience of the curriculum. In P. W. Jackson (Ed.), *Handbook of research on curriculum* (pp. 465–485). New York: Macmillan.

Farrell, E., Peguero, G., Lindsey, R., & White, R. (1988). Giving voice to high school students: Pressure and boredom, ya know what I'm sayin'? *American Educational Research Journal, 25*(4), 489–502.

Fauvel, J. (1989). Platonic rhetoric in distance learning: How Robert Record taught the home learner. *For the Learning of Mathematics, 9*(1), 2–6.

Fauvel, J., & Gray, J. (Eds.). (1987). *The history of mathematics: A reader.* London: Macmillan.

Fehr, H. F. (1951). *Secondary mathematics: A functional approach for teachers.* Boston: Heath.

Fey, J. T., Heid, M. K., Good, R. A., Sheets, C., Blume, G. W., & Zbiek, R. M. (1995). *Concepts in algebra: A technological approach.* Dedham, MA: Janson.

Fischbein, E. (1982). Intuition and proof. *For the Learning of Mathematics, 3*(2), 9–18, 24.

Frank, P. (1957). *Philosophy of science: The link between science and philosophy.* Englewood Cliffs, NJ: Prentice-Hall.

Freudenthal, H. (1973). *Mathematics as an educational task.* Dordrecht: Reidel.

Fuller, R. (1893). *A double discovery: The square of the circle.* Boston: Author.

Gallas, K. (1994). *The language of learning: How children talk, write, dance, draw, and sing their understanding of the world.* New York: Teachers College Press.

Gallas, K. (1995). *Talking their way into science.* New York: Teachers College Press.

Gerofsky, S. (1996). A linguistic and narrative view of word problems in mathematics education. *For the Learning of Mathematics, 16*(2), 36–45.

Gillies, D. (Ed.). (1992). *Revolutions in mathematics.* Oxford: Clarendon.

Goldenberg, P. (1988). Mathematics, metaphors, and human factors: Mathematical, technical, and pedagogical challenges in the educational use of graphical representations of functions. *Journal of Mathematical Behavior, 7,* 135–173.

Good, T., Grouws, D., & Ebmeier, H. (1983). *Active mathematics teaching.* New York: Longman.

Goodlad, J. (1984). *A place called school: Prospects for the future.* New York: McGraw-Hill.

Goodman, N. (1978). *Ways of world-making.* Indianapolis: Hackett.

Goodman, N. (1986). Mathematics as an objective science. In T. Tymoczko (Ed.), *New directions in the philosophy of mathematics* (pp. 79–94). Boston: Birkhauser.

Gormas, J. (1998). *The centrality of a teacher's professional transformation in the development of mathematical power: A case study of one high school mathematics teacher.* Unpublished doctoral dissertation, Michigan State University, East Lansing.

Grabiner, J. (1986). Is mathematical truth time-dependent? In T. Tymoczko (Ed.), *New directions in the philosophy of mathematics* (pp. 201–214). Boston: Birkhauser.

Greenberg, M. J. (1980). *Euclidean and non-Euclidean geometries.* San Francisco: W. H. Freeman.

Hall, R. (1990). *Making mathematics on paper: Constructing representations of stories about related linear functions.* Unpublished doctoral dissertation, University of California, Irvine.

Hall, R., Kibler, D., Wenger, E., & Truxaw, C. (1989). Exploring the episodic structure of algebra story problem solving. *Cognition and Instruction, 6*(3), 223–283.

Hallerberg, A. E. (1977). Indiana's squared circle. *Mathematics Magazine, 50*(3), 136–140.

Hamley, H. R. (1934). *The National Council of Teachers of Mathematics ninth annual yearbook: Relational and functional thinking in mathematics.* New York: Teachers College Press.

Hammer, D. (1995). Epistemological considerations in teaching introductory physics. *Science Education, 79*(4), 393–413.

Hammer, D. (1996). More than misconceptions: Multiple perspectives on student knowledge and reasoning, and an appropriate role for education research. *American Journal of Physics, 64*(10), 1316–1325.

Hanna, G. (1983). *Rigorous proof in mathematics education.* Toronto: Ontario Institute for Studies in Education.

Hanna, G. (1989). Proofs that prove and proofs that explain. In G. Vergnaud, J. Rogalski, & M. Artigue (Eds.), *Annual Proceedings of the International Group for the Psychology of Mathematics Education* (Vol. II; pp. 45–51). Paris.

Hanna, G. (1995). Challenges to the importance of proof. *For the Learning of Mathematics, 15*(3), 42–49.

Hawkins, D. (1974). *The informed vision: Essays on learning and human nature.* New York: Agathon.

Heaton, R. (1994). *Creating and studying a practice of teaching elementary mathematics for understanding.* Unpublished doctoral dissertation, Michigan State University, East Lansing.

Heid, K. (1996). A technology-intensive functional approach to the emergence of algebraic thinking. In N. Bednarz, C. Kieran, & L. Lee (Eds.), *Approaches to algebra: Perspectives for research and teaching* (pp. 239–255). Dordrecht: Kluwer.

Herbst, P. (1998). *What works as proof in the mathematics class.* Unpublished doctoral dissertation, University of Georgia, Athens.

Hiebert, J. (Ed.). (1986). *Conceptual and procedural knowledge: The case of mathematics.* Hillsdale, NJ: Lawrence Erlbaum.

Hiebert, J. (1999). Relationships between research and the NCTM Standards. *Journal for Research in Mathematics Education, 30*(1), 3–19.

Holmes Group. (1990). *Tomorrow's schools: Principles for the design of professional development schools.* East Lansing, MI: Author.

Husserl, E. (1970). The origin of geometry. In *The crisis of European sciences and transcendental phenomenology: An introduction to phenomenological philosophy* (pp. 353–378; D. Carr, Trans.). Evanston, IL: Northwestern University Press.

Inhelder, B., & Piaget, J. (1958). *The growth of logical thinking from childhood to adolescence: An essay on the construction of formal operational structures* (A. Parsons & S. Milgram, Trans.). New York: Basic Books.

Jackson, A. (1997a). The math wars: California battles it out over mathematics education reform (Part I). *Notices of the American Mathematical Society, 44,* 695–702.

Jackson, A. (1997b). The math wars: California battles it out over mathematics education reform (Part II). *Notices of the American Mathematical Society, 44,* 817–823.

Jurgensen, R., Brown, R., & King, A. (1980). *Geometry: New edition.* Boston: Houghton-Mifflin.

Kaput, J. (1995). Long term algebra reform: Democratizing access to big ideas. In C. Lacampagne, W. Blair, & J. Kaput (Eds.), *The algebra initiative colloquium* (pp. 33–52). Washington, DC: U.S. Department of Education.

Katz, V. (1993). *A history of mathematics: An introduction.* New York: HarperCollins.

Kenner, M. (1994). Meta-mathematics and the modern conception of mathematics. In F. Swetz (Ed.), *From five fingers to infinity: A journey through the history of mathematics* (pp. 682–689). Chicago: Open Court.

Kieran, C., Boileau, A., & Garancon, M. (1996). Introducing Algebra by means of a technology-supported, functional approach. In N. Bednarz, C. Kieran, & L. Lee (Eds.), *Approaches to algebra: Perspectives for research and teaching* (pp. 257–293). Dordrecht: Kluwer.

Kirsner, S. A., & Bethell, S. (1992). *Creating a flexible and responsive learning environment for general mathematics student* (Research report 92-7). East Lansing: Michigan State University, National Center for Research on Teacher Learning.

Kitcher, P. (1983). *The nature of mathematical knowledge.* Oxford: Oxford University Press.

Kline, M. (1953). *Mathematics in Western culture.* Oxford: Oxford University Press.

Kline, M. (1980). *Mathematics: The loss of certainty.* Oxford: Oxford University Press.

Koendinger, K., & Tabachneck, H. (1994). *Two strategies are better than one: Multiple strategy use in word problem solving.* New Orleans: American Educational Research Association.

Kramer, E. (1981). *The nature and growth of modern mathematics.* Princeton: Princeton University Press.

Kuhn, T. (1962). *The structure of scientific revolutions.* Chicago: University of Chicago Press.

Kuhn, T. (1977). *The essential tension: Selected studies in scientific tradition and change.* Chicago: University of Chicago Press.

Lacampagne, C., Blair, W., & Kaput, J. (Eds.). (1995). *The algebra initiative colloquium.* Washington, DC: U.S. Department of Education.

Lakatos, I. (1976). *Proof and refutations: The logic of mathematical discovery.* Cambridge: Cambridge University Press.

Lakatos, I. (1986). A renaissance of empiricism in the recent philosophy of mathematics? In T. Tymoczko (Ed.), *New directions in the philosophy of mathematics* (pp. 29–48). Boston: Birkhauser.

Lampert, M. (1985). How do teachers manage to teach? Perspectives on problems in practice. *Harvard Educational Review, 55,* 178–194.

Lampert, M. (1990). When the problem is not the question and the solution is not the answer: Mathematical knowing and teaching. *American Educational Research Journal, 27*(1), 29–63.

Lampert, M. (1991a). *Covering the curriculum one problem at a time.* Paper presented at the annual meeting of the National Council of Teachers of Mathematics, New Orleans, LA.

Lampert, M. (1991b). *Knowing and telling about teaching: Paradoxes and problems in being a school teacher and a university researcher.* Paper presented at the annual meeting of the American Educational Research Association, Chicago, IL.

Lampert, M. (1991c). Looking at restructuring from within a restructured role. *Phi Delta Kappan, 72*(9), 70–74.

Lampert, M. (1995). Managing the tensions in connecting students' inquiry with learning mathematics in school. In J. Schwartz, D. Perkins, M. West, & M. Wiske (Eds.), *Software goes to school* (pp. 213–232). New York: Oxford.

Lampert, M. (1998). Studying teaching as a thinking practice. In J. G. Greeno & S. V. Goldman (Eds.), *Thinking practices: A symposium on mathematics and science learning* (pp. 53–78). Hillsdale, NJ: Lawrence Erlbaum.

Lappan, G., & Ferrini-Mundy, J. (1993). Knowing and doing mathematics: A new vision for middle grades students. *Elementary School Journal, 93*(5), 625–641.

Lave, J. (1988). *Cognition in practice: Mind, mathematics, and culture in everyday life.* Cambridge: Cambridge University Press.

Lee, L. (1996). An initiation into algebraic culture through generalization activities. In N. Bednarz, C. Kieran, & L. Lee (Eds.), *Approaches to algebra: Perspectives for research and teaching* (pp. 87–106). Dordrecht: Kluwer.

Lee, O., & Anderson, C. W. (1993). Task engagement and conceptual change in middle school science classrooms. *American Educational Research Journal, 30*(3), 585–610.

Leitzel, J. (1989). Critical consideration for the future of algebra instruction. In S.

Wagner & C. Kieran (Eds.), *Research issues in the learning and teaching of algebra* (pp. 25–32). Reston, VA: National Council of Teachers of Mathematics.

Lensmire, T. (1994). *When children write: Critical revisions of the writing workshop.* New York: Teachers College Press.

Lester, F. (1994). Musing on problem solving research. *Journal for Research in Mathematics Education, 25*(6), 660–675.

Lester, F., & Garofalo, J. (Eds.). (1982). *Mathematical problem solving: Issues in research.* Philadelphia: Franklin Institute Press.

Mason, J. (1989). Mathematical abstraction as the result of a delicate shift of attention. *For the Learning of Mathematics, 9*(2), 2–8.

Mathematical Sciences Education Board. (1989). *Everybody counts: A report to the nation on the future of mathematics education.* Washington, DC: National Research Council.

McClelland, D. C., Koestner, R., & Weinberger, J. (1989). How do self-attributed and implicit motives differ? *Psychological Review, 96*(4), 690–702.

McConnell, J., Brown, S., Eddins, S., Hackwarth, M., Sachs, L., Woodward, E., Flanders, J., Hirschhorn, D., Hynes, C., Polonsky, L., & Usiskin, Z. (1990). *The University of Chicago School mathematics project: algebra.* Glenview, IL: Scott, Foresman.

McDonald, J. (1992). *Teaching: Making sense of an uncertain craft.* New York: Teachers College Press.

McHenry, R. (Ed.). (1992). *Encyclopedia Britannica* (15th ed.). Chicago: Encyclopedia Britannica Inc.

McNeil, L. (1985). *Contradictions of control.* London: Routledge and Kegan Paul.

Metz, M. (1993). Teachers' ultimate dependence on their students. In J. W. Little & M. W. McLaughlin (Eds.), *Teachers' work: Individuals, colleagues, and contexts.* New York: Teachers College Press.

Miles, P. (1992). An interim goal for school mathematics reform. *Focus, 14,* 13.

Mokros, J., & Russell, S. J. (1995). Children's concepts of average and representativeness. *Journal for Research in Mathematics Education, 26*(1), 20–39.

Morris, W. (Ed.). (1976). *The American Heritage dictionary of the English language.* Boston: Houghton Mifflin.

Moschkovich, J., Schoenfeld, A. H., & Arcavi, A. (1993). Aspects of understanding: On multiple perspectives and representations of linear relations and connections among them. In T. A. Romberg, E. Fennema, & T. P. Carpenter (Eds.), *Integrating research on the graphical representation of function* (pp. 69–100). Hillsdale, NJ: Lawrence Erlbaum.

Moses, R. (1994). Remarks on the struggle for citizenship and math/science literacy. *Journal of Mathematical Behavior, 13*(1), 107–112.

Moses, R., Kamii, M., Swap, S., & Howard, J. (1989). The algebra project: Organizing in the spirit of Ella. *Harvard Educational Review, 59,* 423–443.

Nachmias, R., & Arcavi, A. (1990). A parallel representation of linear functions using a microcomputer-based environment. *Journal of Computers in Mathematics and Science Teaching, 9*(4), 79–88.

Nagel, E. (1956). *Logic without metaphysics.* Glecoe, IL: The Free Press.

National Center for Research in Mathematical Sciences Education. (1993). An algebra for all students. *NCRMSE Research Review, 2,* 1–4.

National Center for Research on Teacher Learning. (1992). *Draft statement: This kind of teaching*. East Lansing: Michigan State University.

National Center for Research on Teacher Learning. (1995). *What's the relationship? Learning to teach subject matter and diverse learners*. Paper presented at the annual meeting of the American Educational Research Association, San Francisco.

National Council of Teachers of Mathematics. (1989). *Curriculum and evaluation standards for school mathematics*. Reston, VA: Author.

National Council of Teachers of Mathematics. (1991). *Professional standards for teaching mathematics*. Reston, VA: Author.

National Council of Teachers of Mathematics. (1994, September). *A framework for constructing a vision of algebra: Working draft* (unpublished manuscript), Reston, VA.

Nemirovsky, R. (1994). On ways of symbolizing: The case of Laura and the velocity sign. *Journal of Mathematical Behavior, 13*(4), 389–422.

Nemirovsky, R. (1996). Mathematical narratives, modeling and algebra. In N. Bednarz, C. Kieran, & L. Lee (Eds.), *Approaches to algebra: Perspectives for research and teaching* (pp. 197–220). Dordrecht: Kluwer.

Nesher, P., & Kilpatrick, J. (Eds.). (1990). *Mathematics and cognition: A research synthesis by the International Group for the Psychology of Mathematics Education*. Cambridge: Cambridge University Press.

Newman, J. (Ed.). (1988). *The world of mathematics: A small library of the literature of mathematics from A'h-mose the scribe to Albert Einstein*. Redmond, WA: Tempus. (Original work published 1956)

Newmann, F. (Ed.). (1992). *Student engagement and achievement in American secondary schools*. New York: Teachers College Press.

Nicholls, J. G. (1989). *The competitive ethos and democratic education*. Cambridge, MA: Harvard University Press.

Page, R. N. (1990). *Lower track classrooms: A curricular and cultural perspective*. New York: Teachers College Press.

Paley, V. (1979). *White teacher*. Cambridge, MA: Harvard University Press.

Perkins, D. (1986). *Knowledge as design*. Hillsdale, NJ: Lawrence Erlbaum.

Peterson, P. L., Fenema, E., & Carpenter, T. (1991). Using children's mathematical knowledge. In B. Means, C. Chelemer, & M. S. Knapp (Eds.), *Teaching advanced skills to at-risk students: Views from research and practice* (pp. 68–101). San Francisco: Jossey-Bass.

Phelan, P., Cao, H., Yu, S., & Davidson, A. (1994). Navigating the psychosocial pressures of adolescence: The voices and experiences of high school youth. *American Educational Research Journal, 31*(9), 695–704.

Phelan, P., Davidson, A., & Cao, H. (1992). Speaking up: Students' perspectives on school. *Phi Delta Kappan, 73*(2), 415–447.

Piccioto, H., & Wah, A. (1994). *Algebra: Themes, concepts, and tools*. Alsip, IL: Creative Publications.

Pimm, D. (1995). *Symbols and meanings in school mathematics*. London: Routledge.

Pollatsek, A., Lima, S., & Well, A. D. (1981). Concept or computation: Students' understanding of the mean. *Educational Studies in Mathematics, 19*, 191–204.

Polya, G. (1945). *How to solve it*. Princeton, NJ: Princeton University Press.

Powell, A., Farrar, E., & Cohen, D. (1985). *The shopping mall high school: Winners and losers in the educational marketplace.* Boston: Houghton Mifflin.

Pycior, H. (1976). *The role of Sir William Rowan Hamilton in the development of British modern algebra.* Ithaca, NY: Cornell University Press.

Pycior, H. (1981). George Peacock and the British origins of symbolical algebra. *Historia Mathematica, 8,* 23–45.

Pycior, H. (1982). Early criticism of the symbolical approach to algebra. *Historia Mathematica, 9,* 392–412.

Ralston, A. (1999). Let's abolish pencil-and-paper arithmetic. *Journal of Computers in Mathematics and Science Teaching, 18*(2), 173–194.

Robinson, A. (1969). From a formalist's point of view. *Dialectica, 23,* 45–49.

Rojano, T. (1996). Developing algebraic aspects of problem solving within a spreadsheet environment. In N. Bednarz, C. Kieran, & L. Lee (Eds.), *Approaches to algebra: Perspectives for research and teaching* (pp. 137–147). Dordrecht: Kluwer.

Romberg, T., Fennema, E., & Carpenter, T. (Eds.). (1993). *Integrating research on the graphical representation of functions.* Hillsdale, NJ: Lawrence Erlbaum.

Rorty, R. (1991). *Objectivity, relativism, and truth.* Cambridge: Cambridge University Press.

Ross, K. (1998). Doing and proving: The place of algorithms and proofs in school mathematics. *American Mathematical Monthly, 105,* 252–255.

Roth, K. J. (1992). *The role of writing in creating a science learning community* (Elementary Subjects Center Series No. 62). East Lansing: Michigan State University.

Rotman, B. (1987). *Signifying nothing: The semiotics of zero.* Stanford: Stanford University Press.

Rotman, B. (1993). *Ad infinitum: The ghost in Turing's machine: Taking God out of mathematics and putting the body back in.* Stanford: Stanford University Press.

Rowe, D. (1996). New visions and old images in the history of mathematics. In R. Callinger (Ed.), *Vita mathematica: Historical research and integration with teaching* (pp. 3–16). Washington, DC: Mathematics Association of America.

Runes, D. (1983). *Dictionary of philosophy.* New York: Philosophical Library.

Russell, B. (1910). *The study of mathematics: Philosophical essays.* London: Longmans, Green.

Russell, B. (1988). Mathematics and the metaphysicians. In J. Newman (Ed.), *The world of mathematics* (Vol. 3; pp. 1551–1564). Redmund, WA: Tempus. (Original work published 1956)

Scheffler, I. (1960). *The language of education.* Springfield, IL: Charles C. Thomas.

Scheffler, I. (1965). *Conditions of knowledge: An introduction to epistemology in education.* Chicago: Scott Foresman.

Schifter, D. (1996). *What's happening in math class?: Reconstructing professional identities.* New York: Teachers College Press.

Schoenfeld, A. (1988). When good teaching leads to bad results: The disasters of "well taught" mathematics courses. *Educational Psychologist, 23*(2), 145–166.

Schoenfeld, A. (1991). Making an informal attack on the unfortunate divorce of formal and informal mathematics. In J. Voss, D. Perkins, & J. Segal (Eds.), *Informal reasoning and education.* Hillsdale, NJ: Lawrence Erlbaum.

Schoenfeld, A. (1995). Is thinking about "Algebra" a misdirection? In C. Lacampagne,

W. Blair, & J. Kaput (Eds.), *The algebra initiative colloquium* (pp. 83–86). Washington, DC: U.S. Department of Education.

Schoenfeld, A., Smith, J., & Arcavi, A. (1990). Learning: The microgenetic analysis of one student's understanding of a complex subject matter domain. In R. Glaser (Ed.), *Advances in instructional psychology* (Vol. 4; pp. 55–175). Hillsdale, NJ: Lawrence Erlbaum.

Schwab, J. (1978). Education and the structure of the disciplines. In I. Westbury & N. Wilkof (Eds.), *Science, curriculum, and liberal education: Selected essays* (pp. 229–274). Chicago: University of Chicago Press.

Schwartz, J. (1989). Intellectual mirrors: A step in the direction of making schools knowledge making places. *Harvard Educational Review, 59,* 51–60.

Schwartz, J., & Yerushalmy, M. (1990). *The geometric supposer* [Computer program]. Pleasantville, NY: Sunburst.

Schwartz, J., & Yerushalmy, M. (1992). Getting students to function in and with algebra. In G. Harel & E. Dubinsky (Eds.), *The concept of function: Aspects of epistemology and pedagogy* (pp. 261–289). Washington, DC: Mathematical Association of America.

Schwartz, J., & Yerushalmy, M. (1995). On the need for a bridging language for mathematical modeling. *For the Learning of Mathematics, 15*(2), 29–35.

Schwartz, J. L., Yerushalmy, M., & Education Development Center. (1985). *The Geometric Supposer* [Computer program]. Pleasantville, NY: Sunburst.

Schwartz, J., Yerushalmy, M., & Education Development Center. (1988). *Visualizing algebra: The function analyzer* [Computer program]. Pleasantville, NY: Sunburst.

Schwartz, J., Yerushalmy, M., & Education Development Center. (1989). *The function supposer: Explorations in algebra* [Computer program]. Pleasantville, NY: Sunburst.

Secada, W. (1990). Agenda setting, enlightened self-interest, and equity in mathematics education. *Peabody Journal of Education, 66,* 22–56.

Sedlak, M., Wheeler, C., Pullin, D., & Cusick, P. (1986). *Selling students short: Classroom bargains and academic reform in the American high school.* New York: Teachers College Press.

Senk, S., Thompson, D., Viktora, S., Rubenstein, R., Halvorson, J., Flanders, J., Jakucyn, N., Pillsbury, G., & Usiskin, Z. (1987). *The University of Chicago School Mathematics Project: Advanced Algebra.* Chicago: University of Chicago Press.

Senk, S., Thompson, D., Viktora, S., Rubenstein, R., Halvorson, J., Flanders, J., Jakucyn, N., Pillsbury, G., & Usiskin, Z. (1990). *The University of Chicago School Mathematics Project: Advanced Algebra.* Glenview, IL: Scott Foresman.

Serres, M. (1982). *Hermes: Literature, science, philosophy.* Baltimore: Johns Hopkins University Press.

Sfard, A. (1995). The development of algebra—confronting historical and psychological perspectives. *Journal of Mathematical Behavior, 14*(1), 15–40.

Sfard, A., & Linchevski, L. (1994). The gains and the pitfalls of reification—The case of algebra. *Educational Studies in Mathematics, 26,* 191–228.

Sharron, S. (Ed.). (1979). *Applications in school mathematics (1979 yearbook).* Reston, VA: National Council of Teachers of Mathematics.

Shell Centre. (1985). *The language of functions and graphs.* Nottingham: Joint Matriculation Board.

Simon, M. (1995). Reconstructing mathematics pedagogy from a constructivist perspective. *Journal for Research in Mathematics Education, 26*(2), 114–145.

Sizer, T. (1984). *Horace's compromise: The dilemma of the American high school.* Boston: Houghton Mifflin.

Sizer, T. (1996). *Horace's hope: What works for the American high school.* Boston: Houghton Mifflin.

Skemp, R. R. (1976). Relational understanding and instrumental understanding. *Arithmetic Teacher, 26*(8), 9–15.

Smith, E., & Confrey, J. (1994). Multiplicative structures and the development of logarithms: What was lost by the invention of functions? In G. Harel & J. Confrey (Eds.), *The development of multiplicative reasoning in the learning of mathematics* (pp. 333–364). Albany: State University of New York Press.

Smith, J., diSessa, A., & Roschelle, J. (1993). Misconceptions reconceived: A constructivist analysis of knowledge in transition. *The Journal of the Learning Sciences, 3*(2), 115–163.

Smith, J. P. (1996). Efficacy and teaching mathematics by telling: A challenge for reform. *Journal for Research in Mathematics Education, 27*(4), 387–402.

Smith, S., Charles, R., Keedy, M., Bittinger, M., & Orfan, L. (1988). *Algebra.* Menlo Park, CA: Addison-Wesley.

Speiser, B., & Walter, C. (1994). Catwalk: First-semester calculus. *Journal of Mathematical Behavior, 13*(2), 135–152.

Stein, S., & Crabill, C. (1984). *Elementary algebra: A guided inquiry.* Pleasantville, NY: Sunburst. (Original work published 1970)

Stevenson, H., Lummis, M., Lee, S-Y., & Stigler, J. (1990). *Making the grade in mathematics: Elementary mathematics in the United States, Taiwan, and Japan.* Reston, VA: National Council of Teachers of Mathematics.

Stigler, J., & Hiebert, J. (1997). Understanding and improving classroom mathematics teaching. *Phi Delta Kappan, 79*(1), 14–21.

Stinson, S. (1993). Meaning and value: Reflections on what students say about school. *Journal of Curriculum and Supervision, 8*(3), 216–238.

Strauss, S., & Bichler, E. (1988). The development of children's concepts of the arithmetic average. *Journal for Research in Mathematics Education, 19*, 64–80.

Sutherland, G. (1984). *Ability, merit, and measurement: Mental testing and English education, 1880–1940.* Oxford: Clarendon.

Thom, R. (1986). "Modern" mathematics: An educational and philosophical error? In T. Tymoczko (Ed.), *New directions in the philosophy of mathematics* (pp. 67–78). Boston: Birkhauser.

Thompson, P. (1994). Students, functions, and the undergraduate curriculum. *CBMS Issues in Mathematics Education, 4*, 21–44.

Tymoczko, T. (Ed.). (1986). *New directions in the philosophy of mathematics.* Boston: Birkhauser.

Usiskin, Z. (1995). Why is algebra important to learn? *American Educator, 19*(1), 30–37.

van Barneveld, G., & Krabbendam, H. (Eds.). (1982). *Conference on functions: Report 1.* Enschede, The Netherlands: Foundation for Curriculum Development.

van der Waerden, B. L. (1985). *A history of algebra: From al-Khwarizmi to Emmy Noether*. Berlin: Springer-Verlag.

von Neumann, J. (1983). The formalist foundations of mathematics. In P. Benacerraf & H. Putnam (Eds.), *Philosophies of mathematics* (pp. 61–65). Cambridge: Cambridge University Press.

Weinberg, S. (1996). Sokal's hoax. *New York Review of Books, 43*, 11–15.

Welch, W. (1978). Science education in Urbanville: A case study. In R. Stake & J. Easley (Eds.), *Case studies in science education* (pp. 5-1–5-21). Urbana: University of Illinois.

Wheeler, D. (1989). Contexts for research on the teaching and learning of algebra. In S. Wagner & C. Kieran (Eds.), *Research issues in the learning and teaching of algebra* (pp. 278–287). Reston, VA: National Council of Teachers of Mathematics.

Wheeler, D. (1993). Knowledge at the crossroads. *For the Learning of Mathematics, 13*(1), 53–55.

Wigner, E. (1984). The unreasonable effectiveness of mathematics in the natural sciences. In D. Campbell & J. Higgins (Eds.), *Mathematics: People, problems, results* (Vol. 3; pp. 116–126). Belmont: Wordsworth International.

Wilder, R. (1986). The cultural basis of mathematics. In T. Tymozcko (Ed.), *New directions in the philosophy of mathematics* (pp. 185–200). Boston: Birkhauser.

Wilson, S. (in press). Mastodons, maps, and Michigan: Exploring uncharted territory while teaching elementary school social studies. *Elementary School Journal*.

Wong, E. D. (1995). Challenges confronting the researcher/teacher: Conflicts of purpose and conduct. *Educational Researcher, 24*(3), 22–28.

Wood, T., Cobb, P., Yackel, E., & Dillon, D. (Eds.). (1993). Rethinking elementary school mathematics: Insights and issues. *Journal for Research in Mathematics Education [Monograph #6]*. Reston, VA: National Council of Teachers of Mathematics.

Wu, H. (1997). The mathematics education reform: Why you should be concerned and what you can do. *American Mathematical Monthly, 104*, 946–954.

Yerushalmy, M. (1997). Emergence of new schemes for solving algebra word problems: The impact of technology and the function approach. *Proceedings of the 21st annual meeting of the International Group for the Psychology of Mathematics Education* (Vol. 1; pp. 165–178). Lahti, Finland.

Yerushalmy, M., & Chazan, D. (1990). Overcoming visual obstacles with the aid of the Geometric Supposer. *Educational Studies in Mathematics, 21*(3), 199–219.

Yerushalmy, M., & Gilead, S. (1997). Solving equations in a technological environment: Seeing and manipulating. *Mathematics Teacher, 90*(2), 156–163.

Yerushalmy, M., & Schwartz, J. (1993). Seizing the opportunity to make algebra mathematically and pedagogically interesting. In T. Romberg, E. Fennema, & T. Carpenter (Eds.), *Integrating research on the graphical representation of function* (pp. 41–68). Hillsdale, NJ: Lawrence Erlbaum.

Yerushalmy, M., & Shternberg, B. (1994). *The algebra sketchbook* [Computer program]. Pleasantville, NY: Sunburst.

Index

About the Author

Daniel Chazan is an associate professor of teacher education at Michigan State University and a graduate of the Harvard Graduate School of Education. As chronicled in this book, in order to research mathematics teaching and learning, he taught algebra for three years at Holt High School. His professional interests include student-centered mathematics teaching, the potential of history and philosophy of mathematics for informing such teaching, the role of technology in supporting student classroom exploration, exploring possibilities for constructive links between educational scholarship and practice, and the preparation of future teachers. Professor Chazan lives in Ann Arbor, Michigan, with his wife, Ronit, and son, Jonah.